ACKNOWLEDGEMENTS

We are indebted to many people for their help with this research and publication, but special thanks are extended to:

* Calderdale LEA for providing the financial support;

* the LEA's Senior Inspector (INSET) and General Inspector (Science) for conceiving the idea of the evaluation and facilitating a rare and much appreciated opportunity for a long-term inquiry into the effects of INSET;

* the two advisory teachers, the high quality of whose work withstood intensive investigation over a long period of time;

* the headteachers and staff of the five case-study schools who showed great patience and hospitality during repeated fieldwork visits and gave their unswerving support to the project, in spite of many competing pressures.

Evaluations are greatly aided by contexts and circumstances that encourage openness, honesty, constructive criticism and reflexivity. The authors would like to record that, throughout the evaluation, these qualities were found to prevail at all levels of the education service within Calderdale. Undoubtedly, they were a major reason why the evaluation was both a privilege and pleasure to conduct.

The Impact of INSET:

The Case of Primary Science

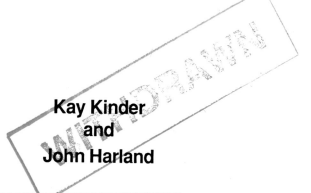

Kay Kinder
and
John Harland

nfer

Published in 1991
by the National Foundation for Educational Research,
The Mere, Upton Park, Slough, Berkshire SL1 2DQ

ISBN 0 7005 1289 6

CONTENTS

CHAPTER ONE

THE STUDY'S CONTRIBUTIONS

This opening chapter discusses how the longitudinal evaluation of one Education Support Grant (ESG) scheme in primary science may be a contribution to the developing field of research into INSET and its impact on teachers.

INTRODUCTION

Several writers have noted that research-based inquiries into the impact of in-service training on teachers' practice - and hence, evaluations of the long-term effectiveness of INSET provision - have seldom been conducted (Henderson 1978, Fullan 1982, and Halpin *et al* 1990). According to Bolam (1987), the reasons for this lacuna in evaluation studies are partly due to the inherent technical difficulties and partly to the lack of adequate funding and resources:

> *If insufficient time and money are allocated to an evaluation, then it is simply not possible to produce a summative evaluation which depends upon such outcome data. On the other hand, it is both easier technically and also less expensive to evaluate context, input and process factors and to produce a formative report which can be timely and useful ...*

> *In consequence, and in spite of the often expressed wish to measure the impact of INSET on teachers' behaviour and pupils' learning, few evaluations actually produce summative output data whereas most do produce formative process data. A wide range of evidence supports this conclusion. For example, ... Day (1986), reported, in a national survey of DES Regional Courses, that while 'All regions conducted some form of evaluation ... this varied from the informal impressionistic ... to the formal report based on the systematic collection of evidence from course members before, during and after the course by an independent evaluator'. It was recognized that although current methods of evaluation assisted in both course improvement and accountability, they did not, on the whole, provide evidence of the long term impact of courses on classrooms and schools. Lack of time and money were cited as reasons why post-course evaluation rarely occurred. (pp. 3-4)*

In recent years, largely as a response to Department of Education and Science (DES) calls for evaluation and monitoring of the effectiveness of INSET under a succession of new funding arrangements (e.g. DES 1986 and 1987), there are signs that, in addition to an increasing number of process-based studies, research into the outcomes of in-service provision is beginning to gather momentum (e.g. Dienye 1987, Harland 1989, Brown and Constable 1989, Halpin *et al* 1990, Hodgson and Whalley 1990, and Parsons 1990). While signalling advances in research into the effects of INSET, they often exhibit the following shortcomings:

*   the researchers may be from the same institution which provided the in-service input;

*   the time-scale following the input is often quite short;

*   using evaluation sheets or questionnaires, the data collected are often based on self-reports only, with few checks on possible discrepancies between teachers' rhetoric and classroom reality;

*   teachers tend to be the only source of perceptions about effects, with few attempts to corroborate their accounts with those of, say, headteachers and advisers;

*   classroom observations and pupil interviews are rare;

*   the institutional context in which teachers are expected to implement changes is often neglected;

*   there is sometimes a wholesale swing towards documenting outcomes with insufficient complementary attention to process factors;

*   the reporting of findings on the effects of INSET often lacks an appropriate conceptual framework for discussing outcomes.

Although the present study remains a small-scale case-study evaluation of the effects of in-service training in one area of the curriculum, Calderdale's bold and imaginative approach to the funding of INSET evaluations created the opportunity and resources to address some of the shortcomings alluded to above. The overriding intention in commissioning the evaluation was to facilitate an in-depth and longitudinal study of the impact of INSET in one particular area of the curriculum - **primary science** - in such a way that a generalizable conceptual framework or model of INSET outcomes may be tentatively formulated and general lessons about the nature of effective INSET may be gleaned. For Calderdale it represented a considerable investment of resources in a genuine endeavour to initiate an evaluation that would tackle the kind of methodological shortcomings described above.

Consequently, as a primary objective, it is hoped that the resulting evaluation has a contribution to make to the developing field of research into the impact of INSET: firstly, as an attempt to tackle some of the inherent methodological difficulties in studying the effects of INSET; secondly, as offering an exploratory and provisional framework for conceptualizing INSET outcomes; and thirdly, as a portrayal of some of the opportunities and problems entailed in trying to bring about changes in teachers' classroom practices through in-service training.

However, even though the main significance of the study is seen in terms of its contribution to the understanding of the impact of INSET generally, other specific aspects of professional development are also addressed. At a subsidiary level, it is hoped that the study of this ESG scheme also has something useful to say about in-service training in the specific area of primary science, the kind of INSET provided by advisory teachers, and the professional development role of school co-ordinators for science. Thus, the study is conceived as offering a contribution in four overlapping areas of discourse:

- conceptualizing INSET outcomes;

- primary science INSET;

- advisory teachers;

- primary subject co-ordinators.

Each of these are introduced in turn.

CONCEPTUALIZING INSET OUTCOMES

One consequence of the paucity of empirical investigations into the effects of in-service training is the lack of conceptual frameworks relating to INSET outcomes. At the start of the evaluation, the most useful typology of INSET outcomes was to be found in the influential paper by the American researchers, Joyce and Showers (1980), whose work was relayed in this country by Bolam (1987) and Hopkins (1989).

As part of a matrix between forms of training and level of impact, Joyce and Showers (1980) describe training outcomes under four categories:

- general awareness of new skills;
- organized knowledge of underlying concepts and theory;
- learning of new skills;
- application on-the-job.

Our original intention was to apply this typology of outcomes to chart the effects of the in-service training we were studying. However, analysis of the accounts of teachers and others about the effects of the INSET scheme, suggested that the nature and range of outcomes were more complex and broad-ranging than that contained in the model advanced by Joyce and Showers. Furthermore, the outcomes evident in our data, but omitted in the American researchers' typology, appeared to have significant consequences for any analysis of the relationship between INSET inputs and impact on teachers' classroom practices. Thus, while Joyce and Showers' notions of 'awareness', 'knowledge and skills' and 'application on-the-job' are readily taken on board as important and empirically substantiated outcomes, the typology derived from the evidence of this evaluation is more extensive. As an example of the extensions to the model, it should be noted that Joyce and Showers' typology implies that the challenge of in-service training is principally concerned with capability and cognitive outcomes. Evidence from our research suggests that there are other factors which have been totally omitted from the classification summarized above. Motivation and value-orientation changes are not considered by Joyce and Showers, yet our study suggests these can be highly influential outcomes which can have a crucial influence on teachers' subsequent practices in the classroom.

Our alternative framework for classifying INSET outcomes - the central focus of this report - is set out in Chapter Six. The typology we offer has a number of affinities with the list of INSET effects cited by Halpin *et al* (1990). However, that study's reduction of the effects of INSET to three broad categories - namely, (i) Teaching, (ii) Organization and Policy, (iii) Attitudes and Knowledge - appears to exclude some important outcomes and runs the risk of failing to distinguish clearly between attitudinal and knowledge effects. Whereas their mainly quantitative techniques have the advantage of drawing evidence from a larger sample of teachers, it is hoped that the qualitative case study methods of this evaluation (with its inevitably much smaller sample) complements their research. An in-depth, longitudinal study allowed for a more detailed exploration of the connections and interdependency between different outcomes, especially in terms of their overall contribution to the end goal of impacting on classroom practice. In this way, it is intended that the analysis of the observed outcomes may go some way to offer INSET planners and researchers the beginnings of a language or conceptual frame for further examinations of the effects - and hence the effectiveness - of INSET.

PRIMARY SCIENCE INSET

In addition to the evaluation's main purpose of offering generalizable insights into effective INSET, the study also hopes to contribute to research in the specific area of INSET for primary science. This is an important area of inquiry, especially in the light of the National Curriculum. Two key reference points in the recent literature on INSET for primary science are Kruger *et al* (1990) and IPSE (1988a, b and c). However, before considering these studies, an earlier paper by Whittaker (1983) provides a timely reminder of the sheer enormity of the problems involved in helping primary teachers to enhance their own levels of understanding in science, as well as to improve their performance in teaching it effectively. Whittaker stressed that primary teachers are mostly not science specialists, and often have low self-esteem in the subject. Consequently, a significant change in many teachers' frames of reference about science was required, yet the paper warns:

> *very few people are capable of deliberately making radical changes in their view of the world; most can modify it gradually, if they are convinced of the value of doing so* (p. 250).

Several central problems are identified: the preferred investigative approach to science lies outside the educational experience of most primary teachers; initial teacher training has not adequately addressed this weakness in primary science; and the vast majority of primary teachers are women who were schooled during a period when girls' science, especially the physical sciences, was often very limited. Hence, there were major obstacles to be overcome in the development of primary teachers' expertise in both the processes of science (e.g. constructing a hierarchical progression of questioning, developing observational and

5

experimental skills) as well as the content of science (e.g. an understanding of scientific concepts, facts and principles).

Whittaker, a college tutor, goes on to describe her involvement in an in-school in-service programme designed to address such problems:

> *In each year, I worked with a linked group of schools, covering the full nursery, infant and junior age-range. The enthusiasm and involvement of the heads was, of course, vital. The schools were offered a total of one and a half days of my time and a small sum of money for equipment. In return, they were asked to ensure that as many teachers as possible took part in the project. I explained to staff meetings that my function was to help to develop science work in the schools, in co-operation with the teachers. I was available for consultation, to help teach classes, to advise on books and resources, or to help in any other way that seemed useful. I explained my approach to primary science, especially the emphasis on practical investigation and on children's ideas and interests, with written work arising only when the children felt they had something to record.* (p. 255)

Foreshadowing later developments in primary science INSET, such an approach has much in common with the whole school emphasis and the highly prevalent use of advisory teachers in the primary science ESG. The benefits which Whittaker considered had arisen from her programme included: more teachers participated and were more confident because it was on their 'home ground'; it was tailored to teacher's individual needs; teachers' awareness of pupils' needs increased; more favourable attitudes towards science were fostered; and the programme acted as a catalyst for staff discussions of the whole curriculum. From a more critical perspective, however, it should be noted that the paper did not include an analysis of any long-term effects.

Turning to the first of the two recent key references on primary science INSET, Kruger et al's paper looks at the INSET provided under the ESG scheme for primary science and offers evidence from in-depth interviews with teachers designed to probe their understanding of particular attainment targets. The authors argue that, in order to prepare teachers for the effective implementation of the National Curriculum, there is a pressing need to provide INSET which would concentrate on developing teachers' own understanding of science concepts.

The publications produced by IPSE, the second key study referred to, provide a crucial context-setting source for the evaluation reported here. The evidence presented in this report is drawn exclusively from a local evaluation of only one authority's ESG scheme in primary science. For the national evaluation of the ESG scheme in primary science, the DES commissioned the Association for Science Education, which set up a project, entitled 'Initiatives in Primary Science: an Evaluation' (IPSE) to carry it out. The IPSE series of publications consists of three booklets and a file of separate papers, which together constitute the findings of the evaluation. The size and breadth of the sample of schemes studied by the evaluation team is particularly impressive.

The IPSE material suggests that the scheme under study here shared many similar features with others implemented elsewhere. Moreover, the scheme demonstrated qualities commensurate with the factors which were reported in IPSE as being considered most significant for success by those with responsibility for managing the ESG schemes, e.g. skilled advisory teachers and a clearly reasoned LEA INSET plan. In most important respects, the central interpretation of the overall effects of the ESG scheme presented consistently by both IPSE (1988a, b and c) and Kruger *et al* (1990) receive further corroboration from our study. All three studies, for example, conclude that, although ESG schemes generally succeeded in raising the profile of primary science:

> *teachers' lack of scientific knowledge was an aspect of the teaching of science which had not been adequately addressed within these training programmes and this omission constituted a problem.* (Kruger *et al* 1990, p. 136)

One such problem, addressed in depth by IPSE (1988c), was continuity and progression in the teaching and learning of science.

Notwithstanding the broad agreement between the three studies, some differences do exist between the studies, and these are worthy of comment because they point to the distinctive contribution that the research reported here can offer. In particular three differences are noteworthy:

(i)   In comparison with the broad global perspective laid out by IPSE - the strength of which is undoubtedly its capacity to draw out general patterns across the ESG scheme as a whole - the present study offers a more sustained and focused look at the problems and opportunities for bringing about changes in teaching primary science through INSET activities associated with a single scheme. It was also possible in this study to follow up the effects of the in-service training to the point of the implementation of the National Curriculum statutory orders for science.

(ii) The IPSE project team explicitly used the typology of INSET outcomes proposed by Joyce and Showers (1980) as a device for researching in-service delivery and effects. Kruger *et al* (1990) imply a similar categorization of outcome types in their paper. By adopting a broader classification and framework of INSET outcomes, which were derived from teachers' actual perceptions of the effects of the in-service scheme, it is hoped that the present study can throw into sharper focus the particular manifestation of each type of outcome for primary science. Outcomes like 'new awareness' or actual impact on classroom practice are depicted with considerable illustrative material.

(iii) Finally, differences also stem from contrasting stances taken on the ideological position of the researcher and evaluator. The IPSE project team, for example, adopt something of connoisseurship model of evaluation and clearly state their criteria for identifying good practice in the primary school. To this extent, they were committed to a particular view of science teaching. Likewise, Kruger *et al*'s (1990) adherence to constructivist views on teaching and learning in science pervades much of their analysis and recommendations for practice. In comparison with these quite value-laden approaches, the stance adopted here was more detached and was less committed, for instance, to any school of thought on effective practice in primary science.

Our brief was to take a 'goals-free' evaluative approach, through which perceived effects - regardless of whether or not they could be defined as 'good practice' or 'constructivist learning' - could be examined in the light of the inputs and messages provided through the ESG scheme. It may well be largely as a result of this more neutral evaluative stance that the whole problem of differences between INSET providers' and INSET consumers' values relating to curriculum and pedagogical issues receives greater emphasis in our analysis than in those of IPSE and Kruger et al.

Hence, to conclude this section, we are in almost total accord with the latter authors' main interpretations of the overall effects of the ESG scheme - e.g. higher awareness but not increased knowledge. However, we feel that the major significance for effective in-service training of value congruence or discongruence between INSET providers and consumers is not afforded the attention it deserves. Accordingly, it is hoped that the research reported here will serve not only to endorse the main findings conveyed by these two key sources on INSET in primary science, but augment and extend them as well by arguing that other key outcomes, such as value congruence in primary science, should be injected into the debate.

ADVISORY TEACHERS

The IPSE team found that the use of advisory teachers was an almost universal feature of the primary science ESG schemes. Consequently, any study of the schemes - and this one is no exception - is bound to open up general issues pertaining to the role and work of a professional group which expanded rapidly in the late 1980s in response to a whole range of ESG initiatives. Within the existing literature, two related but separate strands of analysis are noticeable: one set of issues relates to the employment conditions and careers of advisory teachers (Lofthouse 1987, Petrie 1988, IPSE 1988a, ASE 1990, Biott 1990, and Harland 1990), whereas another agenda addresses the nature of the work undertaken by advisory teachers, particularly their roles in delivering school-based INSET (Sullivan 1987, de Boo 1988, IPSE 1988a & b, Jones 1988, Straker 1988, Webb 1989, ASE 1990, Biott 1990 and Harland 1990). In this present study, a contribution to the latter discussion - namely advisory teachers as INSET providers - is sought in preference to the debate about the employment conditions and career prospects of advisory teachers.

Notwithstanding this focus, the present study unearthed plenty of evidence on the employment and career conditions of the advisory teachers involved. By way of illustration, in the final year of the first stage of the scheme, both advisory teachers were deeply troubled by the apparent lack of career prospects and security of employment. (As explained later, both were happy to take up headship and deputy headship posts at the end of their stints as advisory teachers.) Given the openness of the advisory

9

teachers about their career aspirations and concerns, there was ample material to have written about this aspect of the scheme. However, for several reasons it was decided to concentrate on the advisory teachers' INSET delivery role rather than career-related issues. Firstly, because the evidence relating to the latter closely corroborated our interpretations on the occupational structure of advisory teachers offered elsewhere (Harland 1990), it was felt that there would only be marginal benefits in rehearsing them further here. Secondly, the employment conditions and prospects of advisory teachers are somewhat fluid and uncertain at the moment, and so anything written on the subject could be out of date before the report is published. Finally, the alternative focus - i.e. on advisory teachers' role in delivering INSET - seemed to be more directly relevant to a central remit of the evaluation, namely, examining the outcomes and effectiveness of the INSET provided under the scheme. This decision, however, should not be taken to imply that the issues surrounding the employment and careers of advisory teachers are considered by the authors to be less important or crucial than those concerning their approaches and effectiveness in delivering school-based INSET.

Within the broad areas of the nature of advisory teachers' INSET role, the direction of our focus here is targeted upon the format, process and content of the whole-school inputs, including providing training by the strategy of working alongside resident teachers. A detailed portrayal and analysis of the advisory teachers' approach to their in-service work is presented. In several respects, this can be seen as an extension of another NFER inquiry into the work of advisory teachers (Harland 1990). In the latter report, four modes of INSET delivery by advisory teachers in three different teams were identified:

(i)   provisionary mode ('I will give you')

(ii)   hortative mode ('I will tell you')

(iii)   role modelling mode ('I will show you')

(iv)   zetetic mode ('I will ask you')

The first three modes were conspicuous and regular features of the school-based inputs mounted by the advisory teachers in the present study. The fourth mode - development through a process of asking questions - was not practised by the advisory teachers to any significant degree. Central to the school-based input was the working alongside component, and observations of the advisory teachers in action in the classroom provided an opportunity for analysing this role-modelling mode of INSET. Since the research reported in Harland (1990) did not include any observations of advisory teachers, the illustration and examination of the role modelling mode provided in Chapter Five offers greater scope for reflection on this important form of in-service training than was possible in the earlier study. It is hoped that the analysis of this dimension to the INSET work of advisory teachers constitutes a useful elaboration to previous studies and will be of value to advisory teachers in their own deliberations about their practices.

PRIMARY SUBJECT CO-ORDINATORS

The third subsidiary contribution which we would hope the study could make is to the expanding literature on the capacity (or lack of it) for primary schools to sustain the professional development of their staff through the work of curriculum co-ordinators or leaders. Again, while our current focus is clearly upon science co-ordinators, studies of their counterparts for other curriculum areas suggest that many of the interpretations advanced here are not exclusive to science. The continuities in the findings between this and other studies are summarized in the chapter dealing with the role of the school science co-ordinator (Chapter Seven).

For the time being, it is worth recording that the conclusion reached here about the difficulties which science co-ordinators faced in sustaining professional development in their school is reinforced by the IPSE publications. They conclude:

> *Those ESG projects which relied on the school co-ordinator as the principal agent of change in the schools have often been disappointing. The projects have usually given individual co-ordinators a greater understanding of primary science, leading to development in their own classrooms. However, in many cases this development has not been carried over to their colleagues' classrooms.* (IPSE 1988b, p. 40)
> *Co-ordinator leadership is often unfulfilled because of:*
> - *lack of training*
> - *lack of active support from the head teacher, and*
> - *no relief from classroom duties in order to work with colleagues.* (IPSE 1988a, p. 23)

Whilst confirming these conclusions, the data collected in this study demonstrate the kinds of staff development support which is not usually accomplished or even attempted by co-ordinators, and also what can be achieved by those who give the post a high degree of commitment and professional skill. Finally, it is hoped that the analysis of the problems and obstacles confronted by co-ordinators - including those embedded deep within the prevailing culture of the primary school - can contribute to a realistic assessment of the policy implications associated with the co-ordinator role. This is especially pertinent in the context of National Curriculum implementation.

CONCLUSION AND OUTLINE OF THE REPORT

To sum up, at a subsidiary level the study is intended to have significance for the discussion of issues relating to primary science INSET, advisory teachers' delivery of in-service training and the role of subject co-ordinator in primary schools. Its main aim, however, is to contribute to the general development of the conceptualization of INSET outcomes through reference to the particular experience of one ESG scheme in primary science. Concomitant to this aim, is the tentative construction of a typology of INSET outcomes which, it is argued, could be used to improve the identification of professional development needs, the planning of INSET to meet specific outcomes, and the evaluation of INSET as an audit of its key effects.

The rest of the report is structured as follows:

Chapter Two	outlines the evaluation's methodology and discusses some of the particular problems this methodology had to address.
Chapter Three	describes the scheme in terms of its original submission and broad implementation.
Chapter Four	portrays the General INSET Provision associated with the scheme by giving examples of four different types of in-service activity.
Chapter Five	gives a detailed analysis of the advisory teachers' school-based input.

Chapter Six	presents the typology of INSET outcomes accruing from teacher accounts of the scheme's impact.
Chapter Seven	gives an overview of the self-sustaining component of the scheme, looking particularly at the work of the school science co-ordinator.
Chapter Eight	offers an evaluative update on science practice in the light of the National Curriculum, and then presents a summative overview of the scheme's outcomes. Facilitative and inhibitive factors which account for such outcomes are also discussed.
Chapter Nine	outlines eleven implications for policy to arise from the study.

A note to the reader

The main analytical dimensions to the study commence in Chapter Five. For those readers who are primarily interested in the analysis of the evaluation's findings and their associated implications for policy and practice, a cursory perusal of Chapters Two, Three and Four would be sufficient to gain a picture of the research and background context upon which the main chapters are based. Chapter Two is provided for those readers with an interest in the methodological issues involved in the evaluation of INSET, while Chapters Three and Four are aimed at an audience which requires a more detailed description of the wider issues, conditions and circumstances in which the scheme was operating.

THE EVALUATION

INTRODUCTION

The main purpose of this chapter is to describe the evaluation design and research methods used in the study. First of all, however, it is necessary to offer a very brief outline of the ESG scheme that was evaluated, since without this, it is difficult to comprehend the reasoning behind the research methodology. It should be noted that a more comprehensive account of the scheme and its implementation is provided in the following chapter.

OUTLINE OF THE SCHEME

Essentially, Calderdale's successful 1986 bid to the DES for participation in the ESG initiative, 'The Teaching of Science as part of primary education', consisted of three elements:

- a school-based input from two specially appointed advisory teachers;

- followed by school self-sustaining INSET;

- and the LEA's general INSET activity in primary science.

For the school-based input, twelve schools were to be selected annually by criteria which included '*not at present having a coherent school curriculum policy for Science and Technology*', and would each be involved in 'an intensive half-term programme' consisting of preliminary visits by an advisory teacher; six weekly after-school in-service meetings, for all the staff in the school, held within the school itself, and an advisory teacher working alongside members of the school staff for one day per week.

The submission outlined a further programme of support for the selected schools subsequent to this input, which consisted of supply cover for the release of the science curriculum co-ordinator to develop a school policy;

the provision of £200 worth of equipment, materials and publications to implement the policy; and follow-up visits by an advisory teacher over the following year.

It was stated that the whole-school in-service meetings would '*provide a basis for a programme of further development by the school staff*'. Although the advisory teacher would continue to '*support, monitor and evaluate progress*', the school - and particularly the designated science curriculum co-ordinator - would gradually take responsibility for sustaining the developments.

In addition, the LEA - principally the General Inspector (Science) and the two advisory teachers - would mount a series of INSET activities which would be open for applications from any primary teacher in the authority. These activities would include one day courses for science co-ordinators, two-day residential courses, surgeries and the institution of a self-help group.

In a diagrammatic form, the scheme may be represented as follows:

CALDERDALE'S PRIMARY SCIENCE AND TECHNOLOGY ESG SCHEME

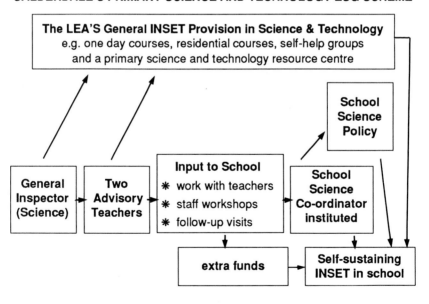

The scheme formally started in September 1986 and operated for three academic years. It was then extended for a further two years.

EVALUATION BRIEF

In Spring 1988, when the scheme had been running for five terms, Calderdale commissioned a researcher at NFER's Northern Office in York to evaluate its impact on schools. The LEA and NFER agreed that the primary focus of the evaluation should be to examine and assess the effect of the scheme on schools that had taken part in the school-based INSET programme. As a secondary focus, the evaluation should also consider the effects of the general and subsidiary in-service inputs.

It was also agreed that three specific objectives identified by the LEA would be met:

(a)   to provide an evaluation of the authority's science scheme in terms of the primary and secondary foci described above;

(b)   to provide an evaluation which would inform decisions on how best to support further development of primary science by means of in-service provision and other suitable means;

(c)   to provide an evaluation which would explore the lessons offered by the science scheme in such a way as to help the authority plan and implement other initiatives (e.g. those funded by LEA Training Grants or other ESGs) aimed at fostering improvements through in-service provision and support.

Four over-arching questions were highlighted as central concerns for the evaluation:

(i)   To what extent were there signs of lasting changes in the primary science practice of the schools involved in the school-based input?

(ii)   What were the main contributory factors accounting for the success or failure of the initiative in different schools?

(iii)   How could factors identified under (ii) be extended or improved to assist further developments in the science programme?

(iv)   Could successful factors identified under (ii) be transferred to other in-service initiatives in the LEA?

The evaluation would be conducted from an independent and detached vantage point, and was to focus on examining the scheme as a whole rather than individual people or institutions within it. Both processes and outcomes of the scheme would be investigated, including unintended as well as intended effects. The evaluation would largely use qualitative case-study techniques and would seek validity in its findings through the triangulation of perceptions and accounts of different participants (e.g. pupils, teachers, science co-ordinators, headteachers, advisers and advisory teachers).

The brief emphasized that, because the scheme was launched well in advance of the evaluation, much of the research required a retrospective approach, particularly in the early phases of fieldwork. Visits to schools selected for these early phases of the evaluation had to be made after they had experienced the main school-based input. Nevertheless, a longitudinal dimension, consisting of pre-, during and post-experience of the school-based input was incorporated into later phases of the evaluation.

The evaluation design was organized around five main phases:

Phase I: a study of general background to the scheme and its mode of working, followed by research in three schools (the 'retrospective' case-study schools) which had experienced the school-based input in the first year the scheme was operative.

Phase II: a study of the expectations and existing provision for science in two schools (the 'prospective' case study schools) due to participate in the school-based input.

Phase III: observation of the school-based input in the two prospective case study schools.

Phase IV: follow-up research in all five case-study schools.

Phase V: follow-up research at a later date in all five case-study schools.

In addition, time was set aside for the researchers to attend the general in-service provision relevant to the scheme. Similarly, time was also allocated for dissemination and feedback sessions with relevant audiences.

EVALUATION DESIGN

In diagrammatic form, the evaluation design can be represented thus:

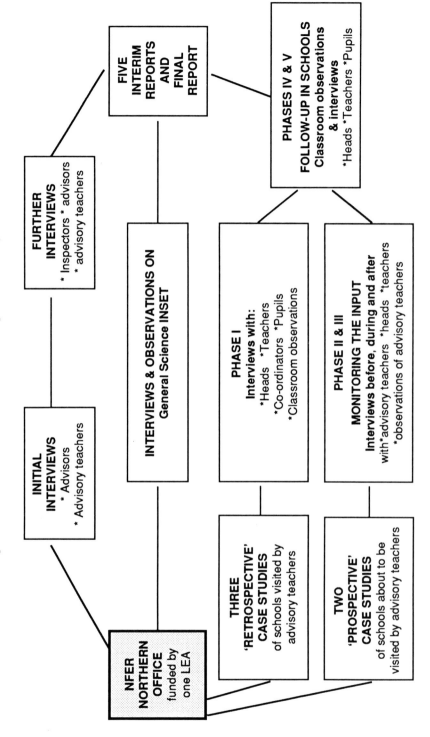

PHASE I: ORIENTATION

The fieldwork for Phase I was conducted during the Summer and early Autumn terms of 1988. During the Summer term, the fieldwork included:

- two group discussions with the General Inspector (Science) and science advisory teachers;

- two long and in-depth individual interviews with each of the advisory teachers;

- in-depth group discussions with advisory teachers;

- interview with General Inspector (Science);

- interview with Senior Inspector for INSET;

- interview with Senior Inspector - Primary;

- collection of central documents (e.g. ESG submission, curriculum policy statements, examples of thematic flowcharts, etc.);

- visits to three 'retrospective' case-study schools during which the headteacher, science co-ordinator and two teachers were interviewed;

- informal conversations with other staff in these three schools;

- collection of school documents (e.g. science policy statements, schools guides).

At the central LEA level, accounts and information were collected on such items as the career of the advisory teacher; their previous experience; the recruitment process; training for the advisory teacher role; deployment of advisory teachers; selection of schools; negotiating contracts with schools; main school-based input and follow-up work; resourcing the scheme; links with other INSET provision; intended aims and criteria for success; degree of impact and quality of outcomes; and perceived factors affecting these outcomes.

At the school level, corresponding versions of these items were incorporated into the interview schedule. In addition, interviews included questions on teachers' previous experience and training; the type and amount of primary science taught prior to the input; early perceptions, expectations and involvement with advisory teachers; perceived aims and emphases of the scheme; initial reactions to main input and other related INSET provision; long-term effects on school, classroom practice, science policy and the role of the science co-ordinator; factors affecting such outcomes; and salient characteristics of the school. In order to allow participants' key concerns and priorities to surface, the interviews followed a flexible format and were not tightly structured.

All three retrospective case study schools were involved in the main school-based input during the Spring term 1987, hence the first visit by the researcher to those schools occurred just over a year after the school-based input. Two of the three were randomly selected from all schools that had taken part in the scheme. The third was deliberately chosen in order to include a larger school in the sample.

One school had a high proportion of children from one particular ethnic minority and was located amidst terraced housing in the inner ring of a large industrial town in Calderdale. Another was sited on the outskirts of this town and drew its intake from large council house estates. The third was a Church of England school in a semi-rural setting some miles from the town.

Early in the Autumn term 1988, return visits were made to these schools. Three classroom teachers were observed and interviewed in each school. In the case of junior age range classes, short recorded interviews were held with three pairs of pupils. The equivalent of three half-days were spent in each school. Additionally, accounts of their work in the three schools were collected from the advisory teachers, and in the case of two schools, the pastoral advisers were also interviewed.

PHASES II AND III: THE 'PROSPECTIVE' CASE STUDY SCHOOLS

Following discussions with advisory staff, two 'prospective' schools were selected and their agreement to take part in the evaluation was secured. They were both to be involved in the school-based input during the second half of the Autumn term 1988.

The following fieldwork was undertaken in these two schools.

1. **Preliminary Visits** (prior to school-based input):

    - observation of the advisory teachers' initial meetings with staff;

    - detailed interviews with the head and each staff member about (i) professional background and previous INSET experiences, with particular reference to primary science; (ii) current classroom practice and the kinds of science planned and delivered to pupils at that time and (iii) their expectations of the school-based input;

    - further interviews with the teachers selected for the 'working alongside' component of the school-based input, to garner their accounts of the whole programme of advisory teachers' preliminary visits;

    - an interview with the advisory teachers about their perspective on the school in the light of their preliminary visits.

2. **School-based Input** (working alongside):

    - five days' observation of the advisory teachers in action with the teachers selected for working alongside;

    - on-going informal discussions with the teachers and advisory teachers about their perspective of the classroom work in progress;

3. **School-based Input** (INSET):

    - observation of three after-school INSET sessions in each school.

The research for Phase III had a final strand of fieldwork, which was undertaken shortly after the completion of the school-based input. This involved detailed interviews (in early 1989) with the two advisory teachers, and the heads and staff of both schools in order to obtain each participant's perspectives on the initial impact of the advisory teachers' work and its perceived effectiveness. Future developments of the scheme, namely the advisory teachers' follow-up visits, the activities of the science co-ordinator and the use of the additional £200, were also considered.

PHASES IV AND V: FOLLOW-UP VISITS

In these phases, the researchers made two rounds of return visits to the five case-study schools: one in the Summer term of 1989 and the final one in the Spring term of 1990. In addition to further interviews with the advisory teachers, the fieldwork in each school typically comprised:

- interview with headteacher;
- interview with science co-ordinator;
- main interviews with teachers;
- classroom observations, including pre- and post- observation interviews, of science co-ordinator and two or three teachers in each school;
- interviews with pupils after observed lessons (1989 only).

These interviews provided opportunities to discuss the development of science practice, in the light of the earlier ESG scheme and any subsequent school-based INSET. In particular, the 1990 visits included consideration of the initial implementation of the National Curriculum core area and focused heavily on the work and impact of the schools' science co-ordinators in delivering further professional development activities.

MONITORING THE GENERAL INSET ACTIVITIES

All teachers interviewed during the follow-up visits were asked about possible participation in any science in-service activities mounted generally throughout the LEA. As it turned out, very few teachers in the case study sample had attended such activities, though most of the science co-ordinators were able to cite at least one such event in which they had participated. Teacher accounts of these activities and the perceived impact on their practice were collected. In addition, the researchers carried out the following fieldwork in connection with the general activities:

- observations of two different residential courses ran by the General Inspector (Science) and the two advisory teachers;

- participant observation of a 'Baker Day' in science provided by the advisory teachers for two other schools (outside the sample of five);

- observations of two National Curriculum training days for science, organized by the General Inspector (Science) and the advisory teachers;

- an interview with one of the key organizers of the self-help group for science co-ordinators.

REPORTS AND FEEDBACK

Five interim and formative working papers were provided over the course of the evaluation. The foci of the earlier papers were determined by the priorities outlined in the evaluation brief; the agenda for the later reports were negotiated with the sponsor.

Prior to circulation within the LEA, all five working papers were validated by returning draft versions to key participants and interviewees. The contents of the interim papers were disseminated by the researchers at several feedback sessions, principally for the authority's pool of advisory teachers.

Consistent with the approach taken in the interim papers, our aim was to use the case-study data to illuminate and not to expose. Consequently, the final report has steered away from the presentational device of detailed school-by-school accounts and portrayals, in order to protect the anonymity of the participants involved. As well as that, in order to concentrate attention on the study's general implications for designing and delivering effective INSET, the interpretive and reporting stance adopted has consistently attempted to formulate and identify overall patterns and trends.

THE SCOPE OF THE EVALUATION

By way of concluding this chapter, four major issues concerning the parameters of the evaluation and its methodology are raised.

(i)   Representativeness of the study?

It should be stressed that the study is limited to an analysis of evidence from only five schools in one LEA. Thus, the grounds for generalizability are weak and, as such, the substantiation of *'findings'* with high levels of frequency and applicability cannot claim to be part of the evaluation's objectives or strengths. Instead, the main purpose of the study was to examine - in depth - the processes and effects of one INSET scheme in a small number of schools so that interpretations and typologies may be generated which could be tested for their wider relevance in subsequent research. In many respects, the study should be viewed as an exploratory and provisional analysis which reaches a number of tentative hypotheses that require empirical verification.

Notwithstanding this limitation, it should be acknowledged that there is little to suggest that the LEA, the one scheme studied, and the five primary schools involved, show characteristics which make them particularly unrepresentative or atypical. The scheme, for example, shared many features with those in other LEAs; it was implemented by two highly proficient and talented advisory teachers who worked in similar ways to their counterparts in other authorities. The schools were selected because they exemplified approaches, settings and problems said to be typical of many schools in the authority. This intuitive sense of the general typicality of the scheme and the case-study schools it operated in, albeit insufficiently rigorous to claim any representativeness, has been broadly endorsed in feedback sessions by advisory staff working in other schools and authorities.

(ii)   The generalizability of primary science INSET?

There are a number of caveats to be considered when using the interpretations of the effectiveness of the primary science scheme to proffer implications and lessons for INSET provision in other curriculum areas and phases of schooling. As Chapter One suggests, science in the primary school has posed a very distinctive set of professional development challenges. Similarly, in comparison with the primary school, the secondary schooling phase presents a different range of INSET opportunities (e.g. whole-school events are harder to mount in secondary schools) and, possibly, a different INSET culture (Kinder *et al* 1991). To avoid the inappropriate transference of ideas from one context to another, the main analytical chapters (six and seven) are deliberately pitched at higher levels of abstraction than the specifics of primary science. The final chapter on policy implications arising from the study is also intended to be a general consideration of INSET relevant to the secondary phase and other curriculum areas.

(iii) Responsive or design-led evaluation?

The evaluation's main aim remained to research the effects of the ESG scheme in the participating schools, even though over the course of the project, several alternative foci for research presented themselves for consideration. Approximately half way through the project, adherence to the evaluation brief meant that the inquiry shifted from the advisory teachers' delivery of the scheme to its longitudinal impact in the case-study schools. At the point of that shift, little further evidence was collected on the extension to the ESG scheme or the subsequent careers of the two advisory teachers. Other interesting possibilities which related to primary science INSET and the ESG scheme emerged - such as the INSET implications of the statutory orders for science or the ever-changing landscape of INSET funding and organization. These were rejected, however, in favour of a continuing focus on the impact of the initial input and the schools' subsequent self-sustaining INSET on teachers' perceptions and practice regarding science. This report reflects that sharp and sustained focus, as delineated in the evaluation brief.

(iv) Methodological problems of a longitudinal study of INSET

Finally, and most importantly, in taking on the issue of the long-term effects of INSET provision, the evaluation encountered the methodological difficulties that any research into learning effects and behavioural changes must inevitably confront. Indeed, for some, these difficulties are perceived to be so severe and invalidating that research into the long-term effects of INSET on classroom practice is viewed to be virtually worthless. Four problems are commonly seen as being particularly debilitating:

(a) gauging the nature and degree of change in teachers' attitudes, knowledge and classroom practices is unreliable and susceptible to differences between rhetoric and reality;

(b) there are insuperable difficulties in disentangling cause and effect, as well as intervening variables, especially over an extended period of time;

(c)   the effects of an INSET scheme may not materialize until after the evaluation has ceased - the so-called 'sleeper effect';

(d)   in a longitudinal study, the form of the original INSET input and its organizational context and climate can undergo such drastic changes as to make any recommendations from the study irrelevant to the new set of circumstances that prevail when the report is produced.

Without suggesting that the project has completely overcome these problems, we feel confident that the methodology adopted has been adequate to reduce the severity of the objections and to provide a study which has empirical validity and educational significance. The four major difficulties outlined above have been tackled in the following ways:

(a)   The reliability of teachers' accounts of change has been strengthened through attention to: rapport building between the researchers and participants; a variety of formal and informal interviews; repeated interviews to check for consistency; use of more than one researcher; and, where possible, corroboration from other participants (e.g. advisory teachers, headteachers). Nevertheless, it is accepted that in recounting their own classroom practices, teachers can feel that they are engaged in evaluating themselves and their professional worth. As a result of the almost unavoidable threat of accountability, it is understandable that many practitioners are liable to distort accounts of their actual practice or at least put the best possible gloss or defensive interpretation on it. Because of this higher probability for rhetoric/reality disparities, the research introduced classroom observations and interviews with pupils in order to gain some more 'objective' purchase on what teachers actually do rather than rely solely on what they say they do. In the vast majority of cases, these techniques helped to ground teachers' accounts in the reality of their everyday practice.

(b)   Using the same variety of interviewing and case-study methods as described above, the researchers found that, providing that the subject under discussion did not place unreasonable strain on their memories, teachers were usually willing and able to give clear and consistent accounts of how different factors and inputs affected their thinking and actions. While not entirely immune from misrecognition or distortion, accounts of the influences of INSET inputs, as relayed to independent researchers are arguably less vulnerable to rhetoric/reality differences, because evaluation of third parties is involved rather than self-evaluative assessment. As a result, the unravelling of perceived influences and effects was not considered to require corresponding 'objectivity' checks (e.g. observation) to those thought necessary for self-perceptions of classroom practices.

(c)   This study included cases of teachers who had experienced in-service activities three years before, as well as tracking those who gave accounts of pre-input expectations, the input itself, initial reactions and impact after two terms and four terms. There was little evidence of significant 'sleeper effects' - i.e. new and potent forms of impact rarely surfaced long after the input had ceased. For the vast majority of teachers interviewed, as the force and memory of an input receded, so did the probability of it having an effect on their thinking and practice.

(d)   That there have been enormous changes in the primary curriculum, the management of schools, and the funding and organization of INSET, since the evaluation started is incontrovertible. The scheme was firmly rooted in a landscape in which many features have vanished or have undergone substantial alteration. Consequently, to lift features and mechanisms straight out of the prevailing context when the scheme started and recommended them for the current climate would be unhelpful to say the least. In an attempt to avoid this, the lessons for INSET that are extracted from the analysis are deliberately pointed to a level of generality which hopefully transcends specific schemes and contexts. Following this approach, we feel that INSET co-ordinators and policy-makers are better equipped to decide how these general principles may be most appropriately applied in any given set of circumstances.

To conclude, while it is readily conceded that the study of INSET outcomes remain an imperfect art (and science), maximizing the contribution that INSET can make to improving the education offered to children requires that evaluations of the effects, and hence the effectiveness, of INSET be attempted. This study does not try to establish directly whether the INSET provided led to an improvement in children's learning (the ultimate goal of INSET providers and, therefore, INSET evaluators). However, it does endeavour to investigate to what extent, and in what ways, a particular in-service scheme had an impact on the participating teachers and their classroom practice. As a product of the study, a typology of INSET outcomes is offered to INSET designers, deliverers and evaluators as a tool for conceptualizing the effects - and hence the goals - of professional development activity.

CHAPTER THREE

THE SCHEME IN ACTION

THE SCHEME AS SUBMITTED

In 1984, the DES invited LEAs to submit bids for participation in an ESG initiative called 'The Teaching of Science as part of Primary Education' which was *'designed to improve the effectiveness and relevance of science teaching for pupils aged 5-11'*. Initially, the programme was to run for three years (1985-88), with the Government contributing 70 per cent to the total costs of each LEA's scheme. In 1985-86, 56 LEAs in England and Wales launched their approved schemes. In the following year, a further 44 LEAs started projects as part of a second round of approved schemes. Calderdale was included in this second round and, as such, its scheme was scheduled to operate from 1986-89. It was subsequently extended for a further two years.

The LEA had unsuccessfully submitted a bid for the first round. Like the second submission, it had been drafted by the General Inspector (Science) who consulted the Senior Inspector (Primary) on matters concerning good primary practice. (For the sake of consistency the title 'inspector' is used throughout the report, although in the early stages of the scheme the term 'advisor' was used in the LEA.) The General Inspector (Science) felt that the main features of the scheme, especially the emphasis on the whole-school approach, had evolved over a period of time. In response to growing demands, more central in-service courses in primary science had been mounted in the early 1980s and these were considered to have been successful in demonstrating to some teachers that science need not be constrained to a 'bunsen burner' image but could be consistent with good investigative and child-centred primary practice. The problem was, however, that these courses were only reaching about a third of the schools and there developed a sense in which they *'were preaching to teachers who were already converted'*. In order to tackle this problem, the General Inspector (Science) began experimenting with school-based courses and it was the perceived success of these that led to the idea of whole-school and in-school forms of INSET becoming a central feature of the ESG submission.

Another major influence on the design of the scheme arose through the involvement of the General Inspector (Science) in the national and regional meetings of the Science Advisers' Group. It was thought that this group was largely responsible for fostering a good degree of consensus on the criteria, priorities and specifications to be found in different schemes.

Reasons for the failure of the first submission are mainly a matter of conjecture but factors which were thought may have had a bearing on the DES decision to turn down the submission included: limited number of LEAs fundable under the DES total budget; geographical spread; and a possible under-estimation of the potential funding and scale of the scheme.

The basic principles and proposals put forward in the successful submission were thought to be very similar to those expressed in the first submission. While the central design features remained virtually unchanged, the second submission, written in the light of the early experiences of the first round projects, put a greater emphasis on the administrative and technical support needed for the scheme. In the second submission, it was also possible to make more explicit use of the job title 'advisory teacher' which, since the drafting of the initial bid, was a concept which had grown in acceptability in the LEA and was perceived to be less threatening than some had initially feared.

What then did the submission say would be implemented through the scheme? Looking to promote long-term curriculum development in primary science, the submission put forward plans for a school-based input, as well as courses of a more general nature. The scheme comprised three elements: school-based input, self-sustaining developments by the school, and the LEA's general in-service provision in science.

The following extract from the submission gives full details of the intentions for the school-based input.

Twelve schools per year will be identified by the Advisory Service for an intensive half-term programme (two per half term). The schools will be selected on the basis of not at present having a coherent school curriculum policy for Science and Technology being implemented by all staff and either having had a record of curriculum development in other areas or be expected, by the commitment of the head teacher, to be able to take advantage of the programme.

Schools will be required to contract with the Authority to undertake the programme as follows: to identify a teacher to act as curriculum leader, to develop a school policy for Science and Technology and to have this policy implemented by all teachers in the school.

The programme consists of:

(1)   Three half-day preliminary visits by an Advisory Teacher.

(2)   Six weekly after school in-service meetings lasting one and a half hours for all the staff in the school, held within the school itself.

(3)   An Advisory Teacher working alongside the school staff for one day per week.

(4)   Six half days of supply cover for the release of the curriculum leader to develop a school policy.

(5)   Six half day follow-up visits by an Advisory Teacher over the following year.

(6)   The provision of equipment, materials and publications to implement the policy.

The Advisory Teachers will have their own area of approximately half the schools in the Authority for the purposes of liaison, visits and working alongside teachers, but both will work together as a team for in-service meetings and courses. This school based input is estimated to take up three days per week for each advisory teacher.

The school-based in-service meetings will aim to remove the anxiety some teachers have regarding science and technology and increase confidence and familiarity with skills and techniques as well as giving an appreciation of the importance of Science and Technology in primary education.

The meetings will predominantly be based on the teachers carrying out themselves activities they could do with their pupils. The content covered will be selected from:

(1)   the process of being scientific

(2)   patterns of classroom organizations

(3)   specific topic areas as examples

(4)   development of scientific and technological skills

(5)   the assembling of resources

(6)   scientific concepts and their development

(7)   assessment and record keeping.

These meetings will provide a basis for a PROGRAMME OF FURTHER DEVELOPMENT OF THE SCHOOL STAFF. Though an Advisory Teacher will continue to support, monitor and evaluate progress, major responsibility for the initiation of the work will gradually pass to the school with an emphasis on the role of the curriculum leader.

The submission described the plans for the general in-service provision in the following way:

In addition to the selective, school-based input, a programme of local in-service training will be established. It will be open to all schools and consist of several components:

(1)   Courses for curriculum leaders in Primary Science and Technology to promote the management skills required in implementing a whole school approach.

(2)   Courses to develop teachers' skills and knowledge in particular areas of Science and Technology.

(3)   The contribution of elements within courses for Heads and/or Governors to exemplify the need for Science and Technology in primary schools.

(4)   Support meetings for teachers where new Science and Technology schemes have been introduced into schools.

(5)   Support meetings for teachers responsible for Science to develop policies for Science and Technology in their schools.

This component, together with general guidance and assistance given to schools including regular 'surgeries' at the Primary Science and Technology Resources Centre is estimated to average one day a week for each Advisory Teacher.

These courses will take place as either meetings after school, residential courses or as day meetings. Supply cover of a hundred days per year is included for this in the proposal.

To support the in-service programme the Science Resources area of the Teachers' Centre will need to be expanded into a Primary Science and Technology Resources Centre to provide materials for in-service courses, act as a reference collection for teachers to consult and evaluate, and to provide loans to schools involved in curriculum development. A full-time technician/clerical assistant will be required to assist in the preparation and administration of the programme. In addition 34 days supply cover is included for teachers to attend regional in-service courses in Primary Science and Technology and 30 days for the release of teachers involved in (5) above to work in their schools to produce a school scheme for Science and Technology.

Schools participating in the above general input will also be provided with equipment, materials and publications on the recommendation of the advisory teachers and General Adviser (Science) to the Senior Adviser (Primary).

To implement the scheme it was proposed that two advisory teachers for science would be appointed for three years on Burnham Scale 3 with Teachers' Conditions of Service. After three years, the LEA would either use different funding arrangements to continue the appointments, which were on a permanent rather than secondment basis, or find suitable alternative posts for the persons appointed. The advisory teachers would be responsible to the Chief Education Officer via the General Inspector (Science), who would oversee the implementation of the scheme. The Advisory Service would provide an induction programme for the advisory teachers 'to promote the necessary skills for in-service training and working alongside teachers in schools'. Additionally, in an effort to foster long-term co-operation between schools, the formation of school groups, preferably based upon the feeder schools for each secondary school, was also proposed.

THE SCHEME AS IMPLEMENTED

Many educational innovations have been found to be ineffective not because they failed to produce the desired outcomes, but because they were never implemented in the first place - or at least they were never implemented in the way submissions envisaged they would be. Consequently, before considering the detailed modes of working adopted by the primary science advisory teachers (see the following chapter), it is necessary to examine the extent to which the scheme as submitted was ever put into practice. All three elements of the scheme can be examined from this angle, though the focus for the evaluation is principally on the school-based input and self-sustaining INSET mounted by schools themselves.

The school-based input
Setting up the scheme
Two advisory teachers, both women, were appointed in September 1986 according to the specifications set out in the submission. They were both recruited from the LEA's own schools with a good record as primary practitioners. Neither of them could be considered 'science specialists' from their initial teacher training experience and neither had occupied senior management posts. Becoming one of the first advisory teacher teams in the LEA, they often found themselves acting as the pathfinders for the growing ranks of advisory teachers that were to follow later.

The line management proposed in the submission was implemented since the initiation of the scheme and appears, from all sides, to have been very effective. The advisory teachers enjoyed a degree of autonomy and flexibility, while the General Inspector (Science) provided regular guidance, management and support.

The induction programme seems to be one of the few proposals set out in the submission which was not implemented to a significant level. It was generally agreed by participants that there had been little initial time for preparation, insufficient preliminary training in advisory teacher skills and not enough formal instruction in the workings and machinery of the LEA.

However, there were mitigating circumstances. Having taken the decision that work would begin in schools in September, there was little available time for a formal induction programme in between the advisory teachers leaving their schools in July and starting work in schools in the new academic year. Both advisory teachers had recently taken courses in primary science which included topics and skills relating to the management of change and emphasized the techniques of working with other teachers to promote science in the curriculum. In addition, being amongst the first advisory teachers in the LEA (only the mathematics advisory teacher preceded them by one year), a stock of experienced advisory teachers from which knowledge and skills could be drawn did not exist in the authority at the start of the Primary Science and Technology (PST) scheme. Later advisory teacher teams received a more formal induction programme from the LEA, including, where appropriate, contributions from the two advisory teachers in primary science. For the latter, however, it was very much a matter of 'learning on the hoof' and sharing experiences with other advisory teachers, including ones working on ESG schemes in other LEAs, as they progressed.

Selecting and approaching schools
The target of 12 schools per year was achieved and, strictly speaking, surpassed in that some smaller schools doubled-up to participate in a joint school-based input, although some did not receive the full six week programme. Although the submission stated that the schools *'will be identified by the Advisory Service'* in practice, schools had a much greater say in voluntarily applying for participation in the scheme than is suggested by this phrase. In both years of operation, schools were sent information about the advisory teacher team in primary science and invited to apply. Members of the advisory service then selected schools from the list of applicants.

Using a selection process which entailed an important element of self-election by schools gave some indication of the commitment of the headteacher - a key selection criterion outlined in the submission. Participants felt that in most cases the stated criteria were applied and this had the desired effect of selecting schools that had not already implemented a coherent science policy and yet were motivated to do so.

An initial proposal that schools could be organized into pyramid feeder groups implied two things: firstly that the groups could be used as a basis for organizing in-service provision and secondly that it may have led to some form of long-term networking between schools. Unfortunately, it appears that the first was difficult to implement for various practical reasons and therefore the foundation for the second was not adequately established. The proposal that each advisory teacher should take responsibility for half the geographical area of the LEA proved impracticable and difficult to co-ordinate with the availability of schools for the six week programme.

One central principle embedded in the scheme was the idea that the advisory teachers, in approaching curriculum development in schools, should remain responsive to the particular needs and organization of individual schools. *'No one method of curriculum organization can be claimed as the only possible method'*, the submission stated. In spite of strongly held personal preferences (e.g. for a topic-based approach), the advisory teachers were at pains to stress that their aims for different schools varied according to the school's professed needs or prevailing circumstances. Most of the teachers interviewed confirmed that flexibility was a characteristic of the advisory teacher team's practice.

The advisory teacher's experience in approaching schools and opening up negotiations with them has, in their view, endorsed the need, which was recognized in the submission, to formulate a contract between the school and the LEA. In some early instances, problems arose because insufficient attention was devoted to negotiating a clear understanding of the contract and the obligations it entailed for both parties. The advisory teachers sought a verbal contract rather than a formally written one.

Preliminary visits to school

Members of staff interviewed in the three 'retrospective' case-study schools corroborated the advisory teachers' accounts of their preliminary visits to schools scheduled to participate in the school-based in-service input. Three such visits were normally made, though depending on the circumstances, some schools could receive two or four visits. These visits were typically used to: identify the school's particular needs in primary science; explain what the scheme entailed and offered; negotiate the contract with the school's senior management; discuss strategies with the science co-ordinator; and meet staff to agree upon learning topics and approaches to the shared classroom teaching component. As with all these phases, a much more detailed analysis of the advisory teacher's preliminary work in schools is presented in Chapter Five.

After-school in-service meetings

The advisory teachers found that a five week programme suited the school calendar more than the original intention of six weeks. Furthermore the sequencing of these five weeks was occasionally adjusted further to avoid busy periods in schools.

The sessions, which were jointly presented by the advisory teachers, typically lasted from 4.00pm to 5.30pm. Once it had been established that the school contracted to arrange for all staff to attend these meetings, the full complement of staff normally took part, except in cases of illness. Some teachers who missed sessions asked the advisory teachers if they could attend a corresponding session in another school's programme. Apart from one session in the LEA's central Primary Science Resources Centre or visits to other schools, the meetings were held in the teachers' own schools. Over and above the standard topics incorporated into every school's programme (e.g. the use of resources, science books, assessment, record-keeping and practical problem-solving tasks for teachers), the precise content was adapted to suit the particular needs and interest of the individual school.

Working with teachers in their classrooms
During the working day before the evening's meeting, one of the advisory teachers worked with approximately four teachers in their classrooms. Interviews confirmed that these shared teaching experiences had taken place and that the advisory teachers were sensitive to the prevailing curriculum organization and teaching approaches within their school and classrooms. The advisory teachers rarely appeared to give 'demonstration lessons', preferring instead to take a team teaching approach in which the advisory teacher would, for example, initiate a problem-solving learning task in science with a group, while the teacher supervised the work of the rest of the class and intermittently observed the work of the advisory teacher and the science group. The teacher would then be invited to try out the science group task with the rest of the class before the advisory teacher returned the following week. The advisory teacher could either remain with each of the four teachers for the full five week programme or change teachers in order to incorporate more staff in the collaborative teaching element. Teachers normally volunteered themselves to work with the advisory teacher though, in some case-study schools, it was noted that teachers could feel compelled into 'volunteering' as a result of group pressures and expectations.

Supply cover
The provision for six half-days of supply cover had been made available

to schools and it had been used for a variety of purposes: e.g. releasing the school co-ordinator to establish a school resources centre for science, to visit another school, or to draft the school's science curriculum policy and recording system.

Follow-up visits

The evidence collected suggests that the intended six-half day follow-up visits by the advisory teacher in the year following the school-based input were not fully implemented. Although all the case-study schools had received some follow-up visits from the advisory teachers, they did not appear to approach the total of six in the following year. Moreover, whereas some of the visits described clearly made full use of a half-day period (e.g. covering for the school science co-ordinator so that the latter could work with other staff), others seemed to be rather less than half a day and less structured. The impression was gained that the follow-up visits did not possess the same clarity of purpose as other features of the scheme. It may well be that the full quota of follow-up visits, as well as their quality, were to some extent a casualty of the scheme's tight schedule and heavy workload for the advisory teachers. Further evidence of this surfaced in the latter years of the scheme, when, in response to requests to visit more schools and to help deliver National Curriculum training, the advisory teachers had a diminishing amount of time for follow-up visits to those schools which had received the main input.

Resources to implement the policy

Each of the schools involved in the school-based input received £200 for science resources. Examples of the resources acquired through these funds included new equipment, such as microscopes and magnets, shelving for the resource centre, and books. The purchasing of these materials and schools' disbursement of the £200 grant was co-ordinated and approved by the General Inspector (Science) with the assistance of the scheme's administrative support worker at the central resources centre.

Whereas the above has looked at the school-based input from a macro level, a portrayal and analysis of the advisory teachers' school-based input at a micro level is offered in Chapter Five.

Self-sustaining INSET in schools: the science co-ordinators

All case-study schools had appointed science co-ordinators (or curriculum leaders, as they are referred to in the submission). None were members of the senior management in the schools. It is important to note that the submission offers few guidelines on the role of the co-ordinators before, during and after the school-based programme. This aspect of the scheme is examined in detail in Chapter Seven.

The general INSET activities

As explained in the LEA's ESG submission, the in-service provision mounted under the general provision was open to schools which participated in the school-based programme, as well as those which had not been involved in the scheme. It included courses in which the advisory teachers had a substantial involvement and those in which they had little or no direct input but which were funded out of the ESG budget. Courses and support group meetings for co-ordinators and teachers included:

- Residential courses;
- One-day courses at a teachers' centre, mainly for co-ordinators;
- One-day courses at a teachers' centre by the General Inspector (Science);
- Self-help group which met once per half term at the teachers' centre and was initiated by the advisory teachers;
- Two-day courses at a local Polytechnic financed by ESG funding.

Examples of these courses and INSET activities are portrayed in the following chapter.

Other activities

The planned Resources Centre was established in a central teachers' centre and was administered by a full-time technician/clerical assistant.

Published schemes, reference books, activity-based books could be loaned and evaluated by teachers before schools committed funds to purchase their own copies. A wide range of materials and items of equipment were collected and made available for inspection and borrowing. Regular surgeries (Monday 4.00-5.00 p.m.) at which the advisory teachers were present to offer advice and loan materials were held, and teachers were able to call in at the Centre on any school day until 5.30p.m. The Resources Centre was also open during the summer holidays.

In addition to running the school-based programmes and making major contributions to organizing and delivering several of the general in-service inputs, notably the residential courses and one-day courses at the teachers' centre, the advisory teachers were also engaged in numerous *ad hoc* visits to non-scheme schools, contributions to other courses or more informal meetings in which they offered guidance and assistance to teachers, including those on the one-term course at a local polytechnic. The advisory teachers were active in attending regular LEA-wide meetings for advisory teachers in all areas of the curriculum and participated in the regional and national network of advisory teachers in science.

IMPLEMENTATION ISSUES

To conclude this review of the extent to which the proposals put forward in the submission were actually implemented, it is considered that there was a high degree of correspondence between what was said would happen and what actually happened in practice. Consequently, a notable feature of the scheme in action, was the absence of any significant gulf between rhetoric and reality. By and large, the main proposals governing both the school-based and general provision were put into effect.

There were, however, some exceptions to this finding. While differences between stated intentions and actuality often represented 'fine tuning' adjustments to practical necessities and changed circumstances, some of the modifications may have had serious consequences, especially the lack of an induction programme and the rather limited follow-up provision and support. Notwithstanding these exceptions, the overall picture of the LEA part of the scheme - the school-based and general provision - is that a carefully structured and coherent design became, in the main, a carefully structured and coherent in-service provision in reality. Whether or not it was an effective provision is the question to which we will shortly turn.

Unfortunately, the reasonably close approximation between intention and actuality was not evident in the school self-sustaining phase of the INSET scheme. This issue will be dealt with in detail in Chapter Seven. Suffice it here to say, that the schools appeared not to have the time, resources, cultural climate, and expertise in the delivery of INSET to take up the baton from the advisory teachers and run with the responsibility for providing continuing professional development in the teaching of science.

Before moving on to consider examples of the delivery of the general INSET provision in primary science, it is worth flagging a number of issues and problems which relate specifically to the implementation of the scheme.

Changing contexts

Over the course of the first stage of the scheme (1986-89) major changes took place which presented new opportunities or posed new problems for the effective implementation of primary science INSET. Professional Development Days, for example, were a new feature on the landscape and their emergence led the managers of the primary science scheme to consider how the ESG programme and Professional Development Days could be made to co-exist to their mutual benefit.

Similarly, the submission was drafted before the procedures for Grant Related In-Service Training (GRIST) and later the LEA Training Grants Scheme (LEATGS) were in operation. Hence, the science ESG scheme, to some extent, can be seen with hindsight to have been conceived and moulded in an INSET context which was very different to that within which it functioned in its final years. GRIST, for example, precipitated major changes in the accounting and administrative procedures for funding INSET. It terminated the practice of categorizing courses as 'approved' or 'non-approved', making it easier to run home-based courses, which were more responsive to local needs. It also facilitated the financing of Thursday-Saturday courses instead of the previous Friday-Sunday residential courses.

Managing the ESG scheme and advisory teacher teams

The scheme had a significant impact on the role and responsibilities of the inspector/adviser in charge of it. In short, it appeared to substantially extend the management and administrative tasks of inspectors and reduced the time they had available for visits to schools. Numerous examples of the management demands could be cited: drawing up submissions; extension proposals and DES monitoring records; representing the scheme on various LEA and regional committees; negotiating the allocation of resources and funding procedures with the LEA's financial department, advisory teachers and schools - e.g. car allowances, supply cover days and the £200 awarded to schools through the scheme; discussing and overseeing the selection of schools; offering support and guidance to the team of advisory teachers and so on. In view of the proliferation of initiatives involving advisory teacher teams, other inspectors doubtless experienced a similar trend. In consequence serious questions about the changing role of inspectors and advisers are raised:

* what were the displacement costs or opportunities foregone of taking on increased managerial responsibilities?

* what were the implications for the 'advisory profession' (and the recruitment to it) of a diminution in the opportunities for conducting school visits and advisory work with teachers - traditionally an aspect of the work which many advisers found the most rewarding?

* for many inspectors and advisers, the emergence of ESG schemes and advisory teacher teams probably constituted their first experience as an adviser or inspector in the management of budgets and personnel - how well prepared for these new demands were they? What level and kind of in-service training was provided to support them?

The careers of advisory teachers

A further issue arising out of the implementation of initiatives which depend on the deployment of advisory teachers relates to questions about the effects of recruiting good practitioners from schools for a limited period - what were the consequences for the schools which the advisory teachers leave behind and what kind of career paths were available to them after they have completed their advisory teacher contract?

As indicated in Chapter One, the advisory teachers voiced some apprehension and uncertainty about their future career prospects and expressed concern over the possible disruption and inconvenience their departure may have caused in schools. They were very aware of the possibility of encountering what other advisory teachers and secondees have described as 'post-secondment blues' (Harland 1990) - there appeared to be a high risk that many positions in schools could become frustratingly constrictive and routine after performing a stimulating, high profile and comparatively autonomous central role for a number of years. Interestingly, though, and contrary to the views expressed in an article cited earlier (Lofthouse 1987), full-blown advisers posts were not pointed to as likely career outlets but senior management positions in schools or initial teacher training were. Although the advisory teachers voiced concerns about their career prospects, especially during their third and final year of operation, it ought to be recorded that both successfully obtained new posts as head and deputy head in two local primary schools.

School involvement in the scheme

A number of complex dilemmas surrounded the problem of deciding on the quantity of schools that should be covered by the scheme and the process by which schools should be brought into the scheme. Two particular issues were noteworthy.

Firstly, the question arose whether the scheme should be based on the premise that effecting significant change in classroom practice often requires intensive and long-term support and therefore should be concentrated in a small number of schools, or whether it should be scattered more widely on the principle that it is better to achieve more limited growth in a greater number of schools. In addition to the school-based programme, it was noted that the advisory teachers visited other schools and provided short INSET sessions on a one-off and *ad hoc* basis for schools not involved in the full programme. The impression was gained (e.g. in interim reports to the DES) that there may well have been certain pressures, perhaps from schools and the DES, to increase the number of schools said to be visited or encompassed within the scheme by counting those with only peripheral involvement. If the policy for going for in-depth quality of impact rather than widespread coverage was to be adhered to, the pressure to use the number of schools involved as a performance indicator needed resisting.

Secondly, the issue arose to what extent schools should volunteer or be selected for the scheme? The advisory teachers and the General Inspector (Science) expressed strong preferences for a system which allowed schools to apply for participation in the scheme. *'We don't choose them, they choose us'*, stressed one of the advisory teachers. Although in circumstances where demand outstripped supply some selection was necessary, the system in practice seemed to allow schools the freedom to decide whether or not they wished to participate. Evaluations of other initiatives lend support to the advisory teachers in that voluntariness and ownership have been found to be key factors associated with effective change. However, the voluntary emphasis may well have impaired the capacity of the scheme to meet one of the uppermost objectives in mind when it was framed - namely, the desire to reach a core of teachers who rarely attend voluntary courses. The scheme as operated elicited the participation of 'reluctant teachers' but only in those schools where senior management, with or without the initial support of the whole staff, was prepared to volunteer the school. The problem of reaching 'reluctant teachers' in schools with 'reluctant senior management' remained unresolved in a system which was totally committed to voluntary self-selection. Some form of constructive pressure, perhaps with greater incentives, may well have been needed.

Differing perceptions of goals and 'needs'

Interviews with the advisory teachers and General Inspector (Science) revealed a substantial degree of consensus on the main aims and intentions of the scheme. They seemed, for instance, to be in agreement upon (*inter alia*):

*   the nature and quality of science (principally science as method) they sought to promote;

*   the emphasis placed on helping teachers with teaching and learning processes rather than providing ready-made materials;

∗   the value of adopting a flexible and pragmatic approach to curriculum development, whereby rather than providing all schools with a fixed and uniform set of prescriptions they preferred starting 'from where the school was at' and operating within its prevailing ways of working;

∗   the advantages of teaching science through across-the- curriculum themes, which were usually mapped out in topic-web diagrams.

Advisory teacher teams lacking such like-mindedness would probably find it more difficult to operate this model of providing INSET including, as it does, the joint delivery of workshops and support.

The main potential source for conflicting goals among all participants (i.e. school staff and the advisory teacher team) seemed to focus on the extent to which the advisory teachers should concentrate purely on pedagogic practices related to science and technology or whether they should allow their concern and guidance to broaden into teaching and learning styles in general. In cases demonstrating evidence of the latter approach, while the overt and 'official' intention was articulated in terms of developments in the science curriculum, a hidden agenda was implemented which had more to do with seeking general improvements in teaching and learning methods than science in particular. Headteachers, for example, sought participation in the scheme in an attempt to encourage some teachers to use more stimulating teaching techniques, regardless of the subject area. Similarly, the advisory teachers considered that little progress could be made with some teachers unless more fundamental developments in general classroom practices and organization were first accomplished.

One question which emerged from this was the degree to which it was practicable to achieve any significant advances in teaching strategies without this wider goal being openly acknowledged and understood by all concerned. Should this kind of 'hidden' and 'wider' agenda be made open and negotiated? It was interesting to note that many teachers were clearly not aware of their 'needs' in the science area until the advisory teachers and the scheme opened up their eyes to the new possibilities it offered - a point which is worth bearing in mind, when in later chapters, we consider a framework for identifying individual professional development needs. Clearly, 'needs' is not synonymous with teacher-only perceptions of 'wants'.

To sum up, the advisory teachers displayed a remarkable degree of agreement as to the main aims and objectives of the scheme. In the main, their views reflected those of the General Inspector (Science), though some interesting differences of emphasis emerged in the later stages of the scheme. These are touched upon in parts of the general INSET provision to which we now turn.

CHAPTER FOUR

THE GENERAL INSET ACTIVITIES IN PRIMARY SCIENCE

INTRODUCTION

Although the LEA's general INSET provision in primary science is not the prime focus of this evaluation, it is worth taking a look at some examples of it as a useful curtain-raiser to the central analyses of the advisory teachers' school-based input (Chapter Five) and the role of the school science co-ordinator (Chapter Seven). By way of illustration, the following examples serve to introduce some of the central messages relayed by the advisory teachers, as well the characteristics of the primary INSET culture, which permeated their approach to in-service training. The depiction of the residential course is especially useful in this respect.

In order to give the reader a flavour of these general in-service activities in science, as well as to raise issues relating to the process of their implementation, four types of provision are illustrated below:

(i)   self-help group
(ii)   input to a Baker Day
(iii)   residential courses
(iv)   National Curriculum Awareness Raising

THE SELF-HELP GROUP

The advisory teachers encouraged the science co-ordinators in the schools which received the school-based input in the first year to establish a self-help group. The advisory teachers took up a facilitating role: encouraging people to participate in the group, offering the Resources Centre for a meeting place and suggesting speakers. Having inaugurated a steering committee for the group, the advisory teachers hoped that their contributions could gradually recede into the background and that the teachers would take over full responsibility for servicing the group. After a promising start in 1987, when approximately 15 to 20 teachers, mainly co-ordinators, attended the termly meetings, the commitment to the group began to decline during the latter part of 1988 and early 1989.

Many of the key instigators left for various reasons (e.g. moves to other schools, different curriculum responsibilities) and others tended to participate in one or two meetings then drift away. One of the main organizers explained that new co-ordinators would come because they wanted some support *'but when they had gained enough expertise to cope, they wouldn't come any more - they'd gain the expertise, then move on'.*

In the early days, a co-ordinator or representative from the three 'retrospective' case-study schools attended at least one meeting. However, apparently typifying the general trend, none stayed to become active members: two handed over the co-ordinator's job to another colleague and the third invested more heavily in her own science course at a nearby polytechnic. At best, after the initial flush of enthusiasm, attendance at the meetings appears to have been sporadic - perhaps reflecting selective attendance depending on the relevance and popularity of the meeting's content and activity.

Issues relating to the role of the science co-ordinator such as the management of change were not dealt with by the group, instead it concentrated on *'the curriculum and on the skills they were trying to teach children'.* One speaker, for example, was invited to talk about her research into *'children's attitudes towards science'.* One session was devoted to discussing school science curriculum policy documents. For another meeting, one of the co-ordinators led a practical session on 'making things', linking science with design and technology. The group also compiled a handbook based on examples of teachers' project work in the LEA. A leading convener of the meetings felt that this booklet:

> *was the biggest thing we did - it was the main impact we had - it went out to many schools - it offered teachers tried and tested examples of projects and activities that we know worked.*

NATIONAL CURRICULUM AWARENESS RAISING DAYS

In the final year of the initial stage of the ESG scheme (1989), there were growing pressures on the advisory teachers to change aspects of their working patterns built up during the first two years. There were increasing demands for more central and uniform National Curriculum training inputs and their agenda for in-service sessions had to take account of the requirements and imperatives of the emerging statutory orders for science. Essentially though, while the vocabulary of the curriculum altered overnight (e.g. statements of attainment, programmes of study, levels, etc), the fundamental message transmitted by the advisory teachers remained intact (e.g. group planning, topic approaches, discovery learning, reassurance etc). These 'steady state' features, as well as more variable ones, were well demonstrated by this brief example from the general provision: a series of three half-day central training events to prepare teachers for the National Curriculum implementation in science.

The National Curriculum awareness raising and preparatory training sessions occurred in the Spring term of 1989 and consisted of three half-day sessions (at weekly intervals) for science co-ordinators at a central venue in the LEA. Like the residential courses described later, the General Inspector (Science) and the two advisory teachers devised and presented the sessions which would be repeated for different geographical zones in the LEA. In the first session, following a talk from the General Inspector (Science) on the latest developments in the statutory orders for science, the two advisory teachers led a discussion and activities designed to show how the attainment targets could be 'fitted into' topics such as 'James and the Giant Peach' and 'Clothes and Fabric'. The second session began with the advisory teachers setting up groups which were given the task of formulating topics to cover Attainment Target 13 on Energy up to Level 5. This was followed by a talk on the latest state of play in the development of assessments for the National Curriculum. The third session included work on record-keeping and implementation strategies for the National Curriculum in schools (e.g. National Curriculum Development Plans and school cluster arrangements). It was envisaged that the co-ordinators would disseminate the contents of the sessions to their colleagues back in school.

The main agenda for the sessions, backed up by copious handouts and booklets, seemed to comprise three elements:

-       **information giving** (e.g. the legal status of governors under the new act, the emerging documents on National Curriculum science, National Assessment, local policies for cluster group arrangements and further training);

-    **introducing/explaining the new vocabulary** - e.g. SATs, programmes of study, levels of attainment etc.;

-    **allaying fears** by advocating that science could easily be incorporated in existing approaches to flow charts and topic webs. The message that it was totally consistent with the methods advanced earlier by the advisory teachers was also conveyed.

In fact, in discussing various options for managing the introduction of National Curriculum science into their curriculum planning and delivery, teachers were encouraged to use the criteria of selecting the method with which they felt most familiar and comfortable. In this way, what surfaced as the preferred method of implementing the statutory orders - namely, the topic web - was perceived to have the key advantage of requiring minimal change and disturbance. In some respects, it appeared that the decision to choose a particular strategy for integrating the attainment targets and programme of study was justified on the basis of VALUE ORIENTATIONS (*'I prefer/ like starting from my usual topics'*) rather than on any intellectual or evaluatory experimentation (*'We need to implement several approaches and evaluate the benefits and disadvantages of each'*). As will be argued later in the study, the significance of such value-orientation should not be overlooked in the planning or evaluation of in-service training programmes.

In comparison with the earlier residential courses and the school-based inputs, the sessions were noticeably more didactic and less lively, with the course members taking on a more passive role. Providers and participants felt that there was too much to absorb in too short a time. In one of the groups observed by the researcher a debate emerged between an advisory teacher and a school co-ordinator. The latter argued that it was nigh impossible to get a group working on a topic which allowed the children to operate at one of four different levels, depending on their individual attainment and needs. Although the advisory teacher maintained, very persuasively, that such differentiation was feasible, it was ironic that no corresponding commitment to differentiation for the professional development of the teachers attending these sessions had been applied. In this case, rather than the medium being the message, it was obviously a case of 'do as I say, not as I do'. Though, to be fair, the available resources most probably precluded the possibility of differentiated programmes of National Curriculum-related INSET.

THE RESIDENTIAL COURSES

After the school-based inputs, arguably the most substantial form of INSET provision organized under the ESG primary science scheme was the LEA's annual residential course. For this reason alone, it is worth considering the organization and delivery process of these courses. In addition, they serve to introduce many of the issues which are later addressed in more detail when a close look is taken at the school-based input.

The researchers attended two of the three residential courses and in focusing on the process of delivery, informal participant observation techniques were used. This involved the researchers 'joining in' or 'going native' for much of the courses' duration, rather than remaining 'outside' the action, adhering to structured or systematic observation or interview schedules. This meant that the material may be described as more 'impressionistic'.

The location and timing of the two observed residential courses (delineated here as course B and course C) followed a similar pattern: they were held at a College of Higher Education in the region, to which the course members were taken by coach on Thursday after school. The courses finished after tea on Saturday afternoon. Course B ran in September 1988 and course C in June 1989. An earlier residential course (A) run in April 1988, had a similar timetable, and though it was not observed by the evaluation team, reference is made to the course programme supplied by the advisory teachers.

Membership of courses B and C numbered approximately 32. Various criteria of selection were mentioned: e.g. *teachers we don't know* and/ or *schools* which had not worked with the advisory teachers, as well as unsuccessful applicants for other LEA science-oriented courses. However, a few previous course attenders were present on each occasion, as well as teachers from schools in receipt of the school-based INSET. Only two teachers from one of the five case study schools attended either course B or C. This certainly suggests that the residentials served the purpose of widening the audience of the advisory teachers' message perhaps rather more than as a follow-up or precursory strategy designed to link with the advisory teachers' school-based work. In course B, a number of pairs of teachers from individual schools were attending - a strategy intended to provide mutual support for the teachers. Course C did not have this criterion apparently because the demand for the course was too high to allow it.

The course programme showed shifting content emphasis in line with impending national imperatives, particularly the implementation of National Curriculum science. Taking a rough notion of nine sessions per course (one: Thursday night; five: Friday; three: Saturday), the main foci of the courses were as follows:

	Course A (Spring '86)	Course B (Autumn '88)	Course C (Summer '89)
Information	2	2	1
Science Knowledge input	-	-	3
Practical/Science process	2	3	2
Topic/Planning	.5	.5	2
Provision perusal	1.5	.5	-
Science through Drama	1	1	-
Presentation and Preparation	2	2	1

Hence, it can be seen how Course C, which significantly was mounted immediately prior to the implementation of the National Curriculum in science, had a much greater focus on topic planning and aspects of science knowledge (physical science attainment targets) than earlier residential courses.

Reflecting the increased emphasis on knowledge and content, and in line with the main aim of upgrading their knowledge of science content, much of Course C was planned by the General Inspector (Science) rather than the advisory teachers. It was pointed out that all the residential courses had been jointly planned by the advisory teachers and the General Inspector (Science) but by Course C there was only one primary science advisory teacher still in post. (The second had taken up her new permanent post in one of the LEA's schools but was returning as a course tutor for this residential.) Significantly, as the remaining advisory teacher felt she could not cover the science knowledge aspects apart from electricity, she had requested the assistance of the General Inspector (Science).

Looking at all the residentials, the forms of INSET led by the advisory teachers included:

(i)   group formation/dynamics exercises

(ii) group planning - topic brainstorming

(iii) practical workshops - experiential approach

(iv) entertainment/presentations

The first and fourth of these indicate a strong emphasis on the social and affective aspects of the residential. For example, concerns were expressed by the advisory teachers at the start of Course C that because practical 'hands-on' experiences and expectations were not being met, the course members were unhappy. This emphasis on learning through practical experiences *'give me something I can use with my pupils'* or *'teach me in a form that I can directly apply to my teaching'* - resonated throughout all the observed in-service activities and signals a very important and pervasive dimension to the primary INSET culture. It is well illustrated in the researcher's fieldwork notes on the C Course. It is worth quoting from these notes at length because they highlight a very important and fascinating tension between the preferred learning mode within the primary INSET culture and an alternative learning mode which is more akin to secondary and higher education and more 'theoretical', 'intellectual' and knowledge-based. Underpinning these notes is a genuine, though not entirely successful, attempt by the course providers to bridge these two expectations about learning and INSET.

'I arrived on Thursday at about 6.00pm, just as the coach [from the LEA] was unloading baggage and teachers. Advisory teacher 1 sorted out rooms, welcomed everyone - she told me as we were finding rooms that the criterion of selection for the course was "people they

didn't know", *"hadn't been on the course before"*, *and this would mean establishing 'the group' would be very important as course members also didn't really know each other. However, it turned out that one or two previous attenders were present also. [The General Inspector (Science) also said that another criterion for selection was unsuccessful applicants to a logo course ...]*

... After dinner, we all congregated in one of the teaching rooms which had black blinds drawn down, two large tables, overhead projectors. [In arrangement, it felt rather like a science lab, with us as the pupils seated around science benches.] The General Inspector (Science) began by welcoming us, and referring to the pre-course questionnaire sent out to participants asking which Attainment Targets would be the preferred focus. Attainment Target 12 had been most popular, but, he said, this needed a course on its own. The chosen attainment targets were LIGHT AND COLOUR, FORCES, ENERGY, ELECTRICITY. Tonight we would be dealing with LIGHT AND COLOUR. He said he wanted to stress very heavily that this was not to be for the children, but was for them - tomorrow afternoon the task would be to turn what they had learned into a form suitable for children.

He introduced and handed over to another course tutor, a secondary teacher who began by referring to and reading from his M.Ed thesis ... on children's misconceptions in science. He had also commented that he "knew a little bit about science", and that he "needed to say to children that he didn't know". By overhead projector, he took us through his tabulations of percentages of his own pupils' mis-views on light and also those of some Swedish researchers, demonstrating children's regression in scientific understanding. He showed us diagrams, on OHP, of experiments on light travelling, reflection, held up pin-hole camera etc. At one point, a teacher asked .. why he wasn't using 'real' experiences of light travelling, like cracks of light showing through the door in the dark, she found all these diagrams of mirrors difficult and wouldn't children too. She was dealt with diplomatically: primary had the time to do this, secondary had a syllabus to get through. The references to children's misconceptions were brought up again and [Advisory Teacher 1] contributed that perhaps after the National Curriculum, and more science, children might not regress so far - he should do all his 'experiments' on pupils' understanding again in a few year's time! I suspect this diffused a moment of tension - there was - if not yet hostile - a very dulled atmosphere among the teachers. They were, it turned out, quite overwhelmed and threatened by this and the next input on COLOUR. One implication was possibly that secondary children's inaccurate scientific concepts were due to lack of/inadequate science teaching in the primary school thus far. The presenter went on to say that children found it difficult to talk about why they held their scientific ideas, even though they could explain what they believed. He stressed it was "important for children to talk" and why worksheets wouldn't do . For me, there was a sense that, with this point, primary teachers were being lectured at on their own patch/forte. The handout on LIGHT was not really referred to.

At about 9.15 the General Inspector (Science) took over, and did a 'lecture' on COLOUR, pointing out the close connection to LIGHT. He began by challenging the audience to identify whether there were in fact seven stripes of colour on a rainbow. Through OHPs and colour filters, in the now [semi] darkened room ... he helped us through understanding principles of the spectrum and filtering and mixing colour, stating that "Filters don't dye the light" etc. It was a lively, extrovert approach/performance [perhaps virtuoso didactic secondary science teaching?] - all OHPs were, he told us, the content of his handout - and he finished with explanation of why mixing pigment was not the same as mixing colour and how filters used in many primary schools would not be successful: they weren't the proper equipment. The session ended with a reference to 'non-statutory guidelines'. He said he had driven to York to collect enough copies for the group, but it turned out most schools had now received copies. Those who had not got copies were encouraged to take one. These were referred to by the General Inspector (Science) on Saturday, in his final talk, but did not feature in the sessions again ... Advisory teacher 1 had three large sheets of paper, with FORCE, ENERGY, ELECTRICITY written on and numbers 1-10: this was for each teacher to select two out of three for tomorrow's session. I noticed at this point that FORCE and ENERGY had most takers, ELECTRICITY least, but because a fair number had already left the room these allocation sheets were not complete, and re-appeared at breakfast the next morning. One or two teachers I spoke to said they already knew about electricity. The first presenter was engaged in a discussion about discovery learning, and was making the point of "needing to

know what questions to ask pupils to lead them to the right conclusion" :
this was to a rather unconvinced looking male course member.

Spread through the bar, there were several groups of course members
- I sat with a somewhat dazed and subdued group by the TV, who were
half watching the tennis. Asked how they had enjoyed it so far, one
said she would "rather have had a go with the filters herself", others
just referred to being tired: it was "a bit much" after a day of teaching
or doing National Curriculum training already this week. Someone
else said that it reminded them of their science lessons - she didn't
understand it then either. Everyone else laughed loudly and
appreciatively at this. I took this to mean that they had all been rather
uncomfortable and fazed by the input - this wasn't what they expected
from a primary science course.

FRIDAY:
Over breakfast I had a seat next to the General Inspector (Science),
and he told me that the intention of the course was to challenge people
first and then give them what they wanted - practical stuff [the warm
glow] - after that: i.e. put what they'd learnt into practice. Another
version he gave was to familiarize teachers with the accurate use of
the vocabulary of science - particularly in the physical sciences rather
than biological ones. Later, he also stated that he had planned the first
evening session as a listening only session as it was thought that after
a day teaching, a practical problem solving session would be too
tiring.

The prime objective of the colour sessions was to show participants
the problems in explaining and understanding what was happening in
order to discourage them teaching it. It is frequently done in Key
Stages 1 & 2 but the National Curriculum places it in Key Stage 4 as
the principles behind it are quite abstract. He, at a later point in the
day, said that he'd planned much of the course programme. He talked
of the average age of the LEA's primary teachers being 35, which
meant they were products of girls-grammar school science teaching
of 20 years ago.

I ended up in the ENERGY group, working with the secondary teacher
in the room that was used the night before. The General Inspector

(Science) was in another room doing FORCE, and the two advisory teachers and new advisory teacher were doing ELECTRICITY in a room on the floor above. Handwritten signs pointed out the directions. About ten teachers sat silently waiting to start. His first comment was that "last night was too much [information]", and in half a morning he was going to cover half a term's work. He encouraged us to "ask questions", children too would rather "cocoon themselves".

He added he was a physicist, and to a physicist it made sense to do force before energy. He then launched into another secondary performance of climbing on desks to illustrate that energy = work and work = force x distance, and writing "energy" tables on OHP for us to complete through his questioning guidance. He had used two volunteers to hold and lift up and down weights etc etc. Someone pointed out that "two lots of work" was confusing to children, "lots of" and "work" meant something else to children. He sympathised, and said could we use "bits of work". I guess he was following the brief to explain science terminologies, and the teacher couldn't carry her point any further. We got to joules and newtons. He showed us various examples of energy -flywheels, steam engines, bells, clockwork toys, solar etc. When ELECTRICITY was mentioned, someone else contributed that primary children should do STATIC ELECTRICITY first: "That's what the advisory teacher says". He agreed. He also showed us a plate of nuts, and said peanuts were good for burning and thus demonstrating energy; digital thermometers; spirit lights; he also referred here to the advisory teacher and her recommendation of night lights. He finished off by going very quickly through the end of his handout booklet which showed "some ideas for Key Stage 2" and examples of what they do in secondary for Key Stage 3.

Advisory teacher 2 had drifted in by this point and as we were encouraged to "have a play" with the various bits of energy examples, she "bent my ear" about the course so far. It was, she said, very worrying the way it had gone. People were very unhappy with the lack of practical work so far and the group wasn't gelling you could tell that by the bar being empty by 11.00 at night! It just wasn't the way they had run primary science courses. They always did getting-to-know-you exercises, and that was important. They were going to rectify it all this afternoon.

It struck me so forcefully, then and throughout the course, how primary teachers are endemically resistant to learning anything unless it is delivered in the modes they themselves teach in - a safe environment never threatening, 'doing' rather than listening. The two advisory teachers were to demonstrate considerable skill and effort in recreating that "protected" primary classroom and staffroom culture for members: both in working sessions and in the social aspects of the course.

Over coffee, it became apparent that a number of people were unenthusiastic about the FORCE session, although the General Inspector (Science) party-piece of pulling a tablecloth from under crockery seemed to cause some comment and amusement. The references to science days at school continued.

The ELECTRICITY session began with advisory teacher 1 doing a getting-to-know-you exercise: first demonstrating the task of telling three things about your neighbour to the group by talking about her new colleage in three sentences, ending up "she doesn't like black-pudding" (breakfast today) and it got a loud laugh. The new advisory teacher then gave three light-hearted pieces of information about advisory teacher 1. The mood of relaxation and security was instantaneous. Advisory Teacher 1 told us that electricity was what she was asked to do in about 85 per cent of schools and that we were just going to "get on with" the activities in the [very large handout] on electricity. (i.e. No way didacticism here!) The handout was not to be done sequentially with children. Advisory teacher 1 and the other two intervened strategically during this discovery learning, a whole-class teaching point on not using rechargeable batteries was made, the rest of the advisory teacher's interactions was constant reassurance and enthusiasm to the pairs of teachers at work on circuits. A good time was had by all.

At lunch - with some of the group - one teacher told us that she now knew that she had told her son everything wrong for his science exam on colour, she's told him about mixing pigment. I asked my neighbour, who was a supply teacher with a science degree and PGCE training, how she'd found the sessions. She said it was "just 'O' level physics really", and then said on further questioning that she wasn't sure how she could use it at all.

After lunch, we all congregated in a room with easy chairs, and the two advisory teachers were in business. First was a party game of find the others with the same scientist pinned on their back. Much fun. Extra labels made for me, the General Inspector (Science) and secondary teacher: we all had to party.

This party exercise thus made the groups who were going to do a National Curriculum planning exercise. Advisory teacher 1 told us that staff needed to plan together now, everyone has something to offer, brainstorming was great, and you can't do it alone - "every idea you have is a good one or else you feel you haven't got a brain at all." She took us through the handout which she had re-written on a flip-chart. This was a way of planning a thematic approach and she made ironic comment on this new vernacular (once it was a project). The exercise of using this planning framework had been done by her and another advisory teacher - a course member - and "it was hard work wasn't it". The prescription - for such it certainly was - was to "think of your project first - just like you've always done: don't get out your National Curriculum and say what am I going to do". They were to plan through to a mini-theme, and some specific activities, state attainment targets and finally get to an introduction to the theme with the children: this was the [five minute] presentation for tonight - tomorrow there'd be a "making and doing" session on a technological aspect of the chosen theme. An example of a planned cross-curricular project on HOMES was displayed. The General Inspector (Science) commented they should remember "Attainment Target 1 should be half of all you do".

... Saturday was making and doing day. I had been asked by advisory teacher 2 to spend some time in the difficult group; and perhaps foolishly - in retrospect - complied. It meant I went native for the morning rather than monitor all the activities and teachers with any thoroughness. However, the pattern was very clear: pairs of teachers (as recommended/instructed) were scattered through the three rooms making a wheelbarrow, an automatic sprinkler, a working lift, a water-wheel, fire-engines, peep-holes with filters, an adventure playground for a gerbil etc. One group (HOUSES) stayed as a unit and made a house, size about a metre, with burglar alarm and pressure points, door bell. Someone had made little pieces of furniture to go inside: hardly FORCE, ENERGY or LIGHT/COLOUR.

The course team floated through the groups, essentially responsive. There was - it seems - very little communication between groups apart from borrowing hole-punches etc. From 12.00, all models were put on display in the Senior Common Room, where today the suitcases were being stored and coffee had been taken. I was extremely surprised, and even more guilty about my choice of role that morning, when it became apparent that there was to be no official feedback or sharing achievements with the whole group. However, the lack of extrapolation and reflexivity equally was the experience of the course's members.

In retrospect, I found this individualization/responsive mode very interesting. If the teaching-primary-teachers-as-they-themselves-teach theory holds, then it raises the question of how they will interpret this approach in their own classroom. At lunch, someone commented that it was alright doing it here, but it had taken them three hours, and could children really be expected to do the same, and had teachers the time.

At lunch the group I sat with repeated some of General Inspector's (Science) comments on colour and force: they had then, I thought, internalized those sessions after all. They were discussing the difference between mass and weight, pigment and colour - and one was the teacher who'd glumly said to me on Thursday night that she wished she could have had a play with the filters. Someone else felt that she now knew she was going to do homes as a topic next term - [because the advisory teachers had given it official recommendation/ status? It was also a point advisory teacher 1 made: the advisory teachers present in the planning groups had had their ideas taken as gospel, and had to devise ways of taking a lower profile - like staying longer at tea].

To put this extract in context, it has to be said that in terms of describing the implementation of the residential courses (or for that matter the vast majority of this ESG scheme's in-service activities), the practical experiential approach to professional development was the dominant *modus operandi*. The inclusion in this course of more didactic and theoretical inputs was clearly precipitated by the perceived requirement to respond to the expressed need by many teachers for help with the knowledge-base underlying the statutory orders for science. Indeed, as the General Inspector (Science) later pointed out, for him *'the nature of the requirement for an input of science knowledge dictated a particular delivery style. The teachers' references to science days at school were correct in that there was an attempt to get the participants up to Level 5 in some attainment targets. The National Curriculum required that words such as 'force, weight, work, energy, power and mass' were used in their scientific sense hence the similarity to an 'O' level physics lesson. Practical work to find out for themselves was not a suitable way to learn conversions.'*

The case of the C course spotlights the dilemma of whether providers of primary INSET should accept the hegemony of the primary INSET culture by working reassuringly within it or challenge teachers to transgress its boundaries, and hence limitations, by recognizing the value of learning in a more reflexive and intellectual mode as well. To accentuate the former is to risk pandering to the type of learning primary teachers are used to. As such, it is likely that teachers' 'wants' will be satisfied but not perhaps their 'needs'. On the other hand, as the case illustrates, to emphasize a more theoretical mode is likely to lead to the alienation of the intended audience. Arguably, one of the main adverse effects of over-reliance on the practical and experiential approach is that it rarely encouraged opportunities for reflection on the processes of science (Attainment Target 1 in the National Curriculum for science.) Thus, while in both B and C courses, there were ample opportunities to 'experience' problem-solving experiments in science and technology, neither course provided a forum for critical and shared deliberation on scientific processes and appropriate pedagogies for developing it. Consequently, the danger remains that teachers will only implement 'what they've done or experienced' in the INSET event, without extrapolating from it on the basis of understanding why and how they have carried out the practical activity.

AN INPUT TO A BAKER DAY

In the Autumn term 1988, two schools joined forces to initiate a weekend course for all its staff in a local hotel. Funded out of the schools' Baker Day resources, the first day was devoted to developments in science and technology, on which the main inputs were provided by the two advisory teachers.

Accentuating the importance of the whole-school approach, the advisory teachers began by telling their audience that they were going to demonstrate how '*to get science out of any topic*' and relate it to the requirements of the attainment targets.

The theme for the day was 'Homes and Houses'. Reminiscent of the activities run at the residential course B, groups of teachers were requested to draw up a topic web showing how the selected theme could cover all curriculum areas, including science. Having '*shared*' their webs, worksheets on the theme, 'Homes and Houses', were circulated and groups were required to use one sheet to carry out at least one experiment. Upon completion of these tasks, there was a plenary session, followed by a talk from the General Inspector (Science) on the National Curriculum for science.

The predilection within the primary INSET culture for practical and experiential learning was manifested throughout the day and, in fact, it appears to have been transferred directly from the residential course B. Indeed, impressed by the activity-based approach used in course B, a science co-ordinator at one of the schools had allegedly persuaded the headteachers not to ask the advisory teachers to give a talk on progression and continuity in science (as originally planned) but rather to invite them to lead teachers into practical experiments. Most of the day was spent in this mode. Once again, the two advisory teachers demonstrated impressive sensitivity and astuteness in spotting potential problems in group dynamics and intervening before situations and morale deteriorated.

In the plenary session, there was a general discussion on how the various practical experiments could be applied in the classroom. Although time was not plentiful, the tenor of the discussion focused on tasks that pupils could be asked to do. In contrast, there was little mention of what knowledge and skills were intended to be taught or how progression could be tackled. When one teacher voiced anxieties about her lack of scientific knowledge and skills, she was told that there may not be a need to understand all the relevant scientific principles so long as the teacher was prepared to discover things with the pupils. This exemplified a pivotal strand in the advisory teachers' philosophy, as well as a convincing reason why many primary teachers find it such an attractive and reassuring message: it offers a plausible 'coping strategy'. Even with only a modicum of rudimentary scientific knowledge and theory, teachers can be made to feel they can cope with the problem of doing science in their classroom.

CHAPTER FIVE

THE ADVISORY TEACHERS AT WORK

INTRODUCTION

The focus of this chapter is a detailed description and analysis of the scheme's school-based advisory teacher input in action. It seeks to address four major questions about the work of the advisory teachers and the classroom practitioners they supported at school level :

* What are the main features of the implementation of the school-based advisory teacher input?

* From teachers' reactions to the work of the advisory teachers, what is the evidence of its impact?

* What factors determine such reactions?

* From the evidence, what lessons can be learned which may contribute to improving school-based advisory teacher activity?

In addressing these questions, by means of description and analysis of two schools' involvement with the ESG scheme, the evaluators fully recognize that they cannot give an account which comprehensively covers the advisory teachers' working methods with, in all, some hundred teachers, in over 30 schools during their three years of school-based activity. Consequently where relevant, reference is made to significant variations mentioned by the advisory teachers in discussion with the research team.

Reference back to the original submission outlined in Chapter Three will show that the school-based input under scrutiny here consisted of an advisory teacher working alongside individual teachers for one day a week, with both advisory teachers giving an in-service session to the whole staff in the evening. This five week programme has been given the nomenclature **THE MAIN PROGRAMME**. PRELIMINARY VISITS by the advisory teachers to the school preceded this Main Programme.

It is interesting to note, at this point, that although the approach and content of the INSET sessions were clearly stated in the submission, no such detail was offered in relation to the 'working alongside staff' component. Yet this development strategy, in effect, constituted a total of at least 20 hours of advisory teacher activity in each school, as opposed to seven-and-a-half hours of INSET. Likewise, the submission did not indicate the substance of the three half-day preliminary visits. Consequently, these aspects of the school-based input seemed particularly important areas for the evaluation to describe and analyse, and form major sections of the chapter. First however, cameos of the two 'prospective' schools where the observation of the school-based input took place are offered, as well as accounts of the state of science in each school. A brief discussion of the wider educational context in which the observed input took place concludes the first section of this chapter.

THE SCHOOLS AND THEIR SCIENCE BASELINES

Following discussions with advisory staff, two 'prospective' schools were selected and agreed to take part in the evaluation. They were both to be involved in the school-based input during the second half of the Autumn Term 1988.

SCHOOL A was a junior and infant school, with around 180 four to eleven year old pupils organized into six classes, two of which were split-age ranges. The school served what was described by the head as 'a wide and mixed' catchment area : some children were bussed in from areas well beyond the immediate vicinity, others lived locally. The parents were mentioned as being particularly supportive of the school and '*keen for their children to do well*'. The building was 25 years old.

The seven staff, comprising five full-time and two part-time teachers, were (with the exception of one temporary part-time teacher) all long-standing : the most recent member had been at the school five years, and all the rest, including the deputy, had worked there for between 12 and 19 years. The head had been in post for eleven years.

The state of science teaching in the school was, according to the head, '*a hit and miss affair ... though the staff may have been doing it without realizing, it was likely to happen by default rather than as a conscious decision ...*'. With regard to the ESG initiative, the head stressed that the staff had '*definitely wanted the advisory teachers to come in, science is our one and only priority*'.

SCHOOL B was a junior and infant school with approximately 200 four to eleven year old children organized into seven classes, three of which were split-age ranges. The head described the school as serving a '*mixed*' community, with most of the children 'materially well-off'. A strong and active PTA gave the school a good deal of support mainly, as yet, in '*financial and social areas*'. Two years previously, the school had celebrated its centenary. The building was split-site : what was termed '*the infants department*' occupied the classrooms of the original school and the juniors were housed in an adjacent but separate two-storey block across the playground.

The seven full-time staff had spent very different amounts of time at the school. One teacher had 20 years experience there, the rest of the permanent staff had been in post for between two and five years. Two of the staff were temporary, one of whom - the supply deputy - was in post only for the Autumn Term until the newly-appointed deputy took up her position in January. The present head had arrived at the school in January 1988, this was his third headship within the authority and he was the second person to hold the post of head at school B in the past three years.

Science teaching was described as 'very patchy' by the head:

> ... *there has been some work in Nature Study of a traditional kind, but very little evidence of the technical or physics side ....*

He also explained that, for him, involvement in the ESG initiative was a deliberate management strategy to build his staff into a team and he had encouraged them to indicate their preference for curriculum development in the area of science in order to qualify for selection to the scheme. Having experienced the school-based input at his previous school, he firmly believed in its potential for fostering long-term corporate and co-operative attitudes, which in turn greatly facilitated curriculum development work in other areas.

Clearly then, though each head depicted their school's science curriculum (or lack of it) in a broadly similar way, the professional climate of the two schools was markedly different. The long-term stability of school A's staff and senior management contrasts sharply with the somewhat disparate 'connectedness' to the school exemplified by the staff of school B. (It should be noted the term 'connectedness' is not meant to imply anything about commitment. It is meant to convey that the staff's familiarity with each other and with the context and culture of the school was likely to be less than in school A.) Such contrasts in staff composition were likely to present different challenges to the advisory teachers' implementation of the school-based input and the long-term development of primary science and technology, as well as provide a useful comparison for the evaluation.

The teachers' own accounts of their science teaching before the ESG scheme, by and large, corroborated those of the heads'. There were one or two notable exceptions in each school, where a teacher described science activities that seemed to carry all the hallmarks of a consciously open-ended investigative approach AND were undertaken on a regular basis. For the rest, four kinds of deficit in their science teaching were apparent or referred to.

First, one or two staff in each school readily admitted that science did not really feature in their curriculum planning or classroom delivery, largely because they had no predilection for it:

... I do very little science, I don't really like it.

... Like many teachers, I steer clear of science, I'm definitely not trained for teaching it.

Second, some teachers implied that in their personal view of curriculum priorities, science was not considered to have anything like the importance of 'the basics'. Thus, compared with maths and language, science was offered less often, in less 'prime' learning times, and sometimes to less children:

... I try to make sure the children do maths, language and art activities every day. We usually do science once a week, but it's not always possible for them all to have a go.

... I concentrate on maths and language in the Autumn Term, and do some science in the Spring and Summer.

... in the mornings I always do maths and language when they're fresh, in the afternoons I do things like history, geography and science.

Third, some reiterated what might be termed the 'subliminal science' rhetoric : '*I'm doing it but I didn't know I was*'. Yet a deficit could still be apparent here: in their more detailed descriptions of science practice, these teachers indicated that, even though the CONTENT may justifiably be given the name of science - more particularly the natural sciences, the specific ACTIVITIES undertaken with children often could not - be described as constituting scientific investigation:

> *... Last year, [in science] we probably did three practical things, but if you count class discussion, TV and looking up information in books, I'd say science took up 15-20 per cent of the curriculum.*

> *... It depends how you classify science. We did a big topic on Autumn, mainly as a class. My science work tends to be done through class discussion. In topic, I write on the board and the children copy it.*

Finally, one or two infant teachers referred to practical activities - water and sand play and baking as examples of their science work. However, in each case it was clear that these were generally undertaken by the children unsupervised or in the presence of a parent rather than the teacher, while the teacher herself concentrated on other curriculum areas, most often language and number work. It may be that without skilled questioning, such activities could not properly qualify as scientific inquiry and investigation. The low investment of teacher time - and teacher-led talk - in such 'science' activities is perhaps another example of the relative status of the subject itself.

Such was the baseline from which the advisory teachers were working. All in all, these teachers no doubt presented a very typical range of attitudes towards the teaching of primary science. Almost universally they had little experience of science in their own secondary education (beyond 'O' level natural sciences) and, other than environmental studies, it had not greatly featured in their initial training. Only three of the 13 recounted undertaking any INSET with a specific primary science focus. It would hardly be an exaggeration to conclude that, prior to the ESG scheme, 'primary science' was not greatly liked, fully comprehended or valued by the majority of the staff from the case-study schools.

THE WIDER CONTEXT

Finally, before seeking to answer the question 'What did the school-based input look like?', it is important to locate the study in its wider educational context. It should be remembered that throughout the Autumn Term of 1988, when the advisory teachers were undertaking preliminary visits to the case-study schools and then, in the second half of the term, implementing the scheme, the Education Reform Act and particularly the National Curriculum, were ever more prominent in the primary sector's consciousness. Schools were receiving the draft proposals, albeit in very limited numbers. Whilst the designation of science as a core curriculum subject undoubtedly assisted the sense of relevance of the ESG advisory teachers' work in the eyes of the participating teachers, it placed new demands on the scheme's content, particularly the after-school INSET component. Teachers, in turn, brought their own agenda of issues and anxieties heightened by the implications of the National Curriculum: assessment, progression, the extent of their own scientific understanding and so on.

At the same time, the increasing pressure from schools on LEAs to provide information and INSET about science in the National Curriculum inevitably had begun to affect the work-load of the advisory teachers, and - significantly - its emphasis. Finally, the advisory teachers themselves, now in the third and final year of their secondment, were beginning to express some concern about securing a suitable placement before LMS affected their re-entry to a permanent post. The precise influence of some of these factors on the school-based input is beyond the scope of this study, but it is nevertheless important to bear them in mind as factors which may have impinged on the work of the advisory teachers and the school-based input. However, it should be noted that at the stage when the evaluation undertook to monitor the scheme in action, the original design of the school-based input had already been remolded to some degree : for instance, the six-week programme in schools had been reduced to five, largely because of problems with school terms. The other components of the advisory teachers' school-based work - particularly working alongside - had evolved into a fairly regular pattern of activity. The looming imperative of the National Curriculum did not appear to affect the design of the scheme or the *modus operandi* of the advisory teachers to any substantial degree. Having established the science base-line and context in which the scheme was operating, we now turn to the depiction and analysis of the school-based input itself. Its three main components, namely:

* the preliminary visits;

* the Main Programme - working alongside;

* the Main Programme - after-school INSET;

are considered separately and in sequence. A final section entitled 'The Sequel: Teacher Reactions' discusses the perceived immediate impact of the advisory teachers' work.

THE PRELIMINARY VISITS

... we don't go in with a list of notes and tick them off, because we found that's off-putting for the staff. We've found it's easier to go in and talk to the staff as though it was a chat ... there isn't a typical first visit, all the visits we do are at various levels because either we know some of the staff or sometimes we don't know any. We know the majority of heads, but some we don't know at all. So there's all those relationships we have to build into. The same information tends to get given out, but its given out in many different ways. Sometimes less threatening than others, sometimes we have to put in extra visits, but we don't know that till we get there. (Advisory Teacher)

The initial visits

The advisory teachers began the school-based input in the half term prior to the main five-week programme of INSET meetings and working alongside. An initial visit to each school took place in order to meet the staff and outline what their involvement in the ESG scheme would entail. Due to unforeseen circumstances, the advisory teachers' normal practice of undertaking this first encounter together, did not happen in one of the two schools, and it was only the advisory teacher involved in the working alongside component who met the staff on this occasion. A visit was made by both advisory teachers later. At the second school, both advisory teachers together introduced the scheme and themselves to the staff. The introductions took place in the staffroom with the staff as a whole during a lunch hour. In one school this had been preceded by a discussion with the deputy which also clarified the nature of the school's involvement.

This initial visit clearly had a number of functions, such as 'PR' and negotiation of the timetable, as well as the presentation of key issues about the school-based input itself.

These issues included the background of the scheme, and a definition of its main aims. It was worded in terms of '*getting the school going in primary science*' and helping each staff member make a '*tiny step forward*' in their teaching of primary science and technology (PST), '*increasing confidence*' and '*helping the teachers to implement the National Curriculum*'. The advisory teachers also said they hoped to show that '*many teachers were probably already doing quite a lot of science ...*', the aim was '*to change and widen teachers' definitions of primary science*'.

An explanation of the working alongside and INSET meetings component was also given. Of the INSET meetings, the advisory teachers explained how these usually began at 3.45 and finished at 5.15. Here, they emphasized that there was no over-running of this weekly one-and-a-half hour programme. In their experience it was usually the teachers who liked to continue. The sessions would be '*practical*', but the first occasion involved an obligatory discussion of what science in the primary school really meant and what was entailed in the science component of the National Curriculum. A visit to the resources centre was another '*fixed*' session, the rest were to be selected from a number of options by the staff themselves, at that first meeting. Attending these meetings was compulsory; the term '*contracting*' was used here.

The staff also received an account of the working alongside component. It was explained that the advisory teachers usually worked with four teachers. In further preliminary visits, the advisory teachers would '*find out where each of the teachers was at in their teaching of primary science*' and together they would discuss what topic the teacher would be undertaking during the school-based input. The advisory teachers would fit their science work into this teacher-determined theme. The advisory teachers explained that they did not like to prescribe a topic ('*This hadn't worked in the past*'), and similarly, they had found a whole-school topic problematic. They commented that teachers liked to have a '*sense of ownership*' of their topic, and that designated school themes were often '*not broad enough for everyone to feel happy with*'. The emphasis and expectation was firmly placed on a topic-based approach to science and it was stated that this was preferred to its '*being taught as a separate subject*. The teachers were made very aware that such was '*the LEA's policy*' for the delivery of science in the primary school. In order to exemplify the kinds of scientific activity involved, some of the worksheets, cards and flowcharts used in previous schools were left for staff's perusal.

The advisory teachers' account of working alongside also covered some details of the teaching arrangements. It was stressed that groups of children were not taken out of the classroom - '*the contract is to work with teachers not pupils*'. The advisory teachers preferred group teaching rather than taking the whole class - though they acknowledged, when this was challenged, that they could demonstrate a variety of approaches. Usually, the advisory teacher took one group of children for science, and the class teacher would be responsible for the remainder of the class. The suggestion given here was to '*have the rest doing something that was not too intensive (of teacher time), nor have activities that kept the others too quiet*', in order to create some opportunity for observation of the advisory teacher in action. The advisory teachers remained adamant about the feasibility of this, even though it was questioned at each meeting, particularly in the case of infant classrooms. The provision of all materials for science activities was the responsibility of the advisory teachers and not the schools', and it was the task of the resident teacher to undertake the same activity with the rest of the class during the week before the next advisory teacher's visit.

The choice of the four teachers was to be left entirely to the schools. It was suggested that the school might like to use some of the scheme's three day supply cover for the individual consultations with the selected 'client' teachers, but neither of them, in fact, took this up.

Finally, at one point in the discussions with each school, the advisory teachers stressed that although there was an obligation attached once the decision to contract in had been made, the staff could still '*opt out*' of the scheme at this stage.

One school also received, on this occasion, some details of the expected outcomes of the scheme - namely, a science policy created together by the staff. It was stressed that this would be a lengthy process.

Each meeting concluded with arrangements for finalizing the dates of the main programme and also the timing of the advisory teacher's next preliminary visit, where a main focus would be a closer liaison with the four selected teachers. However, in one school this was to be done in the context of another whole-staff meeting, with arrangements for further individual discussion still to be finalized; in the other it first involved an open invitation to a lunch-time meeting at the local pub with another date set aside for the individual discussion.

The 'overture' stage

Such was the official agenda of the initial visit to the schools. The second function - namely that of a carefully managed PR exercise - is equally worthy of comment. At this point in the school-based input, issues like the image and mien of the advisory teachers were clearly as critically important as the messages they were there to convey. Further, a strong sub-text about the approved version of teaching of primary science was apparent amidst their rhetoric of flexibility, choice and responsiveness. And, from the advisory teachers' account of the scheme in action to teachers, it was possible to see where the main emphasis of professional development was to be placed. A number of points about the 'overture' stage of the scheme can thus be made.

First, the advisory teachers' discourse and manner seemed designed to convey an essentially non-threatening and reassuring role. The scheme's aims were expressed in modest terms : '*here to help you a little; ... move forward tiny steps; ... at least have a go at primary science; ... give confidence; ... you're [probably] doing a lot of science already*'. The imperatives implicit in the scheme about how to teach science were placed firmly as coming from the LEA or, at this time, the National Curriculum rather than deriving from the advisory teachers themselves - thus again counteracting the potential threat and insecurity their role might engender. The bestowal of workcards, flowcharts etc. not only exemplified the kinds of activity the advisory teachers would undertake in the classroom, it perhaps equally was a signal and symbol of the teacher-friendly, 'nitty-gritty', 'practical' service they could provide.

Thus, the tenor and thrust of the overture stage seemed to be to allow each advisory teacher to establish herself as a trusted and valuable colleague as much as a high status consultant or expert. (Though this was perhaps more evident in the solo visit than when they were working as a pair.) This suggests an acute sensitivity to the conservative, insular culture of many primary staffrooms as well as a shrewd judgment with regard to the appropriate niceties of etiquette in relation to senior management. Similarly, their approach demonstrated an awareness of the enormous threat to some teachers which working alongside posed, recognizing that teaching in primary classrooms has very often been an intensely private activity, one that is rarely observed by or discussed in detail with another professional. It is a testament to the inter-personal skills of the advisory teachers that easy entry to so many classrooms was achieved. The rhetoric of flexibility and responsiveness which was often used by these advisory teachers to describe their practice seems justified in the area of constructing viable working relationships with their 'clients'.

However, there is some doubt, on the evidence of the overture stage, as to whether the same rhetoric can be as readily applied to the implementation of the scheme itself. In many respects the school-based input as delivered was a package, and although some reference was made to identifying and meeting the needs of the school and individual teachers - 'starting from where the teachers were at', it was clear that many aspects of the school-based input remained a pre-set agenda. The advisory teachers were at this stage of the scheme and in these two schools, unwilling to change from the four teacher involvement with the working alongside strategy.

Beyond that, it seems clear that the initial meeting gave no official or extended opportunity for diagnosis of the state of science teaching, general classroom practice or professional relationships within the school. It could be argued that each of these are crucial considerations in any school-based curriculum development work. Though one advisory teacher did make a fleeting observation of all classrooms on this occasion, the purpose of the visit was above all to outline the implementation of the programme, not probe for the realities and hence specific requirements in relation to these three issues. In the event, the advisory teachers proved themselves able judges of the school climate, picking up on a myriad of visual and verbal clues which signal how the staff operated as practitioners in the classroom and how they related as colleagues in the staffroom. It remains the case that this was very much a hidden agenda within the scheme : time was simply not apportioned to this diagnostic activity.

The initial meetings signalled one further divide between the rhetoric of responsiveness and the reality of prescription and routinized practice. Throughout the first encounter with staff, the advisory teachers strongly advocated a particular approach to the curriculum planning and classroom delivery of science: it was essentially a topic-based group activity. It may be a philosophically moot point whether an enthusiastic advocate can also be genuinely responsive to others' needs - at least as the 'needy' themselves define them. In fact, it is more likely that the task the two advisory teachers were set, particularly within the working alongside component of the scheme, was to persuade each teacher client that his/her own definition of need in the area of science teaching coincided with that of the advisory teachers themselves. It is the distinction between the genuinely responsive questions: 'How can I help you? What do you need?' and the persuasive - and perhaps even rhetorical - one: 'How can I help you to see that what you really need is x ...'. The success of the advisory teachers as change agent would thus derive from teachers being persuaded to adapt their practice and also acquire a commitment to those same principles. At the initial meeting, the advisory teachers clearly portrayed the variety of roles they would be undertaking and it might appear that these were an irresistible combination of persuasion strategies: the sympathetic and enthusiastic relayer of imperatives from above, the skillful role-model, the sensitive and encouraging counsellor, the purveyor of practical and accessible support materials. In this way, any lack of success would derive from a teacher remaining unpersuaded and unconvinced by such strategies, instead perhaps feeling (as one put it), '*manipulated*' or believing that their expressed needs were still being overlooked and unheard. The interface between teachers' expectations and how and if the service offered by the advisory teachers actually met them thus becomes a crucial measurement of the scheme's impact - and even its ultimate success.

In order to give an account of this interface, the expectations of the scheme held by the teachers in the two case-study schools is the subject of the next section of this chapter.

Teacher expectations

Shortly after the initial visit of the advisory teachers, the evaluator/ observer undertook a series of in-depth interviews with all staff from both schools with the exception of one absent part-time teacher from school A. Besides details of their own education, teaching career, in-service record and current classroom practice including science, the interview also focused on their expectations of the scheme, and what needs they felt they and their school currently had in relation to the teaching of PST. The timing of this Phase II fieldwork was deliberately scheduled after the initial meeting with the advisory teachers, in order to capture the teachers' projections when the content and design of the school-based input had been clarified for them.

Beyond a small number of general comments on the lines of the advisory teachers' definitions of the scheme's aims: '*giving confidence*' and '*helping me to see if what I'm doing is science*', these teachers' expectations were usually quite specific and on fundamental issues of primary science practice. They were categorizable under four very general headings - guidance was required in some or all of the following:

1.   the appropriate **CONTENT** of primary science;

2.   the classroom **DELIVERY** of primary science;

3.   approaches to **WHOLE-CURRICULUM PLANNING** to include primary science;

4.   developing a **WHOLE-SCHOOL** approach to the teaching of primary science.

Content

Broadly, two kinds of expectation in relation to the content of primary science were expressed. Some teachers defined these simply in terms of ideas:

> ... *I'd like more ideas of what to do with infants ... suitable things.*

> ... *I'm interested in collecting new ideas for things to do, and [in the] ideas the advisory teachers can bring from other schools.*

> ... *I hope they help me find science activities suitable for my age range.*

Rather than acquiring specific, instantly implementable activities for the classroom, others referred to the scheme providing them with an ELUCIDATION of the content of primary science. This second type of 'content' expectation, then, implied that the school-based input would make good a deficit in the teacher's own professional expertise and understanding, and usually in areas they could readily identify themselves:

> ... *I'd like them to do a topic on something I wouldn't normally do ... on the physics side or CDT, it's what I'm weak at and not at all comfortable with.*

... something on a topic I feel less confident in, like electricity ...

... I'd like more help with the physics and technical side ...

... I hope they are going to raise my scientific knowledge ...

There seem important distinctions between these two expectations. One is essentially PROVISIONARY, perhaps in the tradition of 'tips for teachers', with the teacher in effect saying: 'I want to be given ... [something appropriate to do in the classroom]'; whereas the request for ELUCIDATION implies 'I want to be informed ... so I understand better what to do in the classroom in terms of expanding my own body of scientific knowledge'. Clearly, the latter is a more demanding expectation on the advisory teachers and the scheme.

Delivery

All but two of the twelve teachers suggested that one of their expectations of the scheme was in the area of pedagogy. They wanted an EXEMPLIFICATION of science teaching, in effect saying 'I want to be shown ... [how it's done in the classroom]'. Again, there were two distinct pedagogical issues raised. For the majority of the teachers, the need was expressed as an organizational concern, namely, how to undertake teacher-intensive group science activities in the context of managing a whole class:

... the big question is when they've gone away, I worry about what the rest of the class is doing, how to work in groups, I want help in showing that the approach they're illustrating can operate as a reality.

My main interest is in organization, how to do it with the children. What, if they use a group approach, will the rest of the 25 children be doing ...

I'd like to learn the practicalities of how to organize a class to do science effectively ... it's not the scheme itself, it's how to do it without it degenerating into chaos - that's my first priority. At the moment, I'm very dubious about the group approach ...

Two teachers, perhaps precisely because of their doubts about the classroom management implications of group science teaching, wanted exemplification of an alternative organizational strategy:

... I'd like them to show me how to do science with a whole class.

... I'd like all the class to do different science activities in groups at the same time.

It is questionable whether some of these 'exemplification' expectations lay within the parameters of a scheme designed to show SCIENCE teaching, or whether, in fact, several teachers were referring to a need for guidance in the related, but essentially different, area of teaching strategies in general. The advisory teachers were to face this wider pedagogical issue several times. Undoubtedly, the practices they advocated and demonstrated fitted most comfortably in classrooms where 'informal', 'integrated', mixed-curriculum, group teaching was already the successful norm. The challenges involved in accommodating the advisory teachers' recommended approaches in classrooms with more formal, whole-class or individual-oriented teaching styles will be apparent as the case studies unfold.

Beyond this 'macro' pedagogical issue of appropriate classroom management, perhaps surprisingly, only two teachers indicated that their expectation and interest lay in the 'micro' area of teacher interaction with pupils:

... I'd like help with the experimental approach, to see how they approach and organize group work and what they expect from the children.

... I want to see [the advisory teacher] do it with a group, whether its the same as me, whether I'm doing it right.

Quite why such a marked lack of emphasis on the direct observation of the advisory teachers' teaching skills existed among these teachers is unclear. It is at least possible that it was such an obvious point of interest, no mention of it was thought necessary by the interviewees. On the other hand, it is also the case that the introductory visit had not - in either school - involved a discussion of this opportunity for observing 'good practice' at any length nor offered any details of what teachers might usefully look for. As already noted, the emphasis was very much more on the role of resident teacher as 'minder' to the remainder of the class. Whatever the reason for its absence, a better appreciation of the most crucial moments of curriculum delivery, namely classroom exchanges between teacher and pupils, was not a commonly expressed teacher expectation of the scheme. This point will be returned to later in the report.

Whole-curriculum planning

A rather different 'exemplification' expectation of the scheme, expressed by a small number of teachers, was support in the area of curriculum planning or design. They referred to the topic approach, and the place of science within it:

> ... [I want to know] how to fit science in properly ... how to reduce topic work to fit in more science work, whether you have to do that; more and more things are being asked of us, but reading is still my priority. I want to know how you pull science out of a topic so you don't have to do it as a separate lesson.

> ... I hope they will be showing me how science can be fitted in my topic web.

> To be honest, I don't do topics ... I feel they will help to tell me what to do ...

There were enormous differences in the kinds of curriculum planning undertaken by these three teachers, and in their views of the purpose and content of topic work in the primary curriculum. Again, rather like the classroom management issue of group teaching, the thematic/topic approach advocated by the advisory teachers was unfamiliar to some teachers. Indeed, influencing teachers' different versions of whole curriculum planning - and the subject priorities which underpin them - was likely to prove a major challenge for the advisory teachers given the design, official purpose and time limits of the scheme.

Whole-school approach

The majority of teachers of one school expressed an expectation of the scheme which appeared to reflect exactly its long-term aims: the whole-school improvement and STANDARDIZATION of the teaching of primary science. In effect, the 'need' here is 'I want us all to be given/informed/shown...'

> .. I hope, as a result of the course, science will have a more school-wide base ... currently there is nothing structured in the school, there's a haphazard approach. It relies on a teacher's personal knowledge and contacts to find out what's happened before ... I haven't a clue what's been done in the previous year.

> .. I'd like to know how to write a policy, how we can stretch the children and cater for progression ... have variety but avoid duplication.

*.. hope it will give the staff new ideas, and it will inspire us to continue
... there's been quite a lot of science but it's not as visible or evident
as it should be. There's no co-ordination and no scheme ...*

*.. hope we end up with a document which tells teachers what National
Curriculum areas and concepts they have to cover ...*

A closer look at some of these responses, and the use of such terms as
PROGRESSION, STRUCTURE, CONCEPTS TO COVER intimates
again just what high expectations the scheme encouraged. In the pre-
National Curriculum epoch, and at primary level, it was a vocabulary
perhaps more familiar in the teaching of highly codified subjects like
maths. It suggests that, in keeping with its promotion to the third basic,
science - for these teachers - was to be dealt with altogether more
rigorously than in the past. It leaves the interesting question of how far
the school-based input, and the science practice advocated by the advisory
teachers, could satisfy such expectations.

The 'consultancy stage': planning

*... They all have their own problems. I think it really is addressing the
individual's problems rather than the schools.* (Advisory Teacher)

Teachers are very touchy people. (MPG teacher)

Two further preliminary visits were made by each advisory teacher to
their designated school, in order to discuss and plan the 'working
alongside' component of the school-based input with the four selected
teachers. This part of the input might be described as 'the consultancy
stage' - essentially it was the negotiation of the advisory teacher's
projected classroom work, undertaken on an individual basis.

The evaluation team did not directly observe this planning stage and so
this part of the narrative is based on teachers' and advisory teachers'
retrospective accounts. From these, it is evident that although each
advisory teacher undertook a visit before and after the half-term break,
their methods diverged slightly, but quite significantly, at this point.

One advisory teacher's approach was to have a meeting with all four
teachers together, where each teacher's choice of topic was briefly

ascertained. The advisory teacher and teacher then separately planned, over the half-term holiday, the science component and the 'rest' of the topic respectively. After half-term, and shortly before the main programme started, a more lengthy individual discussion (of about half an hour), took place where plans and flow-charts were exchanged and each teacher was invited to select five out of a possible seven or eight theme-related science activities prepared by the advisory teacher. Each teacher was clear about the order in which his/her selection would be undertaken with the children.

The second advisory teacher met each of her teachers individually for about half an hour before half-term, where choice of topic and the possible science within it were discussed. Again detailed planning of specific activities took place separately over half-term, and the second meeting was an altogether briefer exchange of flow-charts and plans. No teacher was aware of the order in which the science work would be undertaken.

Two general points can be made about the 'consultancy' stage, before looking in closer detail at the various participants' accounts.

First, as these individual meetings constituted the remaining part of the preliminary visits, it is clear that something rather less than the three half days of the scheme's original design was spent in the school or with staff. However, the time involved in the advisory teachers' planning and preparation of eight individualized sets of flow-charts, with references to relevant published teacher materials and to appropriate attainment targets and levels of attainment in the National Curriculum may also presumably be counted as part of that total. Indeed, every teacher involved with the scheme gave unstinting praise to the quality, quantity and thoroughness of the advisory teachers' preparations, recognizing just how time-consuming it must have been. Nevertheless, it remains the case that given the importance attached to the topic-based delivery of science, more time for consultation and the sharing of the advisory teachers' planning processes might well have benefited the teachers, particularly in the context of planning for the National Curriculum. Equally, more opportunity for the advisory teacher to explore cross-curricular links and skills in relation to the needs of the particular class she was to work with may have given a more realistic exemplification of planning science within topic-based learning. At this point it is worth remembering that neither school took up the option of using the available supply cover for this 'consultancy' stage.

The second point relates to the differences in the two advisory teachers' timing of the main discussion with teachers. It seemed to signify, or at least contribute to, their taking rather different positions in relation to teachers' planning. The advisory teacher who had a lengthy consultation at the outset obviously acquired an earlier perspective on the teachers' modes of planning. It meant she could, and indeed did on one occasion, take a more interventionist, challenging role in determining an appropriate overall theme and offering basic advice on how to construct flow-charts. Similarly she was able to involve each teacher in preliminary discussions about the science they might like to do, i.e. probe more deeply about their expectations. However, such collaboration proved quite high risk, in that it opened up - for one teacher - further expectations of shared planning and teacher contribution, which could not really be sustained without a good deal more on-going and in-depth discussion.

The second advisory teacher's approach appeared more conciliatory and consumer-oriented. Offering a selection of activities, and making such choices the major focus of the consultation - in the teachers' eyes anyway - seemed to respect the time-honoured autonomy of the primary practitioner, and probably enhance their sense of 'ownership' of the topic. It was an altogether less threatening role. It may not, however, have given the teachers the same opportunity for discussing science in a whole-curriculum context, or for confronting the implications of the recommended topic-based approach in relation to their own planning and teaching.

It also seems that the advisory teachers' role in these consultations was often determined by the experience and relative status - official or unofficial - of the teacher-client. Intervention in planning and discussion on basic matters of classroom organization was much more evident with teachers of low status and relative inexperience than with senior staff or those well established with the age range they taught. These delicate demarcations were something the advisory teachers were acutely sensitive to, as they navigated carefully round lack of confidence or barely disguised hostility, but in turn could presage an inevitable unevenness of influence upon teachers' science practice. This was something the advisory teachers were well aware of, and indeed by this stage of the school-based input, they were already predicting the likely success of their work on the various teachers' practice. Though they were ready to acknowledge that sometimes the development in a teacher's science work was far beyond their initial expectations, it seems clear that teachers' diverse needs in PST really required markedly different amounts of advisory teacher investment.

The teachers themselves, when asked about their views on the preliminary visits and the approaching 'working alongside' component, revealed a range of attitudes towards the advisory teachers and the science activities they had been provided with. These differences seemed to relate directly to the kinds of 'content' expectation of the scheme they had expressed before the consultation stage. It was very apparent that those teachers - in both schools - who had stated they wanted 'ideas' or 'suitable activities', (i.e. their content expectation was 'provisionary' in its emphasis), were entirely happy and enthusiastic about the coming classroom work, and indeed warmly praised the advisory teachers' contributions. On the other hand, those teachers who had expressed their expectations in terms of 'elucidation' seemed, in some cases, considerably more guarded in their approbation, particularly if they had also expressed interest in obtaining a more RIGOROUS approach to primary science. Two teachers particularly voiced some significant criticism:

> *... I don't know, [these science activities] don't really express my idea of science, I can't see very much scientific content in them, it all sounds rather vague ... I'm disappointed by the lack of science and surprised that there's nothing in the ideas, I couldn't have thought of myself. I don't know what concept it's trying to get over.*

> *This [flowchart] doesn't reflect the joint sharing of ideas from our discussion. I wanted to see progression and short-term goals, but there's none at all in the way the advisory teacher has set it out ... I'm not impressed, but the advisory teacher is doing the science part and I must just leave it to her.*

Clearly one underlying issue here is that the two teachers still had a rather different understanding of the nature of PST than that being exemplified by the two advisory teachers. Talk of '... *not seeing the scientific content*' or discussing science in terms of *'short-term goals'* illustrates this quite sharply. It raises the question of whether the professional development potential of joint planning for working alongside was limited because it took place before the after-school INSET meetings, at which definitions of PST would be clearly laid out to the whole staff. Thus, not only increasing the time available for consultation, but also adjusting its timing may have benefited the immediate impact - and working relationships - of some classroom collaborations. This, of course, has implications for the design of the school-based input: an issue which will be returned to later in the report.

One final issue on the planning stage can be raised at this point. The teacher quoted above was not alone in being unsure of the scientific concepts being introduced to her class. Indeed, all eight testified to the fact that the discussions with the advisory teachers had concentrated on the activities that might be done with the children, and did not really feature an extrapolation of any underlying scientific skills and concepts. For some, the evaluator's question on this point was treated as a quite novel and even startling notion. Though National Curriculum attainment targets and levels of attainment had been provided by the advisory teachers, these also did not figure in the teachers' descriptions of the science work they were about to observe.

In sum, as the working alongside component swung into action, the teachers were the (usually grateful) recipients of a set of highly imaginative, thoroughly prepared, theme-related science investigations. However, it has to be concluded that the rationale underpinning this work was not always entirely clear to them.

THE MAIN PROGRAMME: 'WORKING ALONGSIDE' TEACHERS

In this section, we move on to describe and analyse the major thrust of the advisory teachers work in school, namely their classroom-based activity and accompanying INSET sessions. This part of the school-based input has been termed the 'main programme', in that it involved an advisory teacher presence in the client school for a full day a week over a period of five weeks. During this day, the advisory teacher was to teach alongside each of her four selected client teachers in turn (i.e. all available teaching time was utilized); and then, after school, the two advisory teachers together jointly ran the contracted one and a half hour INSET session with the whole staff.

In each case-study school over this five week period, therefore, the advisory teachers worked in classrooms for some twenty plus hours and undertook seven-and-a-half hours of whole-school in-service. (Although in one school an INSET session had to be postponed until the following term because of the school's pre-arranged Christmas engagements.) By monitoring the five week sequence through the two schools (three days in one and two days in another), the researcher observed, in all, fourteen of these classroom sessions, i.e. just over a third of the advisory teachers' teaching programme and exactly half of their joint INSET sessions in each school.

Without doubt, there was a clear and intended link between the two components of the main programme. For instance, during part of the after-school INSET sessions, the four client teachers were to give feedback to the rest of the staff on the science teaching underway in their classrooms. In these sessions also, staff practised science activities that were similar, or even identical, to those being undertaken by the advisory teachers with children. Despite this shared focus on the classroom delivery of science, the two components - and the advisory teachers' modes of operating within them - were distinct and discrete enough to merit separate consideration by the evaluation team. So, although a key issue raised by the main programme's design is how far the working alongside and evening INSET sessions were a cohesive professional and curriculum development package, it is first necessary to examine the two aspects separately.

Working alongside

...I encourage teachers to do science in groups, but you can't just say 'You must do science in groups'. You have to do it in various ways so that THEY come up with the idea that science is better taught as a group lesson. (Advisory Teacher)

'Working alongside', in the context of the present chapter, is a term used to delineate the advisory teacher strategy of teaching pupils in the presence of their class teacher, as a means of directly demonstrating 'good practice'. Whether intended or not, the major investment of advisory teacher time in the working-alongside component seems to signify its pre-eminence as a professional development strategy within the ESG scheme. As already shown, comprehensive preparations and resourcing for the topic-based delivery of science in the four classrooms as well as delicate negotiations with the class-teachers and the school had preceded the advisory teacher's arrival. Each week, the advisory teacher's work comprised four full-length teaching sessions during the course of a school day. In effect, the advisory teachers were presenting a 'role-model' to their client teachers. The exemplification, extrapolation and subsequent emulation of 'good' science practice were undoubtedly three major aims of the classroom-based work - and also the intended professional development sequence.

The advisory teachers were now showing what the classroom delivery of primary science might look like for the express purpose of its being replicated by the client teacher. In the short term, this simply meant the teacher doing the same science activities with different groups of children during the course of the following week. In the long term, it presumably meant the transference or assimilation of the advisory teachers' science teaching skills into the teachers' own practice. EMULATION thus would seem to depend on the teacher's clear understanding of what the advisory teachers were doing in the classroom, and such understanding is likely to relate to - and grow from - the kinds of opportunities created for observation and extrapolation of that classroom practice. So, providing convincing EXPLANATIONS for why they worked as they did might appear to be another key function of the advisory teachers' working alongside role. Given this complex and substantial set of intended outcomes a series of questions emerge:

*   what was exemplified by the advisory teachers as they worked alongside their clients?

*   what were the range of variations in the working alongside arrangements?

*   what kinds of professional development opportunities (specifically the observation and extrapolation of practice) occurred within these different arrangements?

The main focus in answering these questions is first of all the advisory teachers' *modus operandi* in the classroom, looking specifically at HOW teaching responsibilities were shared between the advisory teacher and the client teacher. Given that any variation in teaching arrangements was likely to offer different examples of practice - and therefore different learning opportunities - for the client teacher, it is important to itemize them in some detail. The following typology and analysis of the working alongside arrangements is designed to illuminate a professional development issue rather than give detailed descriptions of the fourteen classroom collaborations observed.

The other major issue of content, or precisely WHAT the advisory teachers exemplified, is addressed subsequently.

Variations in the working alongside arrangements

Two main approaches to the working alongside arrangements were evident from the classroom observations and accompanying informal discussions undertaken by the researcher.

The more frequent arrangement, seen in nine of the fourteen observations, was that proposed by the advisory teachers themselves during the preliminary meeting with the whole staff. Here, they had described how working alongside usually entailed them taking a small group for science within the classroom, while the resident or client teacher's responsibility was to manage the learning activities of rest of the class AND simultaneously observe the advisory teacher in action. Because of the advisory teachers' implicit advocation of this particular division of teaching responsibilities, it seems appropriate to describe it as the scheme's STANDARD approach to working alongside. However, variations in this 'standard' arrangement also emerged during the fieldwork. On a number of occasions, another adult or teacher was present in the classroom as a way of extending the opportunities for observing, or even joining in with, the advisory teacher in action in the classroom.

In contrast, a second approach, (which was illustrated by one advisory teacher in particular) gave evidence of a willingness to forgo the 'standard' working alongside practice if the client teacher wished to be shown other kinds of organization for delivering primary science. Different advisory teacher modes of operating collaboratively in the classroom then resulted, e.g. with the advisory teacher taking responsibility for teaching two or more groups of children and sometimes the whole class. These pupil allocations could be labelled CONCESSIONARY in that the advisory teacher was deviating from her usual, and perhaps preferred, pattern of classroom collaboration in order to accommodate the particular needs and expectations of her client.

So, in table form, the complete range of working alongside arrangements demonstrated by the advisory teachers and their client teachers in the case-study schools was as follows:

Advisory Teacher	Client Teacher	Other Adult or Teacher II

TYPE ONE: STANDARD

1. Teaches small science group	maintain rest of class/observe [advisory teacher]	-
2. Teaches small science group	maintain rest of class/observe	Adult: maintain rest of class
3. Teaches small science group	observe/participate	Adult: maintain rest of class
4. Teaches small science group	maintain rest of class/observe	Teacher II: observe

TYPE TWO: CONCESSIONARY

5. Two [plus] groups	maintain rest of class/observe
6. Whole class/unit	observe/participate

It is worth making two general points before looking in detail at each of these variations, and commenting on their advantages and disadvantages as professional development procedures.

First, this itemization of working alongside arrangements in the two case-study schools, reveals that neither advisory teacher had (or took) the opportunity to observe her client teacher in action other than she was herself engaged in teaching. The pupil allocations were, for instance, never reversed so that the client teacher could undertake small group work in science with the advisory teacher operating as rest-of-class maintainer and observer, although such a strategy has been described in other research studies of advisory teachers at work (see Easen 1990). It suggests that, on these occasions, the advisory teachers adhered strictly to the DEMONSTRATION function of the role-model mode; any 'advice' accruing from the working alongside component was based on their own practice rather than the teacher's. It is worth pointing out that the advisory teachers in subsequent discussion indicated that they too had on occasion reversed the standard pattern of pupil allocation. They pointed out that in other schools, client teachers had taken on small group science work in later sessions of the Main Programme. Significantly, it remained the case that this was at the specific request of the client teacher. Again this suggests that opportunities for advising on the practice of client teachers was perhaps another version of a CONCESSIONARY working alongside arrangement and not an in-built sequential professional development strategy within the scheme.

Second, and closely related to this, it was evident that the advisory teachers and client teachers often had limited opportunities for discussing or reflecting on the demonstrated teaching together. Because the advisory teachers' schedule involved teaching consecutively in four classes throughout the school day, there could usually be only brief interchanges about the shared practice after or before the lesson. (In the case of one school, Christmas lunchtime commitments seemed to affect opportunities for discussion.) It is also worth noting here that where post-session discussions between an advisory teacher and her client teacher were observed, the focus was often the responses of the pupils or the activities they had attempted rather than any detailed review of the advisory teacher's teaching performance. Given the absence of clearly defined criteria or guidelines for observing the advisory teachers' practice, it is at least possible that the teachers had been applying their usual classroom monitoring skills to the advisory teacher's demonstrated good practice and, of course, the agenda here is traditionally children and their work, not pedagogy. At the same time, as the client teacher had responsibility for delivering the same science activities to other pupils, the focus was likely to remain on pupil response.

The significance of these general characteristics of the working alongside arrangements will become apparent as each is now looked at in more detail.

Type One

Advisory Teacher	Client Teacher	Other Adult or Teacher II
Teaches small science group	maintain rest of class/observe [advisory teacher]	-

This is the standard working alongside arrangement described and undertaken by the advisory teachers. Organizationally, the two participants were replicating the mixed curriculum, group approach to classroom management/learning that often prevails in primary schools. The advisory teacher was, in fact, demonstrating the kinds of science group work which can occur when a class teacher is able to create extended 'teaching space' within a session, (usually by occupying the remainder of the class with some learning activity they can undertake more or less independently).

In practice, it was noted that this arrangement frequently offered only serendipitous opportunities for observation of the advisory teacher, being to a large extent dependent on the class-management skills of the client teacher. In several observations, the client teacher seemed primarily preoccupied with monitoring and controlling the rest of the class and could give only scant and fleeting attention to the advisory teacher at work. Factors like the age of children, and which session of the day the advisory teacher worked in the classroom, were also said to affect the observation opportunities in this arrangement. Notwithstanding these external constraints, it became apparent that it was the most proficient classroom-managers who provided themselves with the best chance of appreciating - and therefore subsequently emulating - the advisory teachers' teaching skills. In contrast, those teachers whose classroom organization was in some way problematic (or even just different from this class management style) were more likely to end up not seeing what the advisory teacher was doing in any detail.

Nevertheless, the standard approach to working alongside did have other advantages. Each advisory teacher was clearly and expertly demonstrating 'best' primary science practice, such as open-questioning techniques, how to encourage science process skills, during these extended interactions with a single group. One advisory teacher particularly seemed to have devised a range of strategies for orienting a distant client teacher to the science work underway: encouraging her group to relay to the teacher what they were doing; leaving her group to go and monitor other activities in the class in order to allow the client teacher unobtrusive access to the science activities underway. This last strategy also provided a means by which the advisory teacher could demonstrate the ways in which a class teacher, working alone, might simultaneously supervise a teacher-intensive science activity and the rest of the class. The actual provision of low teacher investment work for the other groups also featured in one standard working alongside arrangement.

Types Two and Three

Advisory Teacher	Client Teacher	Other Adult or Teacher II
Teaches small science group	maintain rest of class/observe	Adult: maintain rest of class
Teaches small science group	observe/participate	Adult: maintain rest of class

These working alongside arrangements were an extension of the standard approach, with the client teacher taking the initiative in obtaining classroom assistance to relieve her of total responsibility for the rest of the class. It was demonstrated in both case-study schools, exclusively by infant teachers, who used parents or a non-teaching assistant (NTA) to supervise other groups. Given this extra support, the teachers were able to take different roles and degrees of involvement with the advisory teacher's group. One became the official scribe for the science group's responses to advisory teacher open questioning; another sat outside the group as an attentive but non-participant observer, making only minimal control contact with her other pupils. Over the five-week period, a third teacher appeared to move from being a relatively distant observer of the advisory teacher in action (maintaining a role of monitoring the rest of the class alongside her non-teaching assistant) to more lengthy and closer participation in the advisory teacher's group work.

Such involvement suggests considerable benefits from the enhanced version of the 'standard' working alongside arrangement. This informal access to the advisory teacher's group work seemed a useful way to build a greater working rapport - and hence professional development opportunities based on shared practice - between the advisory teacher and client. Nevertheless, the constraints of discussion time perhaps prohibited such a partnership's full potential being explored. Equally, procuring non-teaching assistance to take on the maintaining role would perhaps be a less likely option for the teachers of older children.

Type Four

Advisory Teacher	Client Teacher	Other Adult or Teacher II
Teaches small science group	maintain rest of class/observe	Teacher II: observe

This arrangement occurred in School B, and was initiated by the head who organized supply cover on the advisory teacher's working day. He thus freed other staff from their own teaching responsibilities to spend part of a session in the client teacher's classroom observing the advisory teacher in action. In this way, the 'other' teacher was given an opportunity to monitor (or contribute to) - unhampered - the demonstration of skilled science teaching.

While such a strategy would seem to have considerable professional development potential, it is worth remembering that the 'other' teacher had no agreed guidelines for what or how to observe. Perhaps the extreme consequence of this was the researcher noting how one teacher spent much of his time looking at displayed examples of children's completed science work rather than the advisory teacher. Though it is likely he was demonstrating discretion rather than indifference, the absence of agreed protocols and procedures for observation would seem to reduce the effectiveness of this way of monitoring 'best practice'.

Beyond that, the 'other' teacher was never party to post-lesson discussion (except in the whole-staff INSET sessions after school) and, of course, had not been involved in any of the pre-planning. They were thus likely to be observing with less understanding of the intentions underpinning practice than the client teacher. This again would seem to limit the impact of what was seen.

Equally, the classroom presence of another professional (and even the researcher) may have put pressure on the client teacher to be seen to manage the rest of the class proficiently, which in turn would limit and reduce the degree of observation s/he could undertake.

Types Five and Six

Advisory Teacher	Client Teacher	Other Adult or Teacher II
Two [plus] groups	maintain rest of class/observe	
Whole class/unit	observe/participate	

These working alongside arrangements were labelled 'concessionary' because they were usually set up at the request of the client teacher, who explicitly wished for demonstrations of organizational procedures for delivering science other than the standard small group/rest of class allocation. Perhaps significantly, these arrangements, which occurred in both schools, were undertaken only with classes of older children. Equally, from the quote by an advisory teacher which introduces this section of the chapter (... *I encourage teachers to do science in groups, but you can't just say 'You must do science in groups'. You have to do it in various ways so that THEY come up with the idea that science is better taught as a group lesson'*) the advisory teacher's compliance could be interpreted as a professional development strategy which was ultimately designed to demonstrate - by default - how the approach they advocated was in fact preferable.

Clearly, within the whole class/unit arrangement, with all children doing a science activity, the client teacher was likely to have more opportunity to observe the advisory teacher at work (simply by virtue of having no competing teaching/curriculum responsibilities). They could witness a range of management of science learning strategies: whole-class demonstration (advisory teacher as class enquirer), whole class in groups (advisory teacher as group-learning manager), and could - and did - take on responsibility for the science work of one or more group. In this way, the client teacher was given the opportunity to implement the advisory teacher's science activities in her presence.

However, it was apparent that this approach really necessitated establishing a degree of collaboration between advisory teacher and client that the scheme's design and implementation may not have been able to cater for. There was evidence of some confusion about roles and responsibilities within the classroom as advisory teacher and client attempted to work together in this way :

> *Often I wasn't sure what each group was supposed to be doing ... she gave out work cards but I didn't know what they were either, I just had to read them. There wasn't enough TIME, it wasn't lack of thought, preparation or materials. If we'd had the whole afternoon, I could have talked about it at lunchtime ...* (Teacher)

> *Certain things happened that I was mystified about ... one week an entire lesson was changed round. [We'd talked at lunchtime], I said you're quite happy, you know what we're going to do ,... then when it came to the lesson, it didn't work like that, it seemed so odd - the lesson got completely changed round.* (Advisory Teacher)

Such honest reflections perhaps indicate that classroom collaboration as a professional development strategy, which the concessionary working alongside arrangement was in effect moving towards, sat rather uncomfortably with the kind of status and role the advisory teacher had negotiated at the outset. Teacher vulnerability, as THEIR science practice came in view, was a new and delicate dimension. The advisory teacher was more likely to give exemplification of less than best practice.

The standard arrangement, by comparison, allowed the advisory teacher to maintain a low-key non-threatening presence (indeed it may be seen as something akin to WITHDRAWAL in situ), and she could operate with autonomy in the classroom to ensure the science practice offered as a model remained of the highest standard.

What was exemplified?
Having looked at the various working alongside arrangements by which the advisory teachers delivered their classroom demonstrations of

'exemplary' science teaching, the issue of content or WHAT was exemplified in the working alongside component is now addressed. As the previous section has shown, the advisory teachers' responsiveness to their clients' expectations and existing classroom practice could result in major adjustments to the standard pupil allocation and even to the science work originally planned. On occasion, the working alongside sessions were perceived as not entirely successful by either the client or advisory teacher. Of course, such viewpoints cannot be equated with any judgement about the eventual impact and effectiveness of the advisory teacher's work with that teacher. Nevertheless, given these inevitably varied reactions to the advisory teachers' performance, it seems appropriate to take one session which was regarded as particularly effective by all participants, including the researcher, and examine the kinds of content messages that were explicit and implicit in the advisory teacher's classroom activity. The session chosen, out of all fourteen working alongside arrangements observed, is the one where - to put it bluntly - the most school staff saw the most of what the advisory teacher was doing. As such, it seems to qualify for detailed attention. However, it should be particularly noted that the selection of this session is not intended to imply that there were not equally impressive and lauded examples of science teaching being performed by the second advisory teacher.

Illustration of an advisory teacher lesson

The following detailed description of the advisory teacher at work, with additional commentary on her performance, illustrates a fairly typical advisory teacher lesson structure. It starts with an introduction or overture to all the children, and then moves into a teaching strategy - 'the hook' - designed to capture the interest and involvement of the group she was specifically to work with that day. This beginning can also be seen as the advisory teacher, as yet a relative stranger in the classroom, negotiating her acceptability to the pupils. The real substance of the session, i.e. the group science work, commences only after this important prelude.

The advisory teacher was working alongside in a reception class of about 20 children. The topic was LIGHT & DARK and this was the second week of the school-based work. The previous week, the advisory teacher activity had been baking with a group of children. As well as the client teacher, also present was her NTA, a colleague (who taught the middle-infants class) in a non-participating observer role and the researcher.

The session began with all the children sitting in the carpeted area around the advisory teacher, and all adults in attendance. The advisory teacher began by asking the children what they had done since she was last with them, adding that she had been a 'silly-billy' for not remembering to bring the baking powder the week before. The children explained they had made scones and biscuits with the powder in. The advisory teacher asked what difference this had made and they variously replied that it tasted different, was brown, they'd put raisins in this time. The client teacher also interjected, asking what did the scones do in the oven. Someone replied that they rose up and the teacher continued 'Yes, they nearly touched the roof.'

Comment

The Overture

This start appears to skilfully reorientate the children to the previous week's work; allows the advisory teacher to identify her involvement with that work, signalling that she is an approachable, likeable, non-threatening INSIDER in their learning experiences.

The client teacher (CT) orientates the children to one of the main learning points of the previous week.

The advisory teacher went on to tell an anecdote of how once she was baking when suddenly everything went dark, asking the children what they would do. One child suggested turning on the television to see by its light; a girl mentioned candles, and this was immediately taken up by the advisory teacher who invited her to the front, produced a candle, lit it and invited her to blow it out. One boy shouted 'Look at all the smoke going up'.

Comment

The Hook

The personal anecdote is another typical advisory teacher strategy for introducing the session's theme. It successfully catches interest, appearing to come from children themselves, although a carefully prepared series of activities underlies the morning's work - with the advisory teacher, in fact, waiting for the 'cue' of candles.

The advisory teacher then explained that today they were going to do something with candles, adding that the children should remember that if they were not in her group today they would 'get a chance to work on this later' with their teacher. The client teacher read out a list of six names and the rest of the class were sent to their tables to do number work or another free-choice activity. The three boys and three girls sat at a table and the advisory teacher knelt on the floor with them. Within a very few minutes, after orienting the rest of the class to their morning's activities, the NTA joined the observing colleague and the researcher: the client teacher had taken up her position as scribe for the science group, sitting next to a small easel placed nearby.

Comment

The advisory teacher reassures the rest of the class (indicating the client teacher's involvement too). The efficient organization of this classroom meant in fact that children could be left to work self-sufficiently for nearly all the session. The CT and NTA had a virtually unhampered view of the advisory teacher at work.

The advisory teacher began by pulling out an array of candles of different sizes, colour and shape. She was generating descriptions from the children of how they looked, smelt and felt, while the client teacher wrote down (i.e. classified) the children's answers around drawings of an eye, ear, nose which had been pre-prepared on the easel. The advisory teacher led the discussion on how it was inappropriate to taste or listen to the candles, so no words could be placed around the picture of a mouth and ear. The children then were encouraged to count the candles. Throughout this interchange, the advisory teacher's questioning drew in the quieter children of the group, and the client teacher contributed e.g. she introduced terminology like 'wick' which the advisory teacher reinforced.

Comment

The Exemplification

Here science process - CLASSIFICATION of candles - is handled informally and incidentally by the advisory teacher, the client teacher provides back-up. Particular emphasis seems to be given to language and number aspects of science work, with the CT

97

feeling confident enough to join in. The advisory teacher demonstrates her ability to 'share' talk and contributions among children.

The next task the advisory teacher set the children was to make the candles stand up, and in pairs they were given sand, silver paper and plasticine. The client teacher began a new chart 'Making [the candles] stand'. After some free experimentation, assistance was given to the pair with the sand. The advisory teacher asked them to predict what might happen if they added water to their sand and encouraged them to actually get water and attempt to make the candle stand again. She elicited their descriptions of the sand and water substance, and then led a whole group review of the three substances, drawing the children to the conclusion that plasticine, then the wet sand and then silver paper (only for the little candles) were the best materials for making candle holders.

Comment

A problem solving activity provided for the children also exemplifies the kinds of questioning that will elicit children's predictions and then evaluations of their solutions.

The advisory teacher then moved on to produce a box of matches, first discussing the safety aspect with the children, and then asking which part of the candle they would light - thus eliciting the word 'wick' again - and finally lit a candle, encouraging the children to watch and describe the flame (which they all decided was orange) and also directing them to what was happening to the wax beneath the flame. She then got out a glass bowl and began tipping the melted wax into the water, asking the children whether the wax was going to the top or the bottom. Watching this demonstration intently, the children all agreed the wax was staying at the top. Another candle was lit, the demonstration was repeated, and the teaching points of safety with matches, descriptions of flames and wax floating were reiterated. The advisory teacher, at this point, specifically introduced the terms 'floating' and 'sinking', clarifying their meaning by encouraging further prediction and close observation of what happened to the wax drips as they entered the water. All the children, carefully supervised, had a go at holding the candle.

Comment

More language reinforcement is offered: the advisory teacher now developing the CT's introduction of 'wick'. Significantly, at this point, the advisory teacher does not follow up one child's interest in the direction the flame was blowing, instead keeping the group focused on her teaching point on the properties of wax. Again questioning techniques to encourage observation are exemplified: the advisory teacher is able to diagnose children's understanding of the terms float/sink and reinforce appropriate usage, as well as maintain the central theme of wax.

More different coloured candles were lit, one at a time, the advisory teacher now asking the children to predict and then reflect whether the flames were the same colour. She thus established the principle that the colour of the candle does not affect the colour of the flame. The children again identified the flames as orange-coloured.

Comment

Further example of skilful questioning to help children arrive at an understanding of particular principle, with language and learning points simultaneously reinforced.

All the adults present had watched to this part of the session. At this point, the advisory teacher gave the science group an old candle and asked them to draw with it on paper provided. In pairs, they were sent over to the paint area, where the NTA was now installed and asked to paint over their wax marks.

Comment

Throughout the session, other children did not disturb the advisory teacher or other observing adults. It seems particularly valuable for an NTA to be so closely involved in science work and observe the finesse of the advisory teacher's group teaching strategies.

The children returned with their painted paper, the advisory teacher asked questions as to whether they had missed painting bits of the paper and, it was discovered that in discussion with the NTA, one child had - unprompted - come up with the idea of wax being waterproof. As she waited for each science pair to complete their paint work, the

99

advisory teacher continued to work with the remaining four, dropping more wax into the glass bowl, counting the drips and discussing the activity.

Comment

For the client teacher, this child's discovery of wax's waterproof qualities was seen as a major language achievement. The advisory teacher suggested, in discussion afterwards, that following up wax resistance may be one way to progress with the topic. Note how the advisory teacher's feigned ignorant questioning here 'haven't you missed a bit?' encourages explanations from the children of the wax resistance principle.

When all three pairs had reconvened, the discussion was turned to what candles were made of. Gunpowder and plastic were some of the children's suggestions, and the advisory teacher kept pressing them on this. One or two children from the rest of the class had begun to drift over at this point, and one boy contributed 'wax', which the advisory teacher accepted. She continued to elicit talk about wax resisting water.

Comment

The advisory teacher now accepts other non-science children's interest, continuing to reinforce the purpose underlying the painting activity with the whole group.

The advisory teacher's final discussion point - after an hour of working with this group - turned back to the observation of candle flames. After getting the children to describe what the wick was like after it had been set alight, she lit candles with different sized wicks and asked them to compare the size of the flames. The children were helped to discover, with some considerable interest, that the candle with the larger wick had a larger flame.

The session ended here.

Comment

Final comparison-observation task includes a repeat of foci like WICK, FLAME (and its colour), SIZE.

Discussion of issues

Several content issues stand out from this single illustration of an advisory teacher in action, reflecting the dual emphasis on pedagogy and curriculum which the working alongside component specifically exemplifies.

First, the session is a clear demonstration of the finesse and subtlety which characterised both advisory teachers' group teaching skills. The effectiveness of this version of primary science would seem largely to rest in the quality of interaction between the advisory teacher and pupils, and in the capacity of her questioning technique to continually draw children into science process areas like classification, observation, comparison, prediction and inference. Other sessions, undertaken by both advisory teachers, demonstrated similar informal and incidental introductions to fair testing, accurate recording and so on. It seems a sad irony that such consistently virtuoso performances of science process teaching could remain largely un-noted by several client teachers, because of their concurrent classroom management obligations. Appreciating the advisory teachers at work perhaps deserved - or demanded - rather more attention and analysis from the client. The previous point about lack of guidance or criteria for observation is worth reiterating here. Equally, this micro-teaching issue perhaps reinforces how the lack of opportunity for specific discussion, or extrapolation, of the pedagogical skills underpinning the advisory teacher's classroom exemplifications may be a serious omission in the scheme's design.

However, it would be erroneous to give the impression that no client or observing teacher picked up on the quality of the group teaching skills exemplified by the advisory teachers. In all, four of the thirteen teachers - from both schools - chose to refer to their appreciation of this part of advisory teachers' work, though significantly each of these had created or been given the opportunity for observation without simultaneously having sole responsibility for the rest of the class. They spoke in such terms as *'it was nice to listen to another teacher'*, *'the way she talked to the children helped me'*, *'I got the nitty-gritty: how to ask questions to draw out the children's ideas'*. In the case of the candle session, the client teacher indicated she was most impressed with the *'language output'* of the children (rather than mentioning the advisory teacher input that facilitated this talk), and the observing teacher referred to:

seeing how she did it, her techniques of teaching it, they were useful
... I suppose it made me aware of what I should be doing, trying to get
the children to find out rather than giving them the answers all the time
... making them think for themselves and experiment, you guide them
along the right lines, but it's so easy to tell them the answer.

Thus, despite the positive impact of the advisory teachers' classroom work, these teachers' appreciation seemed to remain rather general and lacking in science focus or vernacular. Perhaps this further indicates the value and need for a more detailed extrapolation of the science process underpinning the advisory teachers' observable practice.

A second pedagogical issue which the candle session illustrated was how the advisory teacher presented a particularly condensed version of primary science practice - on this occasion revolving round the 'thematic vehicle' of candles. Several times, in both schools, it was made clear to teachers that the work undertaken by the advisory teacher during the session was not meant to exemplify a single replicable lesson, but rather represented an accelerated succession of science activities which a classroom practitioner might implement over a longer period of time. Notwithstanding this, there may have been a central ambiguity here: subsequent fieldwork frequently detected a tendency for some teachers to assume, and balk at, the idea that primary science involved devoting an hour or so of their teaching time to a single small group of children. In other words, they believed they were being shown a naturalistic, rather than intensified version of science teaching, and hence found the implications for their daily curriculum and classroom management were particularly challenging, if not untenable.

The things she did were impossible without another adult, it was quite
an unreal situation. With a lot of things it's just impossible to sit and
work with one group ... and then there's the thought that you've to go
round and do it with the rest at another time.

I still feel I have the original problem ... if I do it in groups, what
happens to the rest?

A third area which the candle lesson opens up is that of the advisory teacher's demonstrated versions of science curriculum and progression in scientific learning. Quite clearly, the weekly topic-based activities as presented to the children contained an imaginative yet logical, almost

NARRATIVE sequence: Christmas baking leading on to lack of electricity/ candles, on to Christmas lights/electricity and so on. These links were made explicit to the children by the advisory teacher in her amiable introductions each week. Equally, for the client teacher, each activity undertaken was carefully documented in the provided flow-chart and its accompanying work-sheets, and was also linked to relevant National Curriculum attainment targets. The working alongside component could thus be summarized as the advisory teacher simultaneously offering thorough presentations of both child and teacher versions of her science curriculum. This raises again the question, posed initially in the account of the scheme's consultancy stage, as to how explicitly the client teachers themselves were helped to differentiate between the science activities presented to the pupils and the underlying scientific concepts and processes contained within them. For two teachers this remained a shortcoming at the working alongside stage also, as one put it:

I couldn't see the purpose, she wasn't very explicit ... the only way I could think to describe her lesson was learning the technique of doing an investigation, but it wasn't explained to me in that way ...

Thus, despite the fact that the candle session was obviously an example of well-prepared scientific process and enquiry, it would seem that designing effective science activities - like the advisory teacher's questioning skills - remained, during the working alongside component at least, a largely unreferenced and unarticulated expertise. Client teachers may well have benefited from more explicit and lengthy expositions of the particular science process and content contained within the observed activities on offer to their pupils.

Beyond that, the candle session illustrated one further - problematic - aspect of progression as exemplified in the working alongside component. The wide-ranging, thematically-linked activities were very typical of the process-oriented version of primary science which characterized advisory teachers' planning and classroom work. With the exception of key topics like electricity or magnetism (which were always a component within a wider topic such as TOYS, CHRISTMAS), in the main the advisory teachers' work did not convey a sense of children's sequential accumulation of a specific body of knowledge and skills over a period of time (although this had been an expectation of a small number of teachers, particularly those of older children, at the outset). Whilst comment on this approach is beyond the brief of this evaluation chapter, it is worth noting that the advisory teachers' weekly change of pupil clientele may have inadvertently underplayed the significance of diagnosing, developing and appraising children's progress in science process, leaving the impression that simply providing a range of interesting topic-related science activities was the practitioners' first and only responsibility.

However, given the advisory teachers' starting point in this professional development exercise - and it is worth remembering the generally negative attitudes to primary science exhibited by majority of teachers prior to school-based work - it is evident that engendering such an impression must count as a quite considerable achievement, in effect, entirely coinciding with the modest aims of the scheme which were outlined by the advisory teachers at the outset.

THE MAIN PROGRAMME:
AFTER-SCHOOL INSET SESSIONS

... with the 'in-service', we have definite areas we want the schools to do. But instead of going in with a plan, and saying 'This is your in-service', it's far better to look at the school and assess what they think their needs are, to get their needs and link them with what we want to do ... put the two together. We've never failed yet, it needs some jiggery-pokery, but we manage to get in all the things that we have to get in [according to our brief] ..(Advisory Teacher)

This section looks at the series of five INSET sessions, conducted by both advisory teachers and targeted at the whole staff of each school. These took place after school on the day each advisory teacher had worked with their four client teachers, with the contracted agreement that it would involve one and a half hours of teachers' time. In one instance, the advisory teachers worked with the staff of the case-study school and also that of a neighbouring denominational school who were working with another advisory teacher - making an audience of some 20 teachers for most of each session. The after-school INSET in the second case-study school followed the scheme's conventional arrangement of just the existing staff attending. For one of the five sessions, each school visited the Resources Centre.

Undertaking this second component of the Main Programme clearly meant a different role for the advisory teachers: they were moving from the complex and innovative demonstration/ exemplification function, outlined in the previous section, into a more orthodox 'course leader' mode. However, the two basic areas of FORM (how the advisory teachers operated) and CONTENT (what they transmitted) re-emerge as crucial evaluation issues for this aspect of the school-based work, as well as the overarching question about the scheme's design - namely, how far the after-school INSET complemented and cohered with the advisory teachers' classroom-based work.

Responsiveness or standard agenda?

To begin with, though, it is important to register the degree of responsiveness to individual schools' needs, simply because the advisory teachers' rhetoric stressed this aspect of their work. It was stated that staff were able to select the agenda for the after-school INSET at the first meeting. Several teachers volunteered, in follow-up interviews, that they had indeed had that choice:

She asked us what we wanted to do ... she didn't say 'I'll be doing this and this', we had a choice of what we thought was a priority - that was good.

They did ask us what we wanted, that was quite good, that they did ask - but they insisted on the visit to the Teacher's Centre.

However, (as an earlier quotation from the advisory teacher illustrates) there was a number of areas which the advisory teachers were expecting - or expected - to cover. Thus, perhaps inevitably, part of the negotiations at the first meeting involved the advisory teachers subtly vetoing and manoeuvring teacher suggestions to coincide with their own agenda.

The staff sat at one end of the hall and the two advisory teachers stood in front of the projector. One of them began by asking what the staff would like to do for the rest of the weeks, 'what do you want from the course?' She said that obviously they had to go by what the majority wanted and she asked if the participants could talk to their neighbours about their wants. All present wrote down on a piece of paper what they would like and then ideas were shared and put on a flip chart. ... Someone suggested PROGRESSION, and one advisory teacher quickly came in and said they would do progression through a topic. Someone also wanted something on testing and assessment but the advisory teacher put forward the argument that they don't really know what testing will look like so it would be a shame to spend time on this, only to find the Government was saying something different. 'We'll only do work on recording what you've done with a class. (Observer's notes at initial meeting: School A)

It is important to stress that pointing up this apparent contrariety in rhetoric/actuality does not necessarily imply any pejorative or critical judgement. Rather, its significance would seem to lie in demonstrating how the advisory teachers adhered to the IDEA of a teacher's sense of 'ownership' as a *sine qua non* in any professional development activity and how convincing they appeared to be in promoting the notion that the school had contributed to determining what those activities might focus on. It suggests that the negotiation of content for the INSET sessions was a skilful and shrewd strategy whereby, in the shift to a more formal 'didactic' role, the advisory teachers nevertheless were attempting to maintain the semblance of accessibility and responsiveness to staff.

On one level then, the issue of negotiation of content is another example of the advisory teachers finding ways to operate effectively within the ambiguities of their role and the design of the scheme itself. The delicate balance and tensions between delivering pre-determined imperatives on good science practice and offering specific counsel re-emerges and seemed resolvable only by a certain tokenism at this point. The drawback of such partially cosmetic responsiveness may be that some teachers were left with a feeling that their own agenda and expression of need remained unaddressed or ignored. The full significance of this point will be returned to later. At this stage, it is sufficient to register that there seemed to be a pre-set agenda for after-school INSET and that the advisory teachers themselves acknowledged to the researcher that both schools were receiving a very similar five week programme. How the advisory teachers operated (the form of the input), and what they offered during that programme (the content), is now addressed.

The form of the INSET sessions

By and large, it is possible to identify three main and distinct advisory teacher modes of operating in each session. During the contracted one and a half hours, the researcher usually observed the advisory teachers undertaking:

1. the management of feedback sessions, where the four client teachers relayed the work in progress in their classrooms to the rest of their colleagues;

2. a formal/frontal delivery of aspects of primary science practice (often using visual aids);

3. the management of practical science activities or small group discussion exercises often with plenaries.

An initial point to be made here is just how skilled the advisory teachers were in their presentations and interaction management: the team-work delivery was at all times highly proficient and professional - and often commended by their teacher audiences in the evaluation's follow-up interviews. This expertise is likely to stem from the degree of experience (and familiarity with their material and role) which they had acquired by the third year of their secondment.

However, it was apparent that the sessions' crowded agenda inevitably inclined the advisory teachers towards routinizing their performance and operating at a pace which may have limited the degree of genuine interaction and debate. Perhaps the reduction of the number of sessions from the original six to five is significant here, particularly as the dissemination of information about the approaching National Curriculum became an additional but now crucial component of this part of their school-based programme.

Equally, it is important to recognize that the various professional development strategies represented at these INSET sessions - teacher feedback, group discussion, practical activity, formal input and so on - placed very different demands on the audience. The impact and assimilation of CONTENT clearly depended on teachers' capacities to engage effectively in the particular professional development PROCESS by which it was delivered. Thus, for the evaluation team, it was important to register how the teachers responded during the sessions as well as garner their retrospective reactions and judgements.

Client teacher feedback to the whole staff
This component of the after-school INSET represented the most overt link with the working alongside sessions. At the start of most evening sessions, each client teacher reported back to their colleagues about the science work undertaken in the classroom on that day. By and large, the

client teachers seemed to have an open brief as to what to report. The advisory teachers' contribution at this stage was to determine the overall pace of the feedback and offer the occasional supportive comment or a question designed to focus the staff on a particular point of classroom management or science process.

With one notable exception (significantly, in the week following the formal input and group activities on definitions and processes of primary science), the client teachers tended to focus on their pupils' performance and the products of the advisory teachers' work rather than relay any details of the teaching and learning processes underpinning such outcomes.

The feedback component was undoubtedly a useful introduction or ice-breaker for each session, and also - because of the enthusiastic descriptions generally offered by the teachers - seemed to function as a valuable promotion exercise for the advisory teachers' work in general. It may be only a slight exaggeration to say that the client teacher was in effect operating as a convert/missionary for primary science at this stage.

However, the feedback became increasingly marginalized as the programme unfolded, and in some later sessions was dropped altogether due to pressure of time. Generally, most of the teacher audience was quiescent yet attentive and admiring. It was not an activity generating a great deal of group interaction. This may partly have been because of the openness of the brief for the feedback: more definite and mutually-understood criteria may have provided more focused discussion at this point, though clearly the whole exercise was encouraging and establishing the sharing of classroom practice.

Teacher reactions to this component sometimes referred to the fact that it was rushed and several commented that it would have benefited from a week's gap between classroom activity and the feedback. Reference was also made to its diffuseness:

> We just seemed to go on a long time ... teachers tend to go on a lot don't they. We dropped it otherwise we wouldn't have got through. (Teacher)

However, one teacher out of thirteen interviewed specifically pinpointed the feedback as a valuable learning experience, nominating it as a means of providing her with instantly- accessible ideas for her own classroom practice:

The teachers would talk about how the day had gone. I got a lot out of that ... [such as] that might be a good topic to do, or that I'd try it that way or I must remember not to do it like that.

Formal input
The programme of after-school INSET sessions invariably included frontal delivery by the advisory teachers on various aspects of primary science. At this point they were generally relaying versions and imperatives of good science practice from sources such as their own authority's policy statement, the DES, HMI and National Curriculum documentation. It was here particularly they emerged as skilled and seasoned performers, with a shared repertoire that was now finely honed to an extremely effective delivery.

Aims and definitions of primary science, science process skills, topic-based planning for science, the exposition of National Curriculum draft orders for science were all elements of the formal input. These generally preceded or led on from small group discussions with practical exercises to illuminate the issue further.

Thus, whilst delivering imperatives and explicitly recommending practice was a different stance for the advisory teachers from any that they had undertaken so far, no doubt they were able to capitalize on their accumulated good will and credibility at this stage. They seemed particularly effective as assuagers of the general trepidation surrounding the impending National Curriculum. Several staff particularly referred to '*understanding better*' or '*feeling more positive*' about National Curriculum in the light of the advisory teachers' work.

Interactive small group work
The third main kind of professional development strategy managed by the advisory teachers in the after-school INSET sessions was that of small group or paired discussion and practical science activities undertaken by all the teacher audience. This latter INSET form was outlined in the original design of the scheme and was clearly a popular part of the programme - invariably, involvement was high during the prescribed task itself. The advisory teachers were proficient at relaying instructions and

generating an interest in the impending activity, and it always had clear links with the session's general focus or topic. Thus, on one occasion the teachers explored the number of science skills in a particular task (dropping objects) after an advisory teacher input on science process. In another session, they attempted workcards on batteries and circuits after listening to the advisory teachers explain the National Curriculum attainment target on Electricity. Paired work on planning topics round various other attainment targets and undertaking a critique of a class record sheet were further examples of this kind of activity.

Several teachers referred specifically to the small group practical science activities as a valuable professional development exercise, particularly when it was related to an aspect of science knowledge in which they considered themselves to be deficient.

> ... everyone found it useful, it challenged everyone to tackle things we were nervous about since school days .. it was a good way of making us take it on. I enjoyed it ...

> I found out things I didn't realize I knew, that happened a lot. I remembered how to wire up electricity, I could even do a parallel circuit ... I actually understood it, and I'd thought I didn't have much in the way of scientific concepts.

> I liked the practical side rather than the lecture side, when you're doing you learn more than when you sit and listen.

It seems as though the effectiveness of this approach lies in primary teachers' appreciation of undertaking learning experiences that directly parallel those they offer to their pupils - 'do and I understand'. If this is so, then by being highly skilled practitioners, the advisory teachers could virtually apply their usual classroom strategies and be successful as professional developers.

However, one noticeable aspect of this form of INSET was that the advisory teachers often had difficulties in maintaining a similar dynamism and enthusiasm during any whole group discussion and interaction which followed the small group work. The researcher noted several times a tendency for staff to still exchange points only with neighbours during plenaries or just a general desultoriness in the exchange of ideas. This may have been the result of running courses at the end of a school day, or, in the case of School A; the fact that they were sharing sessions with a number of relatively unfamiliar teachers from another school. However, if practitioners by and large are unused to operating - and therefore learning - in a semi-formal interactive forum, it is likely to limit the impact of any content messages delivered by that means.

The content of the INSET sessions

Having taken a brief overview of the range of professional development processes undertaken by advisory teachers during the after-school INSET, it is now appropriate to look at the major content issues which were addressed by this component of the scheme. However, rather than giving a detailed description of the substance of six observed sessions, the chapter offers the following typology which outlines the main areas dealt with by the after-school INSET:

science knowledge   e.g. electricity, batteries, circuits

science process   e.g. delineation of science skills

curriculum planning   e.g. topic approach to science delivery

pedagogy   e.g. grouping and classroom
             management

whole school management   e.g. resources, record-keeping,
             developing a whole school policy

Though such a list depicts the range of content offered by the advisory teachers in their after-school programme, it does not reveal the proportionate emphasis given to each of the various aspects. When this is addressed, it was apparent that scientific knowledge received considerably less attention than process; that pedagogy was dealt with by and large incidentally, whereas issues relating to whole-school management were the main focus of at least two sessions; and that curriculum planning, (i.e. the advocation of topic approaches to science) reverberated throughout most of the programme. When the content range is tabulated against the various process strategies present in the whole INSET programme, including the working alongside component, the emphasis becomes even clearer.

It is important to stress that the following table is a highly interpretive summary, based on the researcher's observation and analysis of half the programme in each school, and is not intended to convey quantitative findings. (✓) indicates the advisory teachers made a particular content area the main and explicit focus of discussion whilst operating in that INSET form. (✗) indicates the content area was given no direct focus and (0) indicates incidental reference by the advisory teachers.

	working alongside	feedback	input	group activity
SCIENCE KNOWLEDGE	✗	✗	✗	✓
SCIENCE PROCESS	0	0	✓	✓
PLANNING/TOPIC	✓	✓	✓	✓
PEDAGOGY	0	0	✗	✗
MANAGEMENT	0	✗	✓	✓

Several points can be made from this collation.

First, and most importantly, the scheme clearly offered a remarkably thorough and comprehensive introduction to the major issues involved in introducing and upgrading primary science.

Second, it is clear that scientific knowledge was not a prominent feature of the programme. On only one occasion did teachers feel they had been given the opportunity to expand their science knowledge, namely in the small group activity focusing on batteries and circuits. By and large, the ESG scheme could be summarized as a celebration of teachers' existing knowledge base (or even that it was acceptable NOT to know), with the 'subliminal science' rhetoric of *you're already doing it* predominating. At this point it is worth remembering that some teachers had specifically anticipated that the scheme would rectify their lack of expertise in the physical sciences.

In contrast, scientific process featured strongly in both components of the main programme. Nevertheless it was possible to detect certain lost opportunities for consolidating the message being delivered. The main omission seems to be that teachers were given insufficient encouragement and guidance in describing their own or the advisory teachers' practice in its process terms. As noted elsewhere, the most innovatory features of the scheme - working alongside and feedback - were ideal occasions for practitioners to begin to articulate and reflect on their work in this way. Though the after-school INSET offered thorough explanations and valuable reinforcement of science skills and processes, the cross-over and connections with the science practice simultaneously underway in the school was, quite simply, underexploited.

From the table above, it is apparent that the major content investment of the advisory teachers lay in the advocacy of topic-based approaches to science. This message was delivered by every form of INSET which the programme offered. Its prevalence may indicate why scientific knowledge could remain such a low-key feature of the programme. As the working alongside section of this chapter indicated, constructing a 'narrative sequence' of science activities was advocated as the appropriate way to deliver progression and continuity in the classroom. Moreover, recommending such an approach undoubtedly kept the idea of primary science 'user-friendly', i.e. non-threatening to the generalist practitioner. Thus, whether intentionally or not, recommending a topic approach seems to be a direct alternative or surrogate for expanding teachers' scientific knowledge base.

The whole issue of pedagogy, both at the MICRO level of interaction with specific pupils and the MACRO level of the management of science learning in the classroom, is shown to have a quite distinctive presence in the scheme. Though it in effect dominated the work of the advisory teachers during the school day, it noticeably did not feature in such INSET forms as small group discussion, plenaries, formal input during the after-school sessions. Only passing reference and recommendations about group approaches to science were delivered at that stage. As the previous section has shown, much the same informal suffusion of advice also occurred in the working alongside component, and undoubtedly this approach, by respecting the autonomy of the classroom practitioner, successfully established a working relationship between client teacher and advisory teachers. However, the teachers' most frequently voiced caveat about the scheme lay precisely in this area: namely that, by the end of the programme, they still required guidance on how to manage the delivery of science in the classroom. Meeting this need, as indicated earlier in the chapter, was - in the main - outside the parameters of the scheme and the advisory teachers' brief. Nevertheless, the scheme's design would appear to offer opportunities and potential for extrapolating the advisory teachers' considerable pedagogical and classroom organizational skills, which could be built into future school-based work.

Lastly, the area of whole-school management of science was dealt with quite thoroughly during the after-school INSET, with formal input/small group activity/plenaries on record-keeping, developing and reviewing a whole school policy. The session on resourcing science held at the Resources Centre demonstrated the coherence of the scheme's design. Here was an opportunity at least for staff to be involved in the spending of the £200 for science equipment which was offered to all participating schools. One or two teachers commented they had found this the least useful session, perhaps signifying more about their own perspectives on and involvement with whole-school issues than the quality of the session itself.

With reference to the £200 grant, the chapter has begun to move beyond its brief to analyse the school-based work of the advisory teachers and on to the issue of the scheme's provision for the development of science within the school after the Main Programme was completed - all subjects dealt with in subsequent chapters. However, one final question about the scheme's design and the advisory teachers' work in school as it pertained to whole-school management is worth making here: namely what of the role of the science co-ordinator? The scheme envisaged a 'passing of the mantle' from the advisory teachers to science co-ordinator, with that appointment taking on key initiatives in developing science policy and practice within the school. As such, it is worth noting what kinds of support or special training and treatment was offered to the co-ordinator before and during the main programme. The answer, from this description of two such programmes, is that there was none. Both co-ordinators were included as one of the four client teachers, but no other official investment in their future work, role and status was made at this time.

One co-ordinator indicated that observing the advisory teachers at work with the whole staff was going to be a useful 'modelling' process for their own work with colleagues subsequently. This modelling of the co-ordinator on advisory teacher roles and activities was, in fact, described as an explicit intention for the follow-up period. One advisory teacher described how she might work with a co-ordinator in her follow-up visit:

I' ll say 'You go and work with the staff as though you were me' , that's to give the co-ordinator confidence when I'm not there ... [and] get them to plan with the staff just like I plan.

Though clearly as 'clients', the two co-ordinators did have opportunity to see what the advisory teachers did, in terms of their own planning and working alongside, they did not have the facility to discuss with advisory teachers any issue concerning 'advising' or working with colleagues at that time.

THE SEQUEL: TEACHER REACTIONS

Before (staff) were frightened to take science on board ... now they've seen what can be done, they're keen to do it ... science was dead in this school till they came. (Teacher)

The final section of this chapter considers the immediate impact of the school-based input. It is based on interviews which were undertaken in the early part of the term after the Main Programme and in which all participants gave their retrospective views of the scheme.

The timing of this fieldwork was designed to capitalize on the recent experience of the advisory teachers' work, but it is important to bear in mind that any perceived initial impact is not necessarily synonymous with the scheme's longer term effect on science practice in each school. A degree of 'fall-off' or dilution of the advisory teachers' influence was a commonly reported occurrence in the 'retrospective' case-study schools. Conversely, any negative comments offered at this stage may not always correlate with the actual (or ultimate) impression which the advisory teachers made on that teacher's practice. Having registered these caveats, the evaluation design intended to capture early reactions to the scheme as an integral component of the longitudinal study.

Without doubt, in the immediate aftermath of the advisory teachers' work, the response of the teachers was overwhelmingly positive. Unstinting praise for the professionality of the two advisory teachers was virtually universal. As well as that, three outcomes were most commonly referred to:

* an increased confidence to teach science, often based on redefinitions of the nature of primary science offered by the advisory teachers;

* greater communication between staff about their classroom work;

* a reappraisal of pupils' capacities and enthusiasm for undertaking science activities.

Each of these is worth looking at in some detail.

Redefinitions of primary science

Typical responses here were:

I realized how much could be done in science at an early age ... she gave me a lot of enthusiasm and confidence and made me realize I was doing more than I thought .... the word science used to frighten me.

I find I'm thinking about science rather than avoiding the issue .... I suppose I had a very narrow definition of science and they've broadened it out.

.... it made me reflect that I do do it: a lot of what I do is science, but it has made me more adventurous.

Such comments seem entirely congruent with the intended outcomes of the scheme as delivered by the advisory teachers at the outset of their school-based work. (Indeed, it is even possible to describe them as a virtually verbatim repetition). It would seem to confirm that the school-based input was, at the very least, a highly successful proselytizing exercise, resulting in teachers' previously negative attitudes to the notion of primary science being converted into positive intentions.

Greater communication between staff

Typical comments here were:

It has certainly stimulated staff discussion, what's gone on in each other's classrooms ... that's been first class.

We all know what each other is doing now, we didn't before - we all just used to do our own little bit ... I hope that continues.

This outcome, particularly identified by the staff of School A, indicates the benefits of whole-school involvement. Often, the teachers described the enhanced communication in terms of informal discussions of classroom practice between individual colleagues. It also seemed that teachers of similar age ranges were more likely to share practice in this way. It suggests that the climate of cordial, low-key interchange established between advisory teacher and client teacher, and then client teacher and rest of staff during feedback, may have acted as a positive model and influence, especially when the school's existing staffroom culture was similarly fraternal. Capitalizing on, or even engineering this 'bonding' of colleagues may be a useful strategy in future programmes.

Redefinitions of pupil attitude
Typical comments here were:

The enthusiasm of the children was amazing, even if they hadn't done any written work at all, they'd got enough out of it: it got their enthusiasm straight away, it had captured their imagination.

... most teachers were happily surprised, they found that most children were capable of a lot more than they had thought.

... I didn't realize how much their little minds could take in and recall.

This response would seem to offer further verification of the value of the advisory teachers' classroom activity. Earlier reports have already suggested that working with the client teachers' own pupils is a means by which the advisory teachers gained professional credibility to corroborate their INSET messages. Interestingly, an important 'credibility criterion' for several teachers in the case-study schools was simply the esteem and affection which the children displayed towards the advisory teacher. However, these comments also corroborate the view that pupils' reactions enhanced staff's appreciation of the recommended/demonstrated practice. If pupils are thus significant and influential agents in their own teachers' professional development, there may be important ramifications in terms of the quantity, frequency and timetabling of advisory teachers' classroom work. Clearly, the five week period of this scheme facilitated successful advisory teacher-pupil relationships.

In sum, the general viewpoint expressed by the teachers and heads of both schools was extremely affirmative of the advisory teachers and the scheme. However, a number of caveats were made: many of which have already been referred to. These often related to gaps in expertise which still remained and the final part of this section explores the major issue of TEACHER EXPECTATIONS of the school-based input and how far these were fulfilled. It was argued at the outset of this chapter that the interface between teacher expectation and experience of the scheme and the advisory teacher's work was likely to be an important factor in determining its impact and ultimate success. Equally, identifying the areas in which teachers wanted further support was intended to provide useful insights for INSET planners and policy-makers. With this in mind, the follow-up interviews also asked the teachers to reflect on the specific expectations they had voiced before the advisory teachers worked in their school. Those expectations, categorised as CONTENT (provisionary and elucidation), DELIVERY (macro and micro pedagogy) CURRICULUM PLANNING and WHOLE SCHOOL APPROACHES, were not surprisingly, recounted as being met somewhat unevenly.

Content

Those teachers who had requested instantly accessible ideas for the classroom (the 'provisionary' expectation) acknowledged that the scheme had amply fulfilled this. References were made to the amount of materials offered and left by the advisory teachers, to the fact that they could now replicate specific lessons that they had observed and to obtaining flow-charts for a theme undertaken by the advisory teachers in another school. In other words, an expanded repertoire of suitable activities was perceived as an outcome of the advisory teachers' work in school. However, if that repertoire's main constituent was the detailed curriculum planning of an outside expert, rather than stemming from a teacher's own (newly acquired) expertise, it may signal a limitation on future science practice and suggest that greater opportunities for the active transfer of advisory teacher planning skills - rather than passive recipience - would be of benefit.

Further to this point, those teachers who had anticipated an expansion of their scientific understanding (elucidation), were generally disappointed, although the session on electricity was referred to positively. Given the low emphasis on scientific knowledge already identified, this expectation was unlikely to be met by the scheme. This clearly left one or two teachers still feeling unskilled:

> *I never knew what I was aiming to do, what concept I was meant to cover - so I know what I've taught by the end of the day. [Unless you do know], you could spend half your day just doing investigations, I might be doing the same concept on every topic, without knowing it, by just picking an activity that links.*

Though a subsequent ESG-funded central course (with a planning contribution from the two advisory teachers) demonstrated an intention to address this issue of the primary practitioner's knowledge base specifically, it may still count as a major area needing attention in future primary science INSET.

Delivery

The major caveat referred to by the teachers was the difficulties of undertaking a form of solo classroom management which would allow the kinds of science practice exemplified by the advisory teachers. This again was a likely outcome given the school-based input's lack of direct focus on the issue of pedagogy. One or two teachers mentioned how they would appreciate the opportunity to see a 'real' teacher delivering investigative group work in a 'real' classroom situation. More opportunities for the EXEMPLIFICATION (and also the EXTRAPOLATION) of good practice, by utilizing the LEA's bank of existing teaching talent, *in situ*, may be a useful additional strategy. Some earlier client schools had, it seems, chosen to make use of GRIST money or their six half days of supply cover (as an alternative to co-ordinator release) to do this. Visits to other schools after the Main Programme were said to be a well established practice by this stage of the scheme. As with the advisory teachers' working alongside strategy, the professional development potential of any demonstration of 'macro pedagogical' or organizational issues involved in delivering primary science is probably best served by first establishing clear guidelines for observation and proper occasions for subsequent discussion.

Whole curriculum planning/whole school approaches

The expectation of help in the planning for science within the primary curriculum was by and large seen to be fulfilled. The advisory teachers' consistent and overt recommendations to 'fit' science into existing topics, and their exemplification of what was referred to earlier in the chapter as 'a narrative sequence' of science activities based around a theme clearly provided the kinds of support most teachers said they were looking for. Equally, it should be remembered that the topic approach to science had been delivered by and expanded upon in every form of INSET within the scheme.

However, for a small minority, this version of whole curriculum planning, and the place of science within it, remained problematic, in that it did not coincide with their own strongly-held views of how science across the whole school and in individual classrooms should look. These teachers were still discussing the need - unmet by the scheme - for *'progression through the years'*, having *'key concepts to teach'* and seeing science as *'a method of investigating a body of knowledge'*. It suggests that their expectation of a new rigour within the science curriculum remained largely unaddressed. Considering that the advisory teachers worked fairly systematically on National Curriculum attainment targets, science process skills etc., it is interesting to speculate why this teacher reaction occurred. It is at least possible that, in some cases and for some teachers, the advisory teachers' efforts to deliver accessible and non-threatening messages underplayed and over-minimized the challenging nature of the practice they were really advocating. In the interests of advancing primary science practice, further INSET at school level may wish to address the issue of escalating the challenge to teachers.

SUMMARY

This section offers a synopsis of the account of the school- based input, and selects key issues to emerge from each of its components.

In the **Preliminary Visits** section, we provided description and analysis of advisory teacher activity before the five week programme began. This included their introduction of the scheme to the schools (designated the 'overture stage') and their subsequent work with individual 'client' teachers (the 'consultancy stage'). The section also considered the participating teachers' expectations of the school-based input and these were categorized under four general headings: the content of the primary science curriculum; classroom delivery; whole curriculum planning; and whole school approaches.

Several key issues were raised about the preliminary visit stage of the programme:

* **ADVISORY TEACHER ROLE AND STATUS**
  The evidence suggested that the advisory teachers' manner, and their explanations of the impending programme conveyed an essentially non-threatening and reassuring role. Their considerable interpersonal skills ensured they gained the trust and confidence of both practitioners and senior management.

* **RESPONSIVENESS TO SCHOOLS' AND TEACHERS' EXPECTATIONS**
  It was indicated that, at the overture stage, the advisory teachers had no [official] opportunity to diagnose the state of science teaching, general classroom practice or professional relationships within the school, though each of these could be seen as crucial issues in any school-based development work. Teacher expectations and their self-expressed needs were not overtly sought at this stage either. It was pointed out that the advisory teachers were able judges of school climate but this was very much a hidden agenda of the scheme and their role.

  The question was raised as to whether the advisory teachers, in their various roles - enthusiastic relayer of imperatives from above, skilful role-model, encouraging counsellor, purveyor of teaching materials etc. - were operating a range of subtle persuasion strategies rather than undertaking a genuinely responsive stance in relation to teachers' expressed needs.

* **OUTCOMES OF PLANNING AND CONSULTATION**
  Significant - albeit subtle - differences between the two advisory teachers' approaches at the consultancy stage were identified, and a general point was made that considerably less than the three half days proposed in the original design of the scheme was spent planning in school with teachers. It was found that although the client teachers were, by and large, well satisfied with advisory

teachers' comprehensive preparations for the classroom- based
work, they were generally unaware of the science skills and
concepts underpinning the planned activities.

In **The Main Programme - Working Alongside** section we considered
the major investment of the advisory teachers' time during the school-
based input: the exemplification of science practice, with its implicit
professional development sequence of extrapolation and subsequent
emulation by the client teacher. This strategy was discussed in terms of
FORM (how the advisory teachers worked in their client teachers'
classrooms) and CONTENT (what was exemplified). A typology of the
various forms of working alongside arrangements was offered and a
detailed description of a single advisory teacher lesson was
used to illustrate the content messages of this part of the school-based
input.

Key issues raised here were:

*   **FORMS OF WORKING ALONGSIDE AND PROFESSIONAL
    DEVELOPMENT OPPORTUNITIES:**
    The evidence signalled a significant relationship between pupil
    allocation, the degree of client teacher's simultaneous classroom
    responsibilities and opportunities for observation of the advisory
    teacher in action. It showed how some client teachers were able to
    give only serendipitious attention to the science activities being
    demonstrated. The issue of an absence of agreed guidelines for
    observation emerged. The discussion also pinpointed a general
    lack of opportunity for any subsequent extended discussion on the
    observed exemplification of 'good' practice.

*   **CONTENT MESSAGES**
    The illustration of one advisory teacher's lesson indicated that the
    typical format of the five week working alongside programme
    comprised an imaginative, 'narrative' sequence of investigative
    science activities, undertaken with different groups of children for
    a full session. In 'content' terms, the report suggested that client
    teachers were thus being offered - either overtly or implicitly -
    particular versions of PROGRESSION, PEDAGOGY and
    CURRICULUM PLANNING (i.e. topic approaches). The
    perceived viability of these content messages was also discussed
    - particularly in relation to pedagogy and planning - as this would

clearly have implications for subsequent emulation and replication by the teachers themselves.

The Main Programme - After School INSET section began with a discussion on how far the advisory teachers were operating a responsive or pre-set agenda in this component of the school-based input. It then moved on to provide an analysis of the form and content of the INSET sessions. Three main advisory teacher modes of operating in INSET sessions were identified and the efficacy of each was considered. The major content areas of the INSET sessions were also categorized: as scientific knowledge, science process, pedagogy, curriculum planning and whole school management. The chapter then offered an interpretative tabulation to highlight which INSET strategies, including working alongside, were used (both incidentally and explicitly) to deliver these various content messages.

Key issues raised were:

* **RESPONSIVE OR PRE-SET AGENDA?**
  The analysis inferred that the advisory teachers were operating a largely pre-set agenda during the after-school INSET, and were very effective at using their interpersonal skills to give the semblance rather than the actuality of a fully-negotiated programme. The INSET package was nevertheless delivered extremely professionally.

* **CONTENT PRIORITIES**
  From the analysis of content messages and INSET strategies, the report showed that scientific knowledge had an extremely low profile compared with science process. In turn, pedagogy was dealt with largely incidentally, whereas the advocation of topic approaches reverberated throughout the whole programme, being overtly delivered by each categorized INSET strategy. Whole-school management issues featured in two sessions. The impact of these variously emphasized content messages upon teachers' subsequent practice is a future evaluation issue. However, the analysis identified a possible major omission in the scheme's design in not fully utilizing the science practice underway in the school to expand teachers' abilities to describe and understand the process

skills being demonstrated. Given that the classroom delivery of science had a major priority in many teachers' expectations of the scheme, it would seem that discussion on pedagogy might also have featured more prominently in the range of INSET strategies employed within the main programme. Finally, the chapter raised the issue of whether the main programme could have clarified the future role of the co-ordinator.

In **The Sequel**, we considered teacher reactions to the advisory teachers' work shortly after the completion of the main programme, first acknowledging the uncertain correlation between immediate response and longer-term impact on practice. Key issues discussed here were:

* **TEACHER DEFINED OUTCOMES**
  Three major outcomes were identified by the teachers:

  - increased confidence to teach science, often based on the redefinitions of primary science offered by the advisory teachers;

  - greater communication between staff about classroom practice;

  - reappraisal of pupils' capacities and enthusiasm for undertaking science.

  In the light of these outcomes, the discussion concluded that the school-based input was, at this stage, a highly successful proselytizing exercise, turning previously negative attitudes into positive intentions. It suggested that the subsequent increased informal discussion or 'bonding' of teachers (particularly those of same or similar age groups) could be capitalized on in future programmes. The significance of pupil response as a stimulus to teachers' acceptance and appreciation of the exemplified practice was also pinpointed.

* **TEACHER EXPECTATIONS FULFILLED?**
  Those teachers who had expressed a need for instantly implementable ideas in the classroom were most positive about the scheme. This raised the question as to whether future programmes

might include greater emphasis on transferring the advisory teachers' planning skills to help teachers become more proficient and independent designers of their own science curriculum. The major omission, for most teachers, was seen as the area of 'macro' pedagogy, i.e. organizing for the solo management of investigative group work as well as efficiently controlling and occupying the rest of the class. Possible strategies were discussed for using some of the authority's skilled classroom practitioners as 'role-models' *in situ*. Another possibility might be to use video material of teachers in action as the focus for critical discussion on what constitutes effective classroom management strategies for delivering science. The problematic issue of expanding the scientific knowledge underpinning primary teachers' practice was acknowledged. With this in mind, the final section indicated that future science INSET may nevertheless need to escalate the challenge to established practice and curriculum understanding rather than seek to work within it.

EMERGING QUESTIONS

Overall, this case study has demonstrated the positive impact of the advisory teachers' school-based work upon practitioners. Consequently, it is important to stress that the following questions should be read as possible pointers to improving a successful professional development strategy.

Preliminary visits

* could consultations with the client teachers have been allocated supply cover in order to maximize the professional development potential of planning science activities alongside the advisory teachers?

* should an agenda and criteria for observation of exemplary science practice have been offered prior to the working alongside strategy?

* could the definitions, aims and philosophy of the primary science practice advocated by the advisory teachers have been fully clarified before the school based input began?

Main Programme: working alongside

* could there have been greater opportunities for observation of the advisory teacher by the client teacher: for instance, utilizing supply cover to take responsibility for the remainder of the class?

* should there have been a more substantial period for post-observation discussion between the advisory teacher and her client teacher built into the working alongside component? Was the balance between exemplification and extrapolation always appropriate?

* could the five week programme of working alongside have included, or built in, transference of responsibility for science group work from the advisory teacher to client teacher in order to ensure support and advice on aspects of the client teacher's own practice?

* could the advisory teacher have demonstrated a version of progression and continuity in science teaching which followed through the development of children's scientific understanding and process skills by working more often with the same group of pupils over the five week period?

Main Programme: after school INSET

* should there have been greater opportunity for analysis and description of advisory teachers' science practice using the terminology of science process skills?

* could there have been a greater use of the range of INSET forms - feedback, small group discussion, frontal input - to discuss the whole issue of pedagogy at micro and macro level?

* could the role and status of the science co-ordinator have been clarified in the discussions of whole- school curriulum developments?

CHAPTER SIX

THE OUTCOMES OF INSET

INTRODUCTION

Having described the scheme in general and examined in some detail the general provision and the school-based input from the advisory teachers, the present chapter now focuses on perhaps the most central question concerning INSET: namely, what happens to teachers' curriculum perceptions and classroom practice in the light of a particular in-service experience?

Given that the quality and effectiveness of in-service provision is likely to benefit if its designers - at the planning stage - are cognizant of probable long-term outcomes, a major function of this evaluation has been to try to provide information and insights about such outcomes which may also have more general applications for INSET design.

As stated in Chapter One, INSET outcomes, particularly in the long term, have been little researched to date. The opportunity provided by the evaluation to study the impact of one in-service initiative on classroom practice for up to three and a half years after the original input is, therefore, a rare and considerable one.

Taking this opportunity, the main purposes of the present chapter are to identify mid- and long-term outcomes and formulate a tentative typology or framework which attempts to contribute to the general understanding of what certain kinds of INSET actually 'does' for teachers. Clearly, in any consideration of the outcomes of an in-service programme which dealt with primary science during that period, close account must be taken of the context and circumstances within which it was operating. A number of factors would seem to have a bearing on its implementation and subsequent impact upon schools and individual teachers:

* primary science was an area of the curriculum about which many primary practitioners held deep reservations, and one which they often readily admitted they neither liked nor understood;

* the role of advisory teachers as an in-service strategy was innovatory and hence unfamiliar to many client schools and teachers;

* the imperative of the National Curriculum loomed into view during the period in which the scheme was operating, and elevated science to its new status of the 'third basic';

* the advisory teachers - and subsequently co-ordinators - were, however, at that time, still working within the long-standing tradition of classroom and curriculum autonomy associated with the primary sector;

* the nature and funding of INSET within local authorities changed year by year.

In sum, a particular mode of operating by the advisory teachers and a distinctive message about primary science resulted, and needs to be borne in mind when generalizing about the impact of INSET practice from this particular scheme. Nevertheless, precisely because the ESG scheme in question offered a thorough introduction to its subject by employing a carefully considered range of INSET strategies targeted towards a very distinctive professional development need, it would seem that the study of its impact could offer particularly useful general conclusions. For the issue of how primary teachers (operating in the pre-National Curriculum climate of a largely self-determined whole curriculum, whole class responsibility) could be helped to integrate a major and, very often, new and threatening subject area into their existing curriculum design and classroom organization has surely ranked as one of the major challenges for INSET planners to date. Hence, identifying and clarifying INSET outcomes in this area, in terms of long-term influences upon practice, should undoubtedly carry important implications for future INSET design in other subjects and phases of education.

The chapter offers an overview of data gathered in all five case-study schools, (Phases I-IV outlined in Chapter Two) and as such is the first summary of the longitudinal aspects of the research. It utilizes all data obtained in the period before the National Curriculum was implemented, and thus attempts to offer insights on the direct effect of the scheme as far as possible. The chapter is based on analysis of the perceptions and classroom practice of over twenty teachers but concentrates in particular on the detailed experience of ten of these teachers.

WORKING TOWARDS A TYPOLOGY OF INSET OUTCOMES

The first task for this part of the evaluation was to interrogate the data collected for the specific purpose of formulating a typology or model of mid- and long-term INSET outcomes. By trawling the available evidence on outcomes for one particular scheme, it is hoped to construct a typology which will be of general use and interest across the full range of curriculum areas, particularly for INSET organizers at both LEA and school level. Before presenting this typology, however, some preliminary points need raising about the approach taken to the identification and categorization of outcomes within the primary science scheme.

Firstly, it should be reiterated that in focusing heavily on outcomes, impact and effects (the latter three terms are used inter-changeably), the present chapter pays little direct attention to the inputs or processes of delivering the in-service activities. In many respects it should be seen as complementing the previous two chapters, which accentuated INSET processes in preference to outcomes. Here the reverse is the case but in the same way that outcomes (e.g. teachers' responses to the work of the advisory teachers in Chapter Five) were not totally ignored, inputs or the delivery process are not completely overlooked here.

Secondly, in adopting a strategy for analyzing the data in order to address the agreed foci of the evaluation, a deliberate decision was taken to concentrate on any outcomes and effects, irrespective of whether they were intended or unintended. Indeed, for the particular purposes of this chapter, distinguishing between intended and unintended outcomes does not warrant priority attention. This means that instead of identifying the intended aims and objectives of the in-service scheme and matching these as key criteria against the evidence of actual outcomes (i.e. a goals-oriented evaluation), this chapter is based, almost exclusively, on an analysis of accounts of outcomes and impact - intended or otherwise (i.e. goals-free analysis).

Thirdly, our approach to drawing up a typology of outcomes has been shaped by the acceptance that, in keeping with the primary science scheme's formal aims and objectives, and with the brief for the evaluation, the ultimate intended outcome of this particular scheme is the development of teachers' classroom practice in science. The typology offered below would probably look quite different if the ultimate goal was, for example, teachers' personal career development or management skills.

Fourthly, in addition to documenting the occurrence of positive outcomes precipitated by the scheme, the analysis has also included negative effects. It has also entailed considering intentions and expectations which were thought desirable as outcomes, but which were adjudged by participants not to have been attained.

Finally, the analysis of the data upon which the typology is based has been conducted with an open mind as to whether the emergent outcomes represent a disparate and disconnected set of effects or whether it is possible to link them in such a way as to draw out a sequential or even hierarchical order. An exploratory consideration of such ordering is presented in the concluding section of this chapter.

A NEW TYPOLOGY OF INSET OUTCOMES

The typology was constructed by collating accounts of outcomes and effects from across the range of participants: teachers, co-ordinators, headteachers and advisory teachers. These accounts were initially grouped under a list of approximately 45 types of statement. At a subsequent stage, this list was reduced to nine broad categories. The definitions and evidence for each of these nine types are presented below:

1. **Material and provisionary outcomes**

2. **Informational outcomes**

3. **New awareness**

4. **Value congruence outcomes**

5. **Affective outcomes**

6. **Motivational and attitudinal outcomes**

7. **Knowledge and skills**

8. **Institutional - strategic outcomes**

9. **Impact on classroom practice**

Material and provisionary outcomes

This type of outcome consists of the procurement of physical resources and services as a result of participation in in-service activities. Challenging somewhat the conventional view that the impact of INSET is exclusively concerned with cognitive outcomes (e.g. the development of knowledge, skills and attitudes), the evidence from the science scheme suggests that material and provisionary outcomes can be very important products of in-service activities. They can have substantial, and in some cases, indispensable, influences on the overall effects on teachers' classroom practices.

Teachers from all five schools testified to the short- and long-term benefits of the material outcomes which resulted from involvement in the scheme, especially from the input from the advisory teachers. The following material resource outcomes were frequently cited as making a positive contribution:

* **use of the central science resources base** - several teachers thought that the INSET session held at the central resources base was particularly useful in that it offered an opportunity to inspect books and resources prior to purchasing their own. Some teachers continued to borrow equipment from this source.

* **time** - co-ordinators, as a short-term outcome, valued the release time (6 x 1/2 days' supply cover) which they received in the aftermath of the advisory teachers' input.

* **workcards** - teachers appreciated the work sheets left by the advisory teachers.

* **equipment** - teachers reported that, having had little appropriate equipment before the scheme, they welcomed and utilized the various items of equipment purchased with the £200 granted to the school. Outcomes in the form of physical resources included clocks, magnifying glasses, weights and even shelving for the resource-base which all schools were encouraged to establish.

* **books** - the £200 was also used to buy science books for teachers and pupils. The acquisition of new books was rated a particularly beneficial outcome by several teachers. By way of illustration, one teacher remarked that the books obtained through the scheme had

made a big difference to his classroom practice; another teacher emphasized the value of books in aiding her practice by saing that '*the books inspired me more than the two advisory teachers*'; a third teacher, who was one of the few teachers to demonstrate progression and continuity in her science teaching, did so by making use of a published scheme in science. Books recommended by the two advisory teachers were often purchased by the schools and teachers reported using these up to two years after the ESG input.

Received messages about the recommended use and deployment of these resources were also identified as outcomes of the in-service scheme. Some science co-ordinators, for example, described how they were using the newly-acquired books in ways which were advocated by the two advisory teachers:

> *I make the workcards myself by using the ideas from the books they suggested we ought to have in school. I always go through those to see what is applicable.*

> *We got some books that gave teachers some initial ideas. These are helpful in getting you thinking in a scientific way ... I've got some books myself and there's a lot in here that I haven't got, and there's some really good ideas that I use. I pick and choose ideas from all sorts of different places in there.*

In one school, however, science books were being used in a manner which conflicted with the advice given by the two advisory teachers. Rather than use a range of books as resources to be 'dipped into' as and when they befit the occasion and purpose, this school used the £200 to purchase a science scheme through which pupils and teachers would proceed in a fairly systematic fashion. This approach was justified on the grounds that progression could be achieved more efficiently and that it would provide a supporting framework to assist teachers who weren't ready to move in one leap to a more open topic approach.

Some teachers had clearly picked up a 'make-do' philosophy from the advisory teachers. One teachers, for instance, stated that the two advisory teachers had shown the staff how to make-do with 'home-made' equipment and worksheets. Another felt that the advisory teachers, by appreciating the limitations of teachers' classrooms, demonstrated how it was possible to work successfully within any given set of physical circumstances. For many teachers, this 'make-do' message had the combined effect of more-or-less maintaining the status quo in terms of existing resource levels and architectural standards within the classroom (apart from the relatively minor effects of the £200 grant), while stimulating teachers to adopt a more positive and determined stance to teaching science within any given set of constraints. To varying degrees, most teachers accepted this position, though predictably nearly all teachers expressed a desire for a substantial increase in equipment and resources, as well as improvements in the teaching environment (e.g. one teacher had to bring her own magnifying glasses for the pupils to use in science as none were available within the school). A small number of teachers were of the opinion that this lack of resources constituted a valid reason why the in-service scheme had produced little impact on their classroom practices.

Material and provisionary outcomes were also apparent in the accounts of the responses to the on-going work of the science co-ordinators. As will be illustrated in more detail in Chapter Seven, obtaining and organizing equipment and books were often described as the main duties undertaken by co-ordinators. One co-ordinator, for example, borrowed items of equipment from the central resource unit for use by other teachers. Another co-ordinator described attending a further science-related INSET course largely in order to procure additional resources for the school. Another co-ordinator described how the question of resources amounted to the main area of discussion between colleagues and herself. Teachers often commented that they felt they could turn to the co-ordinators for help in obtaining particular items of equipment or ideas for worksheets.

To sum up, experience within the scheme indicated that material and provisionary outcomes were important factors in shaping the long-term impact of INSET activities, and hence are key considerations in the design of any in-service provision. The designers of the scheme, and the advisory teachers who delivered it, certainly intended it to have provisionary outcomes - the latter can facilitate changes in teaching repertoires and can be used as strategy for securing the interest and motivation of clients. Headteachers and teachers undoubtedly looked to some in-service activities to produce material outcomes. As a number of teachers highlighted, attending courses which advocate new teaching methods that are dependent on unavailable resources (e.g. computer software programmes or construction materials) can be extremely frustrating and demoralizing. Hence, some teachers would have welcomed more courses on the use of resources, but only if the latter were accessible.

On the other hand, there was clear evidence that merely providing teachers with new resources (both books and equipment) does not itself guarantee an automatic application of them in the form of developing teachers' classroom practices. One teacher in a school, which interestingly had invested its £200 in equipment rather than books, made this point quite bluntly:

> *I wouldn't say I've done anything that I haven't done before because of the new equipment within the school ... I haven't done anything NEW ...*

It seems, at least for most teachers, that in order to bridge the gap between provisionary outcomes and effects on classroom practice, other intermediary outcomes need to be brought into play. For example, some teachers illustrated how books can inspire and stimulate developments in practice - hence, highlighting motivational outcomes. Others, however, demonstrated that the availability of new resources needs to be accompanied by appropriate extensions in knowledge and skills. It is to this broader agenda of cognitive outcomes we now turn.

Informational outcomes

This term is used to denote the state of being briefed or cognizant of the background facts and news about curriculum and management developments, as well as their perceived implications for practice, as a result of participation in INSET provision. It is distinct from outcomes relating to knowledge and skills, which are intended to imply a deeper and more critical UNDERSTANDING of underlying curriculum and management issues and principles.

Several teachers alluded to the informational outcomes of the inputs by the advisory teachers, especially their first after-school INSET presentation, in which it was standard practice to outline national and local policy statements on primary science. One teacher said that this first session informed her about the aims and objectives of primary science and later sessions brought her up to date on developments in record keeping. A co-ordinator approved of the way the two advisory teachers offered insights into the LEA's thinking with regard to science. Teachers in the two retrospective case study schools clearly felt that the timing of the advisory teachers' work in their schools (i.e. late Autumn 1988) was particularly advantageous in helping them tune in and keep abreast of National Curriculum developments. One teacher summarized this point of view:

> *I think a major benefit was that as a school we became beamed into the needs of the National Curriculum somewhat earlier than [some other schools].*

In a similar fashion, teachers were also appreciative of the information they received as feedback from their science co-ordinators. According to teachers' accounts, this included details on National Curriculum requirements, available courses and local policy developments.

Although informational outcomes as products of INSET provision sound at first to be relatively unproblematic, the evidence from the scheme suggests a number of potentially important issues need addressing when planning in-service activities with information transmission as a salient feature. Firstly, there is the question of the neutrality of those who present the information. It should be recognized that it is highly unlikely that the presenters of 'information' will relay news and facts in a totally impartial manner. It seems more likely that 'information' will tend to be selected and transmitted in such a way as to suit, or at least accentuate the priorities and purposes of the person(s) delivering the in-service activity. Secondly, the timing of the passing on of 'information' calls for careful judgement. There were signs that attempts to convey information too early (e.g. on National Assessment) could soon degenerate into swapping the latest gossip. On the other hand, waiting too long could leave teachers unprepared for the practical implications of the developments. Finally, there were indications that informational outcomes tended to be short-lived and rarely, if at all, appeared to have a direct impact on classroom practice. Consequently, the scope for influencing teachers' repertoire could be diminished by INSET programmes or series of in-service school-based days which over-emphasized the aims of passing on information.

New awareness

Virtually all teachers, in discussions about the impact of the scheme, referred to, and used the phrase, experiencing '*a new awareness*'. Thus, up to two years later, they could firmly pinpoint a changed perception about one or more aspects of primary science accruing from the school's initial involvement with the science advisory teachers. The scheme had presented an image of science practice against which they contrasted their previous assumptions and attitudes. That perceptual/conceptual shift was related to some or all of the following:

(i)   **science, so to speak, had 'entered' their curriculum consciousness**

On an individual basis, some teachers acknowledged they had come to recognize they should include science in their planning and commented on the amendment to their design of topic work. Other teachers also referred to a more general 'collective' awareness: it was of great significance that science was now *'talked about'* in the staffroom.

> *I think there's been a greater awareness to put science in, and not to just get carried away with the interest of a topic or English. Everyone's aware they've to think of a science aspect.*

(ii)   **the boundaries and substance of science as a curriculum area had altered**

Beyond acknowledgement of the subject's existence, teachers also referred to a new understanding and image of what primary science entailed - and equally what it did not. They were able, in effect, to slough the stereotyped image of science as *'bunsen-burners'* *'chemistry formulae'* etc. and appreciate it as *'practical'* or *'finding out'* activities which were *'relevant'* and *'fun'*. Learning activities previously designated *'nature-study'* or *'construction play'*, even maths and language work, were now definable as *'science'*.

> *I'm more aware of what I classed as nature study is more science, is coming under the heading of science. People are more aware of things that they are doing is science ... I don't think we used science as a terminology properly - we're probably doing more and labelling it correctly.*

(iii)   **the teacher's way of working in primary science was clarified**

Some teachers referred to their recognition of a particular *modus operandi* in the delivery of science, such as a distinctive style of teacher questioning or certain forms of pupil grouping and classroom organization.

It opened my eyes to what could be done ... I picked up a way of questioning children - to stand back and let them reach conclusions. I picked that up from the advisory teacher.

(iv) a distinctive kind of pupil learning behaviour and attitude was apparent in science

Whether through observation of their own pupils at work with the advisory teacher, or through undertaking identical science activities themselves in the after-school INSET sessions, some teachers indicated their new appreciation of the learning approaches associated with primary science:

It made me aware that pupils learn by finding things out for themselves, it increased my awareness of the importance of practical work.

In sum, 'new awareness' related to teachers garnering a wide range of insights about the content and management of primary science. Sometimes these insights were referred to as CONFIRMATORY, i.e. the image of primary science that had been presented was felt to reassuringly reinforce and replicate the kinds of curriculum activity and teaching behaviour already part of the teacher's repertoire. The redefinition of science practice legitimized current practice:

People who were perhaps worried about their expertise in science have found out they were doing a lot of science anyway, but otherwise there's no difference in our teaching.

For other respondents, the new awareness was INNOVATORY in that they chose to emphasize how this version of primary science was very different from their previous practice and understanding.

However, several teachers - particularly those with previous expertise and experience in primary science - were adamant that this new awareness, though a very noticeable outcome of the scheme, was not in itself sufficient stimulus to ensure any alteration in their colleagues' classroom practice:

I think the main thing that changed was people's awareness. They may not do anything about it, it was the awareness rather than the actual implementation - but obviously that's the first hurdle to get over.

This comment perceptively raises the issue of what teachers actually DO with their newfound awareness. In itself, it must be stressed, changed awareness is no guarantee of changed practice. For closely associated with awareness is a further step of teachers matching the new image of practice against their own pedagogical preferences and curriculum values. It is at this stage that a small number of respondents clearly balked at the momentous upheaval to their established practice which operationalizing primary science as imaged/recommended by the scheme entailed. This being so, a fourth major outcome of the scheme can be identified as VALUE CONGRUENCE.

Value congruence outcomes

Value congruence is a term referring to the personalized versions of curriculum and classroom management which informs a primary practitioner's teaching and how far these come to coincide with INSET messages about 'good practice'. It is a recognition that teachers' classroom practice is always underpinned by their assumptions and decisions about what it is appropriate for pupils to learn and how these learning experiences are best organized and delivered. These assumptions could be characterized as VALUES or a kind of individuated 'code of practice' derived from a range of professional (and also perhaps personal) experiences. Very often such values can be implicit and unarticulated, but no doubt mostly account for the unique qualities of the teacher in action. Hence, any in-service provision attempting to change practice may need to acknowledge the challenge of impacting upon the unique - and discrepant - professional philosophies of its targeted audience. Certain INSET messages, be they imperatives or simply exhortations, may sit unhappily with the teaching style and curriculum content which a teacher has become comfortable with and committed to over a considerable period of time. Alternatively, such messages may closely reflect a teacher's existing philosophy and practice. A third value congruence outcome may be that a teacher is genuinely inspired or motivated to adapt her current curriculum and classroom management to accommodate the new messages.

The science scheme clarifies three particular aspects of practice which appear pivotal to value congruence: closely aligned to the issues emerging in 'new awareness'.

(i) **pedagogical style, i.e. the organization and delivery of children's learning experiences**

The interviews demonstrate that a number of teachers felt the kinds of practice undertaken by the advisory teachers closely replicated their own preferred organizational strategies, while a small minority openly admitted that it did not.

The advisory teacher didn't do anything different to me, she just worked with a group ... if you want to work with a group, that's what you do, it's what I do normally.

They seemed to think we could work in groups, not so much science groups but maybe three different areas of the curriculum - really I prefer a more structured approach, more formal ... if there was lessons I could do a 'Science Lesson', I would.

I'm a chalk and talk man myself.

Unlike the other key aspects of value congruence, there was no evidence, from teachers' accounts at least, that attitudes towards appropriate pedagogy had changed because of the science scheme: neither the advisory teachers' nor the school's own development work appeared to have altered preferences in classroom management style. However, although value congruence was not achieved (or achievable) by the kinds of INSET experience offered by the scheme, it nevertheless came to be openly acknowledged as an issue which affected subsequent classroom implementation.

Influence on teachers' style has got to be fairly limited ... it's difficult to change people from formal approaches to informal ones and it certainly can't be done in six weeks.

Given that discrepant teaching styles appear often to be left unspoken - and hence unaddressed - at school level, an INSET programme which exposes value discongruence in this area may well prove a valuable opportunity for tackling its resolution. The evidence would suggest that neither the school nor the advisory teachers directly took up the challenge, though clearly it was never part of the official brief of the scheme that this aspect of value congruence would be tackled. Co-ordinators particularly expressed a sense of having no influence on colleagues' classroom management and organization.

(ii)　curriculum content, i.e. the kind of activities offered to children

The second major area of value congruence concerned the kinds of learning experiences offered to children as science. Here, a number of teachers reported a considerable shift in their assumptions about what it was appropriate for children to undertake: they came to accept and indeed champion investigative/discovery learning.

The advisory teachers made me believe in doing more practical things with children.

I could see how exciting science can be for children, that it's important for them to discover and do it for themselves ... it surprised me how much they could do.

In other words, the scheme was seen to be able to effect value congruence with regard to the curriculum content of science. One or two teachers indicated that the demonstrated pupil activities were already part of their practice, i.e. their own values with regard to primary children's learning coincided with those which had been demonstrated by the scheme. However, a small number demurred, indicating, for instance, that teacher-defined learning goals remained important or that practical activities were simply unmanageable within the organization strategies usually employed:

For me, the starting point is what are we trying to find out ... I may be old-fashioned, but I have to plan that way - I can't change.

For some teachers, having groups and children up to their elbows in it ... well, it's just not them.

In this way, the close links between teaching style and pupil activity are evident, and raises an important issue for INSET designers: if teachers' preferences as classroom managers ultimately determine the learning experiences of pupils, then achieving value congruence on the former perhaps emerges as one of the greatest imperatives of any curriculum innovation.

(iii)　curriculum design i.e. the way the whole curriculum is planned and the proportionate importance attached to different subject areas

This aspect of value congruence relates to the way teachers define the appropriate balance of subject areas within their whole curriculum. This was an outcome of the scheme which no doubt was crucially influenced by the wider educational context. Teachers anticipated the National Curriculum and the elevation of science to the third core area and very often indicated that the school's involvement with the ESG scheme reflected rather than inspired a revised view of its importance in the primary curriculum. However, regardless of national imperatives, a few teachers referred openly to their value discongruence with current notions of curriculum balance, stating that in their view the inclusion of science still required that *the basics shouldn't be touched* or that particularly language remained their major priority and teaching investment. In sum, many teachers tended to accede to the imperative of science within the primary curriculum rather more than whole-heartedly concur with its ascribed status.

Overall then, value congruence emerged as a major factor in subsequent classroom practice. Certainly, where discongruence was admitted, the teacher's implementation of primary science was also said to be limited. Further to this - and perhaps as a partial explanation - the rhetoric of the scheme had strongly delivered the message 'you're already doing it' i.e. had represented/assumed value congruence as a general pre-condition of the INSET provision, rather than a (problematic) goal. Hence, acknowledging, let alone solving, the possible tensions accruing from a teacher's sense of dissonance with the imaged practice was never officially on the INSET agenda, and may have significant implications for its ultimate effectiveness.

Beyond that, a number of teachers clearly took the value-congruence message of *'you're already doing it'* to validate a version of curriculum innovation which resulted in virtual inertia. Their descriptions of subsequent practice indicated how they felt relieved of the necessity of addressing possible differences between the value systems underpinning their work and that of the advisory teachers. Indeed, they appeared to have sought out from the imaged science practice precisely those aspects which reinforced their own curriculum values and preferences, and continued to 'domesticate' science to that end:

> I was on the right lines anyway, so I don't think anything new came - the important part for me is getting the vocabulary out of them ... what I got out of the scheme was watching the advisory teacher get the language out.

In sum, encouraging teachers to employ and believe the rhetoric of value congruence may also contribute to limited impact on practice. However, as the next two outcomes show, it clearly can be a very popular and positive strategy by which to effect a major aim of the scheme: 'removing anxiety'. The question has to be tentatively raised though as to whether removing anxiety by ignoring the challenge of innovation is always an entirely appropriate professional development strategy.

Affective outcomes

Affective outcomes acknowledge that there is an 'emotional' experience inherent in any learning situation, and that in the case of the ESG scheme, the teachers also felt a particular anxiety accruing from the subject to be learnt. One of the most frequent responses to questions about the impact of the scheme was a reference to the marked decrease in apprehensiveness about science experienced by the interviewee and her/his colleagues. In describing their anxieties prior to the INSET programme, it was also evident that some of these were related to, and in anticipation of, a novel and potentially threatening learning situation: the school-based INSET meant for the first time they would be learning alongside colleagues, having an advisory teacher in the classroom etc. Teachers attributed their positive affective outcomes directly to the scheme and the two advisory teachers, i.e. both message and messengers had effectively reduced projected fears about the demands of the INSET programme and also contributed to an increased confidence to undertake science in the classroom.

However, in describing that increased confidence, several also commented that apprehensions remained:

> I'm still not one hundred per cent confident ... I'm willing to try but don't feel as confident as I should be.

> I still don't feel I'm an expert ... I think I feel inadequate to teach science.

> The course was good at encouraging teachers to put science into topics, but the main fear now is organizing it into lessons on a permanent basis.

Hence, it may be important to distinguish, as one teacher did, between offering short-term reassurance and instilling a more long-term confidence.

Several teachers pinpointed where the source of that lay: deeper knowledge of the subject/discipline of primary science, gained through further INSET experiences. Positive affective outcomes may thus be a useful motivation or a necessary precursor for developing curriculum understanding.

Negative affective outcomes also were apparent from the scheme. Teachers reported - directly or by inference - a range of feelings deriving from their INSET experience which were destabilizing and demotivating. One or two indicated their discomfort with the exposure of the quality of their teaching skills compared to those of the advisory teachers - an ensuing demoralization and 'de-skilling' outcome was apparent. Another teacher felt her involvement with the working alongside component of the scheme was, in effect, a stigma. Her self-image with regards to her practice resisted the notion of needing such a professional development strategy, and in turn she came to resist and even undermine many of the good practice messages delivered by the advisory teachers. There thus seems to be a strong correlation between limited impact on practice and negative affective outcomes. This being so, close account needs to be taken, in any INSET design and delivery, of its effect on the feelings, as well as the conceptual understanding, of the targeted group. The evidence from the ESG scheme would suggest that universal strategies may impact very differently as affective outcomes in the learning experience of the various course members.

Motivational and attitudinal outcomes

One of the strongest outcomes of the scheme reported by teachers was their enhanced motivation to undertake science. A number referred to the enthusiasm of the advisory teachers '*rubbing off*', and '*being stimulated*' by their energy, conscientiousness etc. Typical comments were:

> *The scheme made you want to devote the whole day to science ... the advisory teacher brought in lots of interesting things to do and equipment, it made you want to get hold of those things and try them with the children yourself.*

> *It really rubbed off, you think if they can do it for three classes, well you think you can do it - it makes you look at yourself a little bit ... Are you really doing all you can?*

These teachers were thus recounting a response which could be described as a replication of the advisory teachers' own attitudes and commitment towards primary science. Their motivation was remembered as deriving from an encounter with equivalently highly motivated advisory teachers. The advisory teachers' strategy of enthusiastic encouragement and reinforcement (not unlike the responses of primary teachers to their pupils) paid off in terms of positive affective and value congruence outcomes, with a resulting reputation of the advisory teachers as an almost inspirational factor in some teachers' subsequent practice. The tendency was for such motivation to be described entirely as an outcome in itself: it was rarely, for instance, talked of as originating from an enhanced knowledge base or from a newly acquired pedagogical expertise. This raises the question of what happens to highly motivated practice in the longer term.

In the retrospective case-study schools at least, a commonly perceived outcome of such high enthusiasm was an inevitable evaporation or 'fall off', at both whole-school and individual teacher level. The phrase 'flavour of the month syndrome' was cited.

It's easy to let science drop, there's always something else being asked of us ... there's a tendency to think we've done it.

A similar prediction was made by certain teachers in the prospective schools, although it was stressed some residue of influence would remain.

It was such a high, but even if we drift back we won't drift back so much.

Clearly, in the schools encountering the ESG scheme in its later stages (Autumn 1988), when the National Curriculum imperative was fully apparent, such fall-off was less likely to occur or be acknowledged: motivation and mandate have, after all, a quite distinctive dynamic.

Nevertheless, accounts of a 'dropping-off' of science need close examination and analysis. Detailed attention to the descriptions of individual teachers indicated that for a few, far from 'dropping off' science, the scheme motivated them to undertake further courses, either within the LEA or outside it. Particularly, extra-authority courses were cited as providing additional confidence and subject understanding, which in turn acted as a further stimulus to classroom implementation.

For one co-ordinator, attendance at a course held at a nearby university was seen to both reflect and grant a special status by conferring new insights and information about children's learning in science. This was an incentive for her own classroom practice as well as her curriculum leadership role.

Teachers' descriptions of practice subsequent to further INSET, however, may offer some further explanation of the evaporation phenomena. The main issue to emerge was that the incorporation of science within their whole curriculum meant the initial rush of enthusiasm had inevitably to be tempered by other competing curriculum imperatives. It was not just at a whole-school level that other priorities emerged to overtake a particular initiative, such adjustment also occurred at classroom level.

> *I was enthusiastic after [my term's] course, [I was] like the advisory teachers - but when you're teaching full-time, your enthusiasm wears off because of other pressures.*

For the primary sector especially, with its whole-curriculum responsibility, re-integrating a subject area which has been given special INSET attention in this way may thus need certain accompanying support. Certainly, the importance of follow-up is reinforced but it may also be that teachers would benefit from the very problem of 'curriculum rehabilitation' being made explicit during the in-service programme itself. In this way, any apparent reduction in enthusiasm would not be seen as some shortcoming of the in-service provision or its recipients, but a necessary and inevitable stage in the professional development process.

However, INSET designers and deliverers may also pre-empt fall-off (and curriculum 'domestication' as indicated in the value-congruence outcome) by a follow-up programme that seriously attempts to monitor and support subsequent classroom practice. This would seem to be particularly the case after an intensive programme such as the ESG scheme offered. Though the scheme's design gave a significant role to the school in furthering the development work, evidence would suggest that the school and science co-ordinator were, by and large, unable to provide such support at classroom level (see Chapter Seven). Lack of time, opportunity and status were often referred to by co-ordinators as constraints on their capacity to maintain and monitor the momentum of curriculum innovation in their colleagues' classroom practice. Though - in 1989 at least - they could provide informal advice (when requested), act as 'servicers' of the science curriculum by organizing resources etc, and attempt to replicate the enthusiast role of the advisory teachers, there was a clear sense that their influence stopped at the classroom door. Sometimes it was reported that the informal discussions between staff taking similar age groups acted as a more significant impetus.

In sum, motivation - whether through imperative or inspiration - emerged as a *sine qua non* in any professional development exercise. There may, however, be a need to acknowledge that heightened enthusiasm and deepened understanding are not synonymous and that the pursuance of the former does not necessarily deliver the latter.

Knowledge and skills

As suggested earlier, outcomes involving increases in knowledge and skills are intended to signify enrichments in teachers' understanding of the tenets, principles and issues which underpin curriculum areas and classroom pedagogy. Whereas new awareness outcomes were defined through reference to changed perceptions and images of science, increased knowledge and skills outcomes denote deeper levels of understanding, critical reflexivity and theoretical rationales.

Extensions in knowledge and skills were rarely mentioned by teachers as outcomes of either the advisory teacher component or the work of the science co-ordinator. Virtually the only allusions to such extensions were related to the insights into scientific knowledge and process gained by experimenting with the practical activities included in the evening INSET sessions (e.g. '*I learned about electricity by wiring the batteries up*' or '*I learned how pupils must experience problem-solving activities*'). Even in these cases, however, there was little evidence to indicate that such rather elementary insights, (which actually have more in common with new awareness), were followed up by any more systematic and discursive examination of the knowledge and skills involved.

To a great extent, this lack of evidence to indicate development in teachers' scientific knowledge and skills was a predictable consequence of an in-service scheme which deliberately accentuated affective outcomes (e.g. '*reducing anxiety*' and '*increasing confidence*' were highlighted as priority aims in the scheme's formal submission) at the expense of outcomes relating to increased knowledge and skills. As outlined earlier, the chosen priorities for the scheme can be seen as highly justifiable responses to a rapidly changing context, which included a pressing need to react to the vulnerabilities and insecurities evinced by teachers, who were facing the challenge of expanding a primary science curriculum, as well as a novel and largely untested means of delivering INSET - the advisory teacher. However, there is evidence to suggest that, while in the short term the strategy of allaying fears without a complementary provision to extend teachers' stock of scientific knowledge and skills, may have produced the desired affective outcomes, in the longer-term perspective, teachers' anxieties and fears (hence lack of confidence to implement science thoroughly) re-surface because of their continuing inadequate knowledge and skills base and the shortage of INSET activities and resources to deal with it effectively. One teacher, who two years after the advisory teacher input considered herself highly unqualified and unsuitable to teach science, succinctly and poignantly summarized the feelings of inadequacy intimated by several teachers in the study: '*What I REALLY need is an 'O' level in science*'.

Teachers' accounts often highlighted their sense of inadequacy and unfamiliarity with several areas of knowledge and skills. The main lacunae (in order of priority) were perceived to relate to knowledge and skills concerning:

- scientific principles, theories and facts, including appropriate forms of progression through this body of knowledge;

- the processes of science (e.g. conducting experiments);

- the assessment of pupils' learning in science;

- teachers' self-perceptions of their own professional development needs.

The first of these was by far the most prevalent. Several teachers felt their own knowledge and understanding of physics, chemistry and technology were very limited. Unfulfilled knowledge needs like forces, pulleys and levers were mentioned with some frequency. In addition, many teachers wanted such knowledge to be taught in a form which was compatible and relevant to the age group they taught:

I'd like more courses for infants because it's a very different area and children at that age are very very different. I want to know what's been proven to be working.

Male teachers in the study tended to be slightly more confident than their female colleagues, but even for them having sufficient scientific knowledge at their finger-tips was problematic and often required a conscious effort to 'learn' the appropriate principles immediately before teaching it. One male teacher stated:

... in primary areas [of science] I'm a bit thin on, but you should be able to keep ahead of children in the primary sector.

A degree of irony was revealed in the comments of a female teacher. Two years after the advisory teacher input, she explained that she definitely required more *'facts and principles, otherwise it was a case of the blind leading the blind'*. She now felt that she would appreciate the kind of 'scientific' in-service activity she originally feared the two advisory teachers might provide. According to some co-ordinators, there were other teachers who had not recognized or at least not openly acknowledged, that they needed to strengthen their knowledge and skills concerning scientific knowledge and processes.

Classroom observation evidence lends support to the view that a number of teachers lacked self-knowledge - a self-critical reflexivity through which teachers could identify, and share with colleagues what it is they know and don't know. Limitations in the capacities for self-knowledge and self-awareness were seen as major obstacles to an accurate diagnosis, hence fulfilment, of individual professional development needs and then stimulating an interest in satisfying them in particular curriculum areas (i.e. motivational outcomes). Perhaps many teachers would benefit from in-service provision which focused on imparting the general skills and techniques in reflexivity and the formulation of valid self-knowledge.

The argument that it is not essential for teachers to possess detailed scientific knowledge because they can acquire it through conducting discovery learning experiments with their pupils, was treated sceptically and countered by most science co-ordinators. Firstly, it presupposes that primary teachers have a sound grasp of the processes of being scientific - a presupposition the observational evidence casts grave doubts on Secondly, it implies that teachers, along with their pupils, can find their own way to the collected achievements of centuries of scientific thinking and development. For those teachers, mainly the co-ordinators, who had taken steps to extend their own scientific knowledge and skills, including knowledge about the processes of science, there was a strong conviction that a good grounding in such knowledge and skills was indispensable to effective science teaching. In depicting the qualities needed for teaching science at primary level, one co-ordinator, who had been on an extensive course in science, put the point in the following way:

You've got to know just what to ask, and when to ask it, and when to leave well alone and let them [i.e. the pupils get on with it] ... you know. And if ... you see this is where I feel, certainly in the fourth year, our school would be better if we had a science expert, because a science expert knows where they're leading the children to. Whereas someone like me can fill in and take the children so far, but I'm not sure of the overall end in view all the time. Whereas somebody with a science background would be - well, this [activity] would be leading on to work on this, or I will ask these questions that will guide the children along those lines and come to the right answer in the end.

This co-ordinator, like most of the others, went on to argue the case for a more intensive and longer in-service input on scientific knowledge and skills. They stressed the crucial lesson that raising awareness (see 'new awareness' outcomes) is in itself insufficient - a point which would seem to have a relevance to INSET planners far beyond the particular constraints of the science scheme.

To conclude this section, then, there was significant evidence to indicate (i) that merely raising awareness had minimal direct impact on practice, (ii) that affective outcomes (e.g. reducing anxiety) could be short-lived if underlying problems and needs were not addressed and (iii) that, for many teachers, significant developments in class practices would seem to necessitate - almost as a pre-condition - significant developments in their scientific knowledge and skills. Clearly, the form of INSET provision most suited to achieving knowledge and skills outcomes requires careful consideration. As a final observation, thus far, little evidence has emerged to suggest that the science co-ordinators have the opportunities or capacities to provide in-service activities capable of developing teachers' knowledge and skills. Neither the co-ordinators themselves nor their colleagues reported help along these lines as a salient part of the co-ordinators' role.

Institutional strategic outcomes

The model of outcomes advanced by Joyce and Showers (see Chapter One) is limited to the effects of in-service teacher education programmes on INDIVIDUAL participants. In contrast, the evidence from the science scheme reveals that in-service provision can have an important collective impact on GROUPS of teachers - in this case, whole schools - and that such a corporate outcome can have a constructive influence on teachers' efforts to change their own individual practice. This view is consistent with a number of writers on INSET who have noted (i) that in-service provision is likely to be more effective if it is related to current organizational changes and developments in the school and (ii) that individual teachers' attempts to innovate following an in-service programme have a greater chance of succeeding if they are shared with sympathetic, knowledgeable and supportive colleagues and supervisors (eg Dias *et al* 1988). Here, the term 'institutional strategic outcomes' is used to capture these organizational and group effects of in-service provision.

Regularly reiterated by the two advisory teachers, the emphasis on whole-school or group outcomes was a novel feature of the science scheme, which undoubtedly produced important and advantageous effects on a school's consciousness and discourse on science. Similar testimonies to raising the level of group discussion on science as those already alluded to in the 'new awareness' section were reported by several teachers. According to most interviewees, both the advisory teacher's input, and the on-going work of some co-ordinators, led to more talk around the school about science, more science displays and increased expectations. Some, however, pointed out that latterly these effects seemed a more direct result of the National Curriculum changes than the in-service scheme. One co-ordinator highlighted what she saw as the importance of the whole staff addressing curriculum developments as a corporate activity:

The scheme [i.e. the advisory teacher input] stimulated us altogether. It gave us more confidence to incorporate more practical science. This area of the school needed a boost. We couldn't have done it individually - everyone needed to benefit from the scheme together. This 'combined way' was new for this school. What was new was all trying some thing at the same time. This was good .... There would have been reduced involvement by some teachers if the scheme had not been aimed at the whole school. If only some of the staff had been

involved, an 'us and them' situation would have developed - teachers
not involved would have said the 'thems' can get on with the science
since they've been on the course. The whole school approach puts
pressure on every teacher to do something.

Her latter point clearly signals the potential for whole-school outcomes
precipitating the knock-on effect of stimulating or reinforcing motivational
outcomes. Hence, the advisory teacher input by *'focusing all the staff's*
attention and thinking in the same direction' can be seen as producing a
'herd effect' through which some of the more reluctant members were
moved in that same direction by virtue of the pressures created by the
dynamics of the group's overall positive response. Some teachers
volunteered the observation that the advisory teacher's involvement
made an important contribution to whole-staff cohesion and bonding
which had benefits far beyond the specific concerns of science. Indeed,
a head of one of the 'prospective' case-study schools identified this wider
uniting impact as one of his main motives for seeking the involvement of
the advisory teachers in his school.

This emphasis on whole-school or group outcomes was accompanied by
a firm intention to influence organizational and strategic developments
within a school. The scheme provides illustrations of three main
(institutional) strategic outcomes: the establishment of a science co-
ordinator, a record-keeping system and a school science curriculum
policy statement. Together these constituted the mechanisms through
which it was hoped that the schools would pursue a self-sustaining
support system for professional development in science. Consequently,
the three key strategic developments should be seen as both (first phase)
outcomes of the initial advisory teacher input and in-service processes
aimed at stimulating and reinforcing (second phase) outcomes such as
effects on classroom practice.

Since the next chapter deals exclusively with the capacities of schools as
institutions to sustain the developments, it is not proposed to dwell on
them here. Suffice here to note that the predominant work undertaken by
the co-ordinators comprised obtaining and organizing resources,
administering a record-keeping system and feeding back to colleagues
reports of science in-service and planning meetings attended. Some co-
ordinators reported that the implementation of the science statutory
orders at Key Stage 1 had increased the level and perceived status of the

functions they perform (e.g. meeting with other science coordinators to agree a common framework of 'topics' for primary schools within a pyramid group). However, in interviews describing their role, no co-ordinator volunteered they had responsibility for the professional development of their colleagues. Similarly, in-service activities were rarely organized by coordinators. In explaining the limited contribution of co-ordinators to staff development, interviewees pointed to the organizational and cultural constraints which inhibit coordinators from taking up directive and interventionist roles like the design and delivery of school-based INSET. Lack of time and limited resources, including further INSET support, were also mentioned as constraining factors.

Clearly the science scheme, principally in the form of the advisory teacher input, successfully PRECIPITATED certain whole school and strategic outcomes, for example the establishment of science co-ordinators. However, these initial outcomes have had little further impact on teachers' CONTINUING professional development and hence their classroom practice. This may well relate to the fact that science co-ordinators have encountered numerous problems - time, status, staffroom culture - which undermine an effective development role. Most significantly, there was a tangible sense in which the ownership of responsibility for sustaining the INSET provision for science had not been taken up by the schools. It often appeared not to have entered the school consciousness. As one deputy headteacher remarked:

We were not aware that the responsibility for developing science, and its related INSET needs, had been handed over to the schools.

Perhaps more needs to be done to encourage schools to accept that the responsibility for teachers' professional development now rests firmly with them, though inevitably in the wake of ERA, INSET policies and practice will have to compete with all the other imperatives now vying for teachers' and headteachers' (highly stretched) attention. It also raises the issue of whether the initial advisory teachers' input should have focused on whole-school outcomes even more than individual ones, and over a longer period of time.

Impact on classroom practice

This final, and perhaps most crucial outcome in the typology refers to any changes or developments in teachers' classroom delivery of science that can be attributed to the various components of the ESG scheme. For us, it represents the ultimate goal of all the earlier outcome types, as well as a separate type in its own right. It differs from previous outcomes in that any analysis focusing on what teachers DO obviously has to be based on observations of practice as well as the teachers' own accounts. Educational research and evaluation has long recognized that there can be a problematic distinction between how teachers describe their practice and how their classroom activity actually appears to outside observers. Though a major function of the evaluation's data collection and analysis was to garner teachers' PERCEPTIONS of the impact of the scheme on their science work with children, it also clearly necessitated a rigorous examination of the teachers in action. To this end, classroom observations and interviews with teachers as well as pupils were undertaken at various stages of the project. Preliminary analysis of the practice and perceptions of ten of these observed teachers, (i.e. two from each of the case-study schools), thus form the basis of this section of the report. It draws particularly on data collected in the summer term of 1989, using semi- structured observation techniques and recorded post-observation discussions with both teachers and pupils.

Two general points need to be made before looking in detail at the classroom practice outcomes of the scheme.

First, as a methodology, it has to be acknowledged that a pre-arranged observation of a single session is likely to induce some sort of 'show' lesson. The evaluators viewed any inevitable special preparation as a useful indicator or demonstration of how the teachers conceived and executed a particular version of 'good science practice`. However extraneous or similar to 'normal' (unobserved) practice, each teacher would still reveal a great deal about the personal interpretation of how s/he OUGHT to teach primary science subsequent to the input of the ESG scheme. In the event, most teachers testified to the typicality of what was seen; or openly referred to how it differed. Pupil interviews tended to corroborate the typicality (or otherwise) of what they had been asked to undertake.

Secondly, generalizing from the close study of ten teachers' practice in order to detect any significant incidences or patterns of impact must inevitably underplay the individuality of their work. Certainly such a study cannot relay a full picture of their teaching repertoire. Nor, given the complexity of the influences on a teacher's practice, can it make categorical cause and effect judgements relating to the scheme's impact. Nevertheless, a concomitant correlation between teachers' responses to the scheme, their curriculum rationales and observed teaching behaviour was detectable, and it is hoped these tentative and interim conclusions offer useful general insights into the 'practice outcomes' of INSET provision.

In looking for these correlations, a number of key questions were applied to the analysis of the full range of data on teachers' classroom science activity after the ESG scheme. The aspects of practice it was felt were particularly important to monitor were:

* the frequency/amount of science being undertaken by teachers;

* the intentionality and planning underpinning the science activities provided for pupils;

* the organization and management of those activities in the classroom;

* the nature of the interactions between teacher and pupils.

These issues were selected because it was felt that the scheme had offered strong messages (or clear images) about each: topic approaches, group teaching, investigative learning, science as process had all featured in the INSET work of the advisory teachers, and in the recommended policy-making and resourcing of the schools subsequently.

Frequency
In 1989, all teachers testified to the fact that since the ESG input they were undertaking science regularly and/or more frequently, though the National Curriculum imperative was clearly influential here, and in some cases infiltrating teachers' value systems quite subtly.

I do do a lot more science but I sometimes wonder if it's because I have to do it, I know we've got to do the science and the children NEED to do it, and love doing it, but I wouldn't say it's particularly because we had the advisory teachers in school.

Others affirmed that they felt they were doing more science because it was now clearly part of their personal curriculum conceptualization or

154

planning 'framework':

Oh yes, I'm doing more, before I didn't realize I was doing science half the time, you just planned your flowchart ... now, I'm looking specifically for the science ... (we didn't put things in boxes before, it was just TOPIC wasn't it, you didn't think if you were doing geography, maths, science ...).

Though all teachers found it hard to quantify the precise amounts of science they undertook, partly because of the cross-curricular nature of their work, there was considerable variation in the capacity to specify when and how much science was undertaken. Two teachers chose to emphasize how scientific learning now equalled maths and English - in importance at least. Others stressed that it formed one or two sessions per week of the children's timetable. This was sometimes achieved in the concentrated form of a science-orientated topic for several weeks rather than being a regular on-going component of each topic.

In these discussions attempting to quantify science work, it was generally the case that those who highlighted the 'confirmatoriness' of the advisory teachers' message (*'They made me realize I was already doing science'*) were more imprecise about the degree to which - and the occasions when - science was underway in their classrooms. This seemed particularly the case with the three infant teachers who emphasized that their nature/environmental studies work was now re-classifiable as science. Disentangling science from language and number work was seen as very problematic. Another teacher indicated he felt he did more science work, but also stated that this involved him *'telling the children, and them listening'*. A colleague in the same school stated that she *'didn't know whether the amount had increased, but my consciousness of the way it should be done, with children finding out, certainly had'*. In sum, questions about frequency and amounts of science opened up considerably diverse and discrepant definitions of what constituted science practice. There was certainly evidence that natural sciences still dominated some teachers science work.

It also seemed, particularly from pupil interviews undertaken after observations of the lesson, that several of the teachers were not presenting children with regular opportunities for the kinds of practical investigative work which they were demonstrating on the day of observation. One fourth year pupil explicitly stated that the only previous time such science activities had been undertaken was when the researcher/ evaluator had last been present in the classroom, adding:

We've only ever had two or three lessons, you can't say you really like a subject if you've only done a few lessons.

Other younger pupils' comments also testified to the limited amount of practical work involved in their science curriculum:

We don't do much experimenting ... so I haven't much practice, it's kind of like playing and I haven't got to learn it yet.

Science is writing and seeing things grow and looking at small animals and fishes .. (in science) you just put them on the table and look at them but to-day we tested things.

Teachers' planning
All teachers had planned their science as a component of a topic, and some indicated that this approach was a result of the scheme:

The advisory teacher taught me how to bring in more science into my topic.

I'm doing a lot more science work through topic since the scheme.

Rather than being attributable to the scheme, some indicated that specification of curriculum areas was a noticeable development in their planning procedures for topic work directly because of the National Curriculum.

Just lately we've done it under actual subject headings ... language, maths, science and art and craft are the main headings .. simply and solely because we've to match it to the attainment targets .. whereas normally you'd just have done a flow-chart and covered everything without labelling it.

Others indicated that this type of planning constituted no change to their normal practice.

In terms of planning specific science work within the topic, it was clear that those teachers who had utilized and pre-researched ideas from text books, workcards or teacher materials had a clearer sense of progression and skill or concept development than those who had devised their own science activities. Equally, those whose topic had an obvious science orientation, such as electricity or structures, were able to present a sequence of learning activities. Where teachers tried to work within more broad or idiosyncratic themes such as water or a geographical country (which had been that teacher's holiday location), especially without recourse to teacher materials/resources, the work undertaken often appeared to have little recognizable primary science process or content. In other words, the rhetoric of *'you can get science out of any topic'* seemed sometimes to be taken too literally, without proper recognition of the rigorous planning and preparation it may involve. Encouraging a far greater familiarity with, and even more respect for, existing teacher materials may have helped here. Only one teacher specifically mentioned this had been an outcome of the scheme:

The scheme made you put a bit more effort into planning, you've got to get down to it, look in the books, sort out your experiments, sort out the progression ... it helped me to prepare.

In sum, encouraging teachers to become critical, selective 'plagiarists' of teacher materials seems a more helpful strategy and emphasis than the comforting rhetoric of *'you're already doing it'*.

In response to questions about what they hoped the children would learn from the science activities undertaken, teachers generally emphasized three different aspects:

* the investigative learning/problem-solving opportunities for children;

* some specific science concept or process;

* the language development opportunities inherent in the work they were doing.

These intentions and aims were clearly reflected in the kinds of learning experiences offered to the children, and in the teacher activity and questioning that accompanied the pupils' work. Moreover, it became apparent that the different emphases given to the purpose of the science work sometimes reflected the kinds of messages teachers felt they had picked up from the scheme. Thus, two teachers who provided problem-solving on the theme of 'Structures' both indicated they felt the main message of the scheme was children 'finding out' and 'discovering' for themselves. Those who elected to stress that the scheme had confirmed their existing practice, significantly, relayed a rationale which concentrated more on language development and vocabulary acquisition than specific aspects of science. And it was those teachers who were most conscious of the challenge to their own scientific knowledge engendered by the scheme and the National Curriculum who tended to describe the learning in their children's work in terms of particular science processes (e.g. accurate recording, fair testing) and/or knowledge (e.g. 'air pushes up', differences in electrical circuits). However, it is important to point out that many other variables such as age of children taught or the teachers' pre-existing understanding of and predilection towards primary science may also have contributed to these variations in rationale.

In answer to the question of impact on teachers' science curriculum planning and intentionality attributable to the scheme, it seems that variations in teachers' intended learning outcomes testify to markedly different ways of interpreting and internalizing INSET messages. INSET designers and deliverers may thus find it beneficial to provide themselves with opportunities for giving close attention to those various message-constructs of the target audience. A better understanding of how INSET messages are reconstructed and remembered by recipients may give important clues as to how they will be operationalized subsequently. Such information may also be a vital component in any school-based development work. It was noticeable in the course of the three year evaluation that teachers did not change their initial perception of the key message of the scheme.

The Organization and Management of Science
Having looked at the scheme's impact on teacher intentionality and planning, the analysis now focuses on its outcomes in relation to the organization of science in the classroom.

It is at this point that the caveats about 'special' lessons become most relevant, and certainly the evaluators received numerous indications that teachers were making particular efforts to set up exemplary science sessions e.g. the rest of the class well briefed and involved in self-sustaining activities. Half of the sample used extra support - in the form of parents, Language support teachers, non-teaching assistants resulting in a number of sessions which seemed direct replications of the working alongside arrangements the teachers had previously been involved with (i.e. one teacher with exclusive responsibility for science group(s), the other maintaining the rest of the class). Certainly, most teachers created enough teaching space to work for up to 95 per cent of the session with their science group(s). (The children engaged in science activities only once totalled more than half the class; a science group usually consisted of between four and eight children).

In discussion, most teachers indicated they had received strong messages that science should and could only be delivered by group teaching situations, though for some this was a pedagogical approach they already were fully committed to, whereas others felt it was a divergence from their own preferences. No one was a committed or enthusiastic convert to group teaching. All indicated the problematic nature of investing their teaching time in science activities while simultaneously providing constructive and demanding work for the rest of the class. Two mentioned discipline problems, others the difficulties of avoiding interruptions and learning inquiries from other children whilst trying to work with a science group. The good practice imaged by the advisory teachers seemed to remain an unresolved pedagogical dilemma. Interestingly, the two teachers with the most expertise in primary science, garnered from advanced study, demonstrated organizational strategies quite distinct from those exemplified by the advisory teachers. Both, working solo, had only one small group undertaking practical science activities and each spent no more than 25 per cent of their total teaching time with that group, usually in short, highly-focused interactions lasting one or occasionally two minutes. This contrasted with the lengthy and sustained investments in science which most other teachers attempted to undertake on the day of observation.

Overall, it would seem that the impact of the scheme on teachers' organizational strategies was quite distinct. Whilst there was a uniformity in teachers' understanding of the received message, the imaged practice of high teacher-investment in group learning was sometimes regarded as neither acceptable nor feasible. Organization of science in the classroom remained a genuine problem for even the most skilled practitioners. It may suggest the need for more discussion and support - at school level particularly - in order to provide teachers with a fuller repertoire of teaching strategies that would assist effective implementation.

Teacher-pupil interaction

This final section looks at the area of micro-pedagogy and asks what impact the scheme may have had on the science-related interactions between pupil and teacher.

In Chapter Five, it was indicated that the advisory teacher input largely dealt with science knowledge and process implicitly rather than as a direct focus, though the working alongside component provided quality examples of questioning skills related to science process. Process skills had also featured in the first INSET session. Several of the policies developed in school subsequently also provided clarification of the key process skills associated with science. How far these illustrations inform teachers' practice is the issue under consideration.

Analysis of teacher-pupil interactions in the ten classrooms demonstrated that there was a close connection between the purposes articulated by the teacher and the ensuing focus of discussion. Thus, the teachers who emphasized the language development inherent in their science work tended to ask questions which elicited and reinforced vocabulary; those stressing a particular science concept encouraged and led their pupils to reiterate that principle (perhaps sometimes at the expense of listening to children's own interpretations and understandings); the two teachers focusing on structures/problem-solving used questions to guide children to solutions.

With the notable exception of the two practitioners who had undertaken advanced study, there was a marked absence of attention given to scientific recording and to the application of science process skills. Children were generally asked to write about or make a drawing/diagram of their science work as a postscript to the activity. Accurate measuring, prediction, fair testing were often not featured, indeed one teacher was heard to say '*don't tell your friend the answer, otherwise it's not a fair test*' (i.e. 'test' was implicitly misunderstood by the teacher, not just the pupils, as a form of assessment rather than experiment).

Nevertheless, all teachers employed questioning as their major pedagogical strategy. Nearly all were skilled at managing and drawing discussion from their pupils. However, the main - and consistent - omission in the classroom work of all those whose only science INSET experience was the ESG scheme can best be conveyed by the reflections of one of the teachers who had undertaken advanced study:

The process skills that form the basis of our policy I try to keep in the front of my mind both when I'm planning and when I'm assessing what children have done and what I think they've learned ... if you learn nothing else from the science course at [the local polytechnic] ... you learn those [process skills]. And in a way I use them unconsciously, because it's been drummed into me over four years ... and I think unconsciously is the word ... I have to make it more conscious, but it is always at the front of my mind in planning and assessing.

In all the discussions on and observations of practice, the rest of this sample of teachers demonstrated very little CONSCIOUSNESS of process, suggesting, in the words of T. S. Elliot, that on some crucial aspects of primary science practice, they may have '*had the experience but missed the meaning*'.

Thus, the analysis of observations of teachers' science practice up to the summer term of 1989 raises one final issue.

Though teachers' perceptions and/or rhetoric indicated the elevation and integration of science into their curriculum design, their practice seemed to testify to a reliance on existing pedagogical skills and curriculum predilections UNLESS further INSET was a feature of their recent professional experience.

The advisory teacher input and the subsequent school-based development work would seem to have underplayed the identification and implementation of process skills associated with the most effective primary science practice.

AN ORDERING OF OUTCOMES?

In constructing and illustrating a tentative typology of nine INSET outcomes, it will be clear that certain outcomes can have a knock-on effect for others, e.g. PROVISIONARY outcomes can he highly MOTIVATING. Beyond this, it is possible to conclude that some of the first eight outcomes rank as being more contiguous with the ninth and final outcome - teachers' changed classroom practice - than others. A sequence, or even hierarchy, of outcomes seems to emerge from the analysis and be implicit within the text. The chapter now attempts to frame the nine constituents of the typology into an order of significance for changing practice, although some general points or caveats need to be registered initially.

First, the ordering is even more tentative than the typology itself. It is descriptive, not prescriptive and intended to contribute to the debate on effective INSET, certainly not resolve it. This is particularly so as it is based on an analysis of the longitudinal perspectives and practices of only ten primary teachers from the five case-study schools.

Second, this ordering takes changed practice as the ultimate goal of INSET provision, although we recognize that some INSET clearly is not always targeted to that end. The purpose of certain INSET experiences may be limited to only one or two outcomes such as information transmission or awareness raising.

Third and closely related to this, the significance of certain outcomes may be diminished or increased by the existing practice (and values) of a particular INSET recipient. For instance, the science scheme was inevitably going to impact very differently upon a teacher who was already committed to, and competent in, providing investigative learning opportunities than one who was more comfortable with formal and didactic approaches. If some INSET outcomes, in effect, already exist in the practice (or attitude) of an INSET recipient - and hence do not have to be achieved by the INSET provider, the ordering can also be seen as a kind of general 'map of preconditions' for effecting the implementation of any recommended practice. Individual teachers' professional development is thus likely to require different routes or outcome-emphases.

Using the evidence of the PST scheme, the outcomes outlined in the report seem to fall roughly into the following order of significance for the ultimate outcome of impacting on teachers' practice:

INSET	
3rd Order	PROVISIONARY : INFORMATION : NEW AWARENESS
2nd Order	MOTIVATION : AFFECTIVE : INSTITUTIONAL
1st Order	VALUE CONGRUENCE : KNOWLEDGE & SKILLS
IMPACT ON PRACTICE	

In this way, the evidence would suggest that INSET experiences which focus on (or are perceived as offering) only third order outcomes - transmitting information, raising awareness, offering materials or resources - are least likely to impact on a teacher's practice unless other (higher) order outcomes are also achieved or already exist. Motivation and the closely related affective outcomes seem particularly important here, and indeed they may move a teacher from a new awareness or from being the mere recipient of new materials to actually attempting implementation. However, without other accompanying (first order) outcomes, any lower order outcome's ultimate impact on practice is likely to be limited or temporary. It would seem almost truistic to conclude that teachers have to genuinely acquire - and also believe in - substantive skills/ knowledge offered by INSET provision in order to effect change. First order outcomes are, however, equally dependent on a range of lower order outcomes - especially motivation. Institutional outcomes could be a particularly effective way of sustaining motivation and consolidating and extending skills/knowledge, though the evidence clearly indicates that within the existing culture of some primary schools this did not occur. (The next chapter deals with this in greater detail.)

In sum, attempting to order INSET outcomes highlights their complex inter-dependency. Moreover, as was noted in the introduction of the chapter, the ordering of outcomes may be very different if impacting on practice is not the goal of a particular INSET activity. Equally, it is entirely possible that another researcher, INSET designer or recipient considering their experience of effective INSET may find the order offered here to be inconsistent with their conclusions: the tentative and exploratory nature of the typology is thus reiterated.

INDIVIDUATED OUTCOME-ROUTES

In this final section, the notion that INSET experiences impact differently upon different recipients can be illustrated by plotting five of the ten teachers' accounts of the effects of the science scheme on their subsequent classroom practice in and attitudes to primary science. These accounts revealed that each teacher had experienced a unique permutation in the number and type of INSET-outcome: a finding that suggested the whole idea of an 'individuated outcome-route'. Juxtaposing this outcome-route against the teacher's descriptions of their science work (as well as the researcher's own observations), in turn, reinforced the conclusion that certain outcomes become particularly crucial if changed practice is the INSET goal.

Beyond that, the illustrations may suggest that if certain outcomes are initially 'missed' by an INSET recipient, deliberate action to re-introduce them may need to be taken by those with responsibility for professional development (at school or LEA level) in order to ensure the practice-change which is required. This in turn implies that INSET providers need to know in some detail how their INSET activities are received. The timing and focus of any canvassing of audience reaction to courses may need to shift to garnering detailed information on these individuated outcome-routes rather than only collecting audience opinion/evaluation of the input itself.

Below, the five teachers' subsequent practice and outcome- routes are summarized. In order to honour confidentiality, a common stylistic devise in educational writing has been employed and all four have been referred to as 'she'. The outcomes delineated for each teacher are those which the respondent herself referred to as a positive effect of the scheme, the omission of certain outcomes denotes its absence in the teacher's accounts of the course's impact.

TEACHER A

PRACTICE:

Referred to a continuing preference for formal teaching approaches, and the pre-eminence of 'the basics' in the curriculum offered to children. She indicated openly that the scheme had minimal impact on her classroom work - very little science was done before, and only a little more after the scheme. Any science activity was usually undertaken as a whole-class teacher-led discussion. Classroom observation corroborated teacher's continuing unfamiliarity with investigative, group learning.

OUTCOME-ROUTE:

3rd Order   PROVISIONARY : NEW AWARENESS
(innovatory)

2nd Order   (INSTITUTIONAL)

1st Order

These third Order outcomes were the limit of the positive outcomes referred to by Teacher A. No positive second Order outcomes were mentioned (although the after school INSET was enjoyed): the teacher claimed to remain 'unhappy' about teaching science and was made conscious of the enormous gulf between advisory teacher's practice and values and her own. However, the co-ordinator was said to provide resources and 'chivvy along', hence a possible institutional outcome.

Thus, Teacher A's outcome-route broke down at the lowest level and evidence of impact on practice was negligible.

TEACHER B

PRACTICE:

In her first year of teaching a younger age-group of children, Teacher B claimed to be doing *'nothing different'* because of the PST scheme or the accompanying £200 worth of science equipment which school had elected to purchase. However, she acknowledged it had helped her to recognize that the advisory teacher's version of primary science was already part of the curriculum experiences she offered to children. Classroom observation indicated a strong emphasis on encouraging descriptive language rather than accurate skills in science process.

OUTCOME-ROUTE:

3rd Order	PROVISIONARY : NEW AWARENESS (confirmatory)

2nd Order

1st Order	VALUE CONGRUENCE

This teacher explicitly referred to negative second Order outcomes: she indicated the scheme had given insufficient attention to her particular macro-pedagogical needs or to the implementation of her preferred topic. The school and co-ordinator were not seen as providing any additional support for classroom practice beyond availability of equipment. Value-congruence was claimed, largely due to the absorption of the INSET message 'you're already doing it'. However, a lack of engagement with, or awareness of, the need to implement new science process skills resulted. This particular outcome-route, with its omission of second Order outcomes and perhaps inappropriate linkage of those designated third and first Order, exemplifies an extreme example of curriculum domestication, to the point of inertia.

TEACHER C

PRACTICE:

Teacher C expressed a strong sense of the looming national imperative to deliver science in the primary curriculum. She was particularly concerned about her continuing lack of scientific knowledge, and made extensive use of the teacher materials and workcards provided by the £200. She acknowledged that she may have *'picked up a way of questioning children in science'* from the advisory teachers, but found their notion of facilitating children's problem-solving inconsistent with her own limited knowledge and confidence. Within an efficient classroom management strategy that ensured she could invest a good deal of time with her science groups, she offered investigative scientific activities based on commercial workcards. However, the concepts appeared to have been rather too sophisticated for the age-group - and, by her own admission, to some extent the teacher herself!

OUTCOME-ROUTE:

3rd Order	PROVISIONARY : NEW AWARENESS
	(confirmatory)

2nd Order	MOTIVATION : AFFECTIVE : INSTITUTIONAL

1st Order

This teacher had an altogether more complex and positive response to the scheme. All thirds Order outcomes were referred to: availability of teacher materials; insights and information on the 'LEA policy' for primary science and the reassurance of the message that her Environmental Studies work already contained a good deal of science. In turn, these third Order outcomes were said to have activated second Order outcomes which, though initially very positive, were also acknowledged to be relatively short term. Ultimately, the National Curriculum imperative maintained motivation to undertake science, as well as support from the co-ordinator. Lack of scientific knowledge was seen as the major stumbling block to a genuine valuation of science in this teacher's curriculum; a conscientious tokenism was the admitted result.

TEACHER D

PRACTICE:

Teacher D expressed a growing confidence and interest in teaching science since her involvement in the PST scheme, and had been particularly inspired by the children's enthusiastic response to practical, problem-solving activities offered by the advisory teachers. The work-books bought with the £200 were a highly valued source of ideas for ensuring progression in the investigative/problem- solving work she now was fully committed to providing. Taking on the co-ordinator role had facilitated further course attendance (both within and beyond the LEA) which in turn confirmed her commitment to practical, discovery learning in science. Observation corroborated this commitment to a role of open-questioning within genuine problem-solving activities.

OUTCOME-ROUTE:

> **3rd Order**   **PROVISIONARY : NEW AWARENESS**
> **(innovatory)**

> **2nd Order**   **MOTIVATION : AFFECTIVE : INSTITUTIONAL**

> **1st Order**   **VALUE CONGRUENCE : KNOWLEDGE & SKILLS**

Nearly all outcomes prevailed in this teacher's descriptions of her subsequent practice and values relating to primary science. The interplay or knock-on effect of third, second and first Order outcomes was particularly apparent: from an initial realization of, and interest in, the distinctiveness of children's scientific learning, she went on to undertake the role of co-ordinator and seek out further knowledge and information about primary science. Achieving the first Order outcomes then in turn reactivated second Order outcomes: a particularly dynamic professional development path had clearly resulted from the scheme.

TEACHER E

PRACTICE:

Teacher E stated that the scheme had *'sparked off interest again'* in science (adjudging that it was an altogether better INSET experience than a previous primary science course she had attended). She commented on how she and the advisory teacher *'taught the same and talked the same'*, and how she had felt considerably more confident that many of the group activities she provided for her reception class were now definable as science in the light of observing the advisory teacher in action. The commercial scheme purchased by the school was sometimes a source of additional ideas for science activities, as were the worksheets and activities presented by the advisory teacher. Classroom observation indicated a highly proficient classroom manager, with a commitment to 'first hand experience' and children learning through structured play. Considerable skills in group discussion with pupils was also evident: the emphasis of her topics remained the natural sciences, with an emphasis on encouraging children's accurate observation and descriptive language.

OUTCOME ROUTE:

| 3rd Order | PROVISIONARY : INFORMATION : NEW AWARENESS (confirmatory) |

| 2nd Order | MOTIVATION : AFFECTIVE : (INSTITUTIONAL) |

| 1st Order | VALUE CONGRUENCE : |

This teacher had a particularly positive response to the scheme. The degree of congruence evident between her practice and that recommended and imaged by the advisory teacher resulted in high motivation and increased confidence. The school's co-ordinator did not figure as offering significant support (partly because the co-ordinator was a top junior teacher) but informally talking about science in the staffroom was said to have helped maintain the initial stimulus of the school-based input - hence the possible institutional outcome. Teacher E's enthusiasm and receptivity for 'new ideas' meant that the provisionary outcomes accruing from the scheme were particularly appreciated. This outcome- route demonstrates how the different order outcomes can all contribute to science being easily accommodated into the existing curriculum, values and classroom organisation of a skilled early years teacher. In this case, the advisory teacher's 'you're already doing it' message appears to be an apt confirmation of a teacher who was already highly committed to experiential learning and always eager to expand her teacher repertoire.

By way of conclusion, it is important to repeat a point made in the introduction: this chapter was conceived as a 'goal-free' analysis of INSET outcomes, and as such, criticism of the science scheme - or the Advisory Teachers who ran it - was not intended. For the purposes of the chapter, the scheme itself stands as a back-cloth, and it is the recipients of the INSET who are spotlighted. Nevertheless, given the range and quantity of outcomes accruing from the PST scheme, it is hard not to conclude that it will stand as an example of a particularly effective form and strategy of professional development. Though, like most prototypes, it may be capable of betterment, the extremely positive effect it had on teachers' appreciation of primary science is indisputable. It would also seem that the advisory teachers themselves, intuiting and acting upon the importance of MOTIVATION as a crucial INSET outcome for changing practice, deserve particular acclaim.

Before considering the implications of the typology for practice (see the final chapter), we examine in more depth the second key strand in the INSET design: the schools' self-sustaining provision for professional development.

CHAPTER SEVEN

SCHOOL SELF-SUSTAINING INSET: THE ROLE OF THE CO-ORDINATOR

INTRODUCTION

The perspective of this chapter concentrates exclusively upon the development work in science which was undertaken by schools themselves following the advisory teacher input. Particular attention is given to the role and activities of the school's curriculum co-ordinator for science.

Two considerations underpin this evaluation focus. First, the original design of the ESG scheme gave particular emphasis and support to schools' own development work, and the evaluation's fieldwork programme was designed to take close account of this. Commentary on the self-sustaining aspect of the INSET scheme was always seen as a vital component of the formative feedback. Second, presenting a longitudinal study of schools' development strategies was felt to have an increasing relevance, given the rapidly changing educational context of delegated INSET funding and curriculum innovation nationally.

It should be noted that the present chapter, like all the others, seeks to honour the confidentiality and anonymity of the case-study schools and individuals within them. It is also important to stress that the evaluation's function was not to 'measure' individual schools' progress in developing science in the light of the ESG scheme - indeed its methodology was not designed to substantiate any such measurement. Consequently, as the present chapter is constructed to illuminate issues (and avoid exposing individuals), it may seem that the individual efforts and activities of some teachers or co-ordinators have not been comprehensively portrayed. However, it is hoped that the achievements, conscientiousness and commitment of those undertaking the co-ordinator role in the five schools are still fully conveyed in the text.

THE ESG SCHEME AND THE SCHOOL

The original design and submission of the LEA's ESG scheme specifies a strategy of co-responsibility for developing science in the participating schools. The section entitled '*School Based Input*', begins with a clear statement that a school's commitment to '*curriculum development*' was to be both a criteria of selection and a contracted outcome:

> *... Schools will be selected on the basis of not at present having a coherent school curriculum policy for Science and Technology being implemented by all staff and either having had a record of curriculum development in other areas or be expected, by the commitment of the headteacher, to be able to take advantage of the programme.*

> *Schools will be required to contract with the authority to undertake the programme as follows, to identify a teacher to act as curriculum leader, to develop a school policy for Science and Technology and to have this policy implemented by all teachers in the school ...*

(Calderdale's Submission for Education Support Grant, 1986-7)

The submission indicates that, following the advisory teacher school-based input, the LEA would provide '... *six half days of supply cover for the release of the curriculum leader to develop a school policy' and 'the provision of (£200 worth of) equipment, materials and publications to implement the policy ...*'. It then goes on to demarcate the degree of advisory teacher and LEA involvement in participating schools' subsequent development work:

> *... [School-based in-service meetings] will provide a basis for a programme of further development by the school staff. Though an Advisory Teacher will continue to support, monitor and evaluate progress, major responsibility for the initiation of the work will gradually pass to the school with an emphasis on the role of the curriculum leader.'* (ibid)

The submission also indicated that the general provision would provide support meetings for science policy development and also target courses '*for curriculum leaders in PST to promote management skills in implementing a whole-school approach*'.

In sum, the scheme's design carried a clear intention that the LEA's programme of professional development (i.e. school-based and general in-service activities) would foster whole-school curriculum development and policy-making. In turn, reference to having '... *this policy implemented by all teachers in the school*' implies that the school has a significant responsibility for ensuring its development work impacts upon science practice at classroom level. Influencing colleagues' classroom delivery of science thus would seem to become a key role of the science curriculum leader. In this way, the aims of curriculum development begin to elide with - and become indistinguishable from - those of professional development.

A key evaluation issue to emerge from the design of this ESG scheme is, therefore, whether the curriculum management and development strategies of the school (with particular reference to the work of its science co-ordinator), can constitute an effective way to advance the classroom practice and curriculum perceptions of its staff. Ultimately, given the emphasis and wording of the submission, it is the supposition that curriculum development will deliver professional development which is under scrutiny.

Given the brief to study the ESG scheme from the perspective of its longer-term impact on the classroom practice in participating schools, four key questions for an evaluation of its self-sustaining component emerged:

* what kinds of development activity did the schools, and especially their curriculum leaders, subsequently undertake in science?

* what sort of impact did this have on the practice and curriculum perceptions of its staff?

* what factors appeared to account for this impact?

* what general implications can be drawn on the most effective strategies for self-sustaining professional development within the primary school?

PERSPECTIVES ON THE ROLE OF
THE CO-ORDINATOR

One of the key aims was to remove the [school's] dependency on outside support ... from this point of view, the co-ordinator role was critical. The intention was that co-ordinators would be able to take up the responsibility for the impetus and drive behind the project. The role of the co-ordinator is a key one for the evaluation. (General Inspector - Science)

The identification of a curriculum leader as a key strategy for developing science practice in the primary school has, so to speak, an impeccable pedigree. For more than a decade, many 'venerable' sources - HMI in the 1978 survey *'Primary Education in England'* (GB: DES 1978) and also in their illustrative surveys of First and Middle Schools (GB: DES 1982 and 1983), The Cockcroft Report (1982), House of Commons Select Committee (GB: Parliament 1986), National Curriculum Council (1989) *'Framework for Primary Curriculum'* and so on have all averred the importance of the role and equally recognized factors which limit or assist its functioning as an effective whole-school influence. Co-ordinators' lack of time and/or expertise; the issue of their status (or 'standing') and social relationships within the school (GB: DES 1978); limiting the role to (solely) *'the provision and organisation of teaching materials'* (GB: DES 1983) have all been identified as prohibitive factors in whole-school development work. As recently as 1989, HMI commenting specifically on primary school science co-ordinators summarized:

... while many co-ordinators influence the work in some classes other than their own, only about one in five succeeds in influencing the work throughout the school.
(GB: DES 1989, para. 29)

They went on to stipulate some by now standard qualities of *'influential'* co-ordinators, and the kinds of management strategies associated with effective staff development:

... in general, those [co-ordinators] who are most influential are knowledgeable about science and ways of teaching it, are accepted by their colleagues as capable teachers, are possessed of good inter-personal skills, and are well supported by the head. Schools which

have good arrangements for staff development typically make use of all the teachers who have responsibility for curricular areas. Such teachers regularly organize discussions and workshops and are frequently called on to give advice. Some heads release co-ordinators in turn by teaching their classes; this allows the co-ordinators to work co-operatively with other teachers and it emphasises the importance of their role; (ibid)

On one level, this chapter's key research issue, i.e. the question of how co-ordinators can contribute significantly to the professional development of colleagues, would seem to have been *a priori* answered by such prescriptive statements. 'Good' staff development, according to HMI, results from co-ordinators operating in a way that approximates with a typical advisory teacher role - offering workshops, advice and classroom support from the basis of a recognized expertise in their subject area and in their general classroom practice. However, HMI's additional 'finding', reported in 1989, was that only one in eight of co-ordinators do undertake the strategy of working alongside other teachers (compared to one in three *'acquiring and organising resources'*). This raises the question of why nearly 90 per cent of primary science co-ordinators are not able (or perhaps even willing) to take on such an overt advisory teacher role, and therefore, by implication, whether it can ultimately be seen as an entirely realistic expectation. Given that so many co-ordinators are apparently functioning in an altogether more modest capacity, it may be timely to review and reappraise what kinds of contribution this makes to their colleagues' science practice.

While those who recommend policy have acknowledged the pivotal but problematic role of co-ordinator, a further perspective comes from the research community. Throughout the late seventies and eighties, their burgeoning interest in the culture and social relations of the primary school has also already part way answered this question of what constrains the professional development capacities of the co-ordinator. Their characterization of the primary sector's traditions of teacher as generalist with classroom autonomy, and a lack of formal hierarchy among staff (with authority recognized and invested only in the headteacher) was clearly at odds with any notion of an 'expert' fellow staff-member expecting (or expected) to change the classroom practice of her colleagues. Studies of the co-ordinator role in whole-school curriculum development by Campbell (1985), Rodger (1983), and Primary Schools Research and

Development Group (1983) identified a greater acceptance of the good practice promoted by HMI with regard to collaborative and collective approaches to curriculum planning, but significantly their conclusion reinforced the limitations of co-ordinator influence on practice. Teachers and co-ordinators alike mostly expressed preferences for 'an informal rather than directive consultant role' (Rodgers 1983), and for *a quietly concerned colleague, ready to help if asked ... rather than ... the teacher expert as an agent of change, alert to innovations in primary education and determined to make a contribution to the professional development of colleagues'* (Primary Schools Research and Development Group, p. 98). Campbell noted that this study's findings indicated how teachers were more likely to ask for help in matters relating to schemes of work and school policy rather than teaching methods and classroom practice. He concluded:

> *[the profession] was aware of the potential benefit to the school of a shift in the exercise of authority to teachers with subject expertise, but were perceptive about the repercussions on the quality of staff relationships and fearful of the loss of informality and reciprocity in professional exchanges.*
> (Campbell 1985, p. 159)

Of course, the context and content of curriculum development has undoubtedly been revolutionized since these studies in the early eighties. Yet, the question of how far - or even whether - the cultural norms of the primary sector have shifted to accommodate a greater responsibility for professional development remains.

A perspective from a different source and one, so to speak, closer to home, comes from the advisory teachers responsible for implementing the school-based input in the present study. They were acutely sensitive to the delicate and complex role of co-ordinator operating as an agent of change and development. In interviews which discussed their views on the role of the co-ordinator within the scheme, they recounted the kinds of advice which they offered to teachers taking up the post and also defined the characteristics of 'good' and 'bad' co-ordinators. Being former co-ordinators themselves, and the recipients of a 40-day course on science co-ordinator role, they offered astute insights and prescriptions. Generally, the picture that emerged from these discussions was that the success of the school self-sustaining component of the scheme rested first on a co-ordinator's enthusiasm and commitment: *'it's no good if they've not chosen the job, if it's been thrust on them'*. The advisory teachers also identified qualities remarkably similar to those advocated by HMI:

    ✱   **Sensitivity and inter-personal skills**
        a good co-ordinator notices people who are struggling and tends to go in in a nice way, doesn't put people down. (Advisory teacher.)

    ✱   **Qualities of leadership:**
        it's a question of whether they've a personality suitable for taking on a leadership role and the problem of staff relations; (ibid)

    ✱   **Willingness to extend their own expertise and a carefully judged demonstration of that expertise**
        they can have too much knowledge, [it can seem] they've got so knowledgeable and they turn other people off. (ibid)

Strategies advocated or approved by the advisory teachers, like '*identifying an ally ... one other person to work on*' or helping out with other classroom chores (such as display), indicated a soft-pedal approach intended not to overtly challenge classroom autonomy or informal staffroom relationships.

However, they too stressed the need for access to the classroom practice of colleagues to ensure effective co-ordinatorship:

> *If you want to get teachers working as co-ordinators, they need time to work with other teachers and to function as good practitioners. A good co-ordinator inspires the rest, goes into other classes and acts as a developer.* (ibid)

Undoubtedly, it was for this reason that the advisory teachers often undertook a covering role on their follow-up visits to allow (and set the precedent for) co-ordinators to go into colleagues' classrooms. Yet they acknowledged that the feasibility of the working alongside/ professional development strategy was not always guaranteed:

> *... the problem is that finding these [good developer co-ordinators] is rare, and there's always the danger that when you do find them, they'll get promoted and move on anyway.* (ibid)

Thus, the local perspective of two people closely involved in the ESG scheme replicates the national 'findings' of HMI published over a year later.

In sum, even before examining the specifics of this ESG scheme, it is possible to conclude that the co-ordinator as a professional developer remains inherently problematic and the versions of good co-ordinator practice promoted both nationally and locally appear to be relatively rare in practice.

This needs to be borne in mind when, in the sections that follow, the report looks at the work of co-ordinators in the five case-study primary schools over the period of the last two or three years. It will be clear that their role often fell short of this 'ideal' practice: hence the question of why this is so, and what they have actually achieved is in some need of addressing.

THE WORK OF CO-ORDINATORS

My job is to make sure we don't drift back into the attitude "We've done science - what next?", I've got to keep saying "SCIENCE". (Science Co-ordinator)

This section provides an overview of the main kinds of activities undertaken by co-ordinators in the five case-study schools.

First there is a brief narrative or 'cameo' account, of co-ordinator activity in each of the five case-study schools, from the period immediately following the advisory teacher input up to the Spring term of 1990. The source of this information is the schools' co-ordinators themselves and also their headteachers. There then follows an analysis of the range of activities currently undertaken by the co-ordinators and the perceived impact on colleagues' practice. It concludes with brief accounts of any other PST development work undertaken by the schools or individual teachers, and the LEA support available for science co-ordinators particularly during the first two terms of the school year 1989-90.

The Cameos

School A

School A received its ESG school-based input in the Spring Term 1987.

Following the school-based input, the co-ordinator for Environmental Studies added the responsibility for science to her brief, and used four of the six half-days of supply cover working on the ordering of teacher materials and sorting out existing science equipment. Visits to other schools also took place, and she attended the LEA's INSET day for science co-ordinators. The advisory teacher's follow-up visit gave her the opportunity to work in her colleagues' classrooms. No other occasion presented itself for this to be repeated. A draft of the amended existing science policy was produced with the head and presented to the staff for discussion. It included a new recording sheet for staff to give account of their science work.

In the Spring Term of 1989, the science post was separated from Environmental Studies and taken up by an ex-probationer with specific initial training in primary science. This teacher attended the LEA INSET for co-ordinators on National Curriculum issues, as well as a course on children's learning in science held at a local university. Information, especially on planning with National Curriculum documents, was fedback to the whole staff, to the school's science working party and particularly to those individual or teams of teachers most closely connected with National Curriculum implementation. A single science resource area was set up.

During the Autumn Term 1989 and Spring Term 1990, the co-ordinator continued to lead a science working party which was producing a new school science policy and deciding on appropriate resource expenditure, including how to create a package of science resources for individual classes. On one Baker Day, advisory teachers for National Curriculum core areas were brought in. The science advisory teacher discussed the science policy with the working party and then the whole staff (this approach was repeated with the maths and English policies being produced by two other working parties).

As the co-ordinator now had an allowance post for record keeping, devising new ways of recording science activities was also undertaken. Responsibility for selecting new teacher materials involved the co-ordinator in bringing a range of commercial schemes to the staff's attention at weekly staff meetings. Staff in adjacent year groups were organized to work out the details of designated National Curriculum topics, using a spiral planning model the co-ordinator had come across during one of her INSET days. Course attendance had continued, the co-ordinator selecting INSET designated for middle infant teachers in order to help her supporting role, as well as more advanced courses. School procedures for feeding-back were employed. Informal liaison with secondary school, advisory staff and attendance at the LEA's self- help group were also undertaken.

School B

School B received the school-based input in January 1987.

Following the school-based input, the deputy head took on the role of co-ordinator. A resources area was set up and equipment and teacher materials were bought using some of the school's own budget, as well as the ESG funding of £200. A visit to another school was undertaken to help determine the most suitable arrangements for storing equipment. Four of the half days of supply cover were used to consult with staff and write a science policy as well as draw up an assessment sheet. Two half-days were used for working alongside in two teachers' classrooms, and demonstration lessons were given. An LEA residential weekend course on science was also attended.

A second teacher was appointed to the co-ordinator post as the deputy was subsequently required to write and implement a language policy for the school. This co-ordinator's tenure was brief and a third teacher took up the role in June 1988.

The third co-ordinator maintained responsibility for the ordering and upkeep of resources. During the school year 1988-9, LEA INSET for co-ordinators on the National Curriculum was attended as well as the course on children's scientific learning at a local university. Information in the form of specially prepared handouts was fed back to the whole staff. The staff were organized into year groups and began the process of cataloguing the schools' resources that matched the attainment targets and levels of attainment in the National Curriculum statutory orders for science. This work continued in Baker Days at the beginning of the 1989-90 school year and also involved the co-ordinator (along with deputy head) in devising new recording and planning sheets, and updating the school policy document. A cycle of school-wide topics to cover attainment targets was instituted, and this too was led by the co-ordinator and deputy head. During 1988-9, a limited amount of working alongside a probationary teacher also was undertaken.

In Spring Term of 1990, a new 'fourth' co-ordinator was appointed following the departure of the previous incumbent. This ex-probationer was given support by the deputy head during the first term of tenure. The LEA's National Curriculum training was attended, and fedback. The co-ordinator indicated that attending out of school-time INSET, including the self-help group, was difficult due to family commitments.

The appointment of a +B allowance post for National Curriculum developments was also planned at this time.

School C

The ESG scheme's advisory teacher input occurred in School C in Spring Term 1987.

Following the school-based input, a scale 1 teacher undertaking an advanced education course in science took on the role of co-ordinator. Discussions on a school policy for science began, two half day visits to other schools took place, but illness prevented further follow-up visits by the advisory teacher to provide opportunities for working alongside. However, the LEA course for co-ordinators and the self-help group had been attended.

By the Summer Term of 1989, the resource area was further developed, with additional teacher materials and equipment, and a science policy had been written by the head and co-ordinator together and fedback to staff for approval. The co-ordinator was given supply cover to discuss with each staff member their current science practice and perceived needs with regard to resources and other matters of classroom implementation. Meetings between the local high school and its feeder primaries had been attended, and the co-ordinator then became involved with a GRIST financed scheme between the feeder primaries to evolve a National Curriculum related scheme of work for 5-11 science. This involved four teachers from the feeder schools working together for five days, using school-financed cover arrangements. Further GRIST-funded days were used in the Autumn Term for the co-ordinator to contribute to the completion of the scheme.

Throughout each year, the co-ordinator fedback information picked up at the advanced course, particularly on National Curriculum science issues.

Both informally and at staff meetings, suggestions were offered on such matters as possible recording systems and assessment procedures.

School D

School D's school-based input took place in the Autumn Term of 1988.

Following the school-based input, the one teacher said to have attended previous LEA science INSET and to have shown an interest in teaching science, agreed to take up the role of co-ordinator. The six half-days of supply cover were used in centralizing the school's existing science equipment and teacher materials, and organizing the purchase of additional resources. This involved the co-ordinator visiting a neighbouring school and the Resources centre to determine the most suitable purchases. No follow-up visits were possible because of the advisory teacher's National Curriculum training commitments, but in the Summer Term of 1989, the advisory teacher did return to work with members of staff who had not been involved in the working alongside component of the original input. The co-ordinator attended the National Curriculum training and the self-help group. No attempt was made to create a school policy during this year: lack of familiarity with the newly arrived Statutory Orders was said to make this an inappropriate task at the present time. Similarly, the school indicated it was 'waiting for help' with a recording system.

During the Spring Term of 1990, working parties for the three core areas were set up, with the science co-ordinator said to be taking the lead in making a science policy and working out the most appropriate allocation of topics to deliver science statutory orders across the school. Responsibility for the school's science resources was maintained. The co-ordinator attended an LEA technology INSET, and fedback informally what had taken place.

School E

School E received the school-based input in the Autumn Term of 1988.

A long-established member of staff took on the role of co-ordinator and spent the three days of supply cover creating a science resource area. Responsibility for ordering some £500 worth of science equipment was also undertaken. During 1989, the LEA course for co-ordinators on National Curriculum was attended, and also a course on assessment at a local university. It was said that there was no formal feedback of these courses, and that there were no specific meetings on science following the scheme. No follow-up visits from the advisory teacher occurred, due to the latter taking up a full-time appointment elsewhere in the authority. The co-ordinator indicated that she was attempting to trial matching her own topic work to attainment targets and levels of attainment. No policy was written: it was decided to adopt the authority's science policy statement, with slight amendments suggested by the co-ordinator. One reason given for this decision was that the school had elected to use a commercial scheme whose upper primary component was still unpublished. Hence, devising a cross-school structured scheme to incorporate this teacher material remained a future task. It was the headteacher who worked closely with the prospective Y1 teacher on National Curriculum implementation.

During 1989-90, the co-ordinator continued to maintain the science resources, having added responsibility for maths resources to her brief. Baker Days at the beginning of the school year were used for staff to work in adjacent year groups and devise the topics they would like to undertake in order to deliver the Statutory orders. In these discussions, no particular role or responsibility for the co-ordinator was mentioned.

THE CO-ORDINATOR ROLE

The longitudinal cameos indicate a similar range of co-ordinator activities, if perhaps noticeable differences in the degree of rigour and energy with which they were undertaken. However, the main focus of this chapter is also concerned with determining the boundaries of the role, and - equally importantly - noting what sorts of activity seem to lie beyond a co-ordinator's brief. It should be noted that the main reference for this section is data collected on the role as undertaken immediately prior to and during the first two terms of National Curriculum implementation.

From the evidence, it is clear that among the five schools:

* no co-ordinator undertook to deliver any form of formal INSET or workshop for her/his colleagues;

* there was only one example of working alongside outside of the occasions when the advisory teachers elected to cover for a co-ordinator in their follow-up visits;

*   monitoring practice was seen as beyond a co-ordinator's brief.

The main activities said to be undertaken were:

*   establishing and maintaining a science resource area;

*   garnering details (including INSET attendance) on current issues and developments in science, and providing informational feedback;

*   contributing to whole-school science planning and policy making;

*   offering informal advice and encouragement.

Thus, despite evidence of their considerable talent and expertise as classroom practitioners, one of the most obvious forms of professional development apparently available to schools, i.e. the direct transmission or exemplification of 'in-house' science teaching skills, barely featured in the co-ordinator repertoire of the case-study schools. Co-ordinators were not called upon to demonstrate their classroom expertise with regards to science in any official capacity. Equally, without any responsibility for INSET delivery or for regularly working alongside, there was no direct opportunity for the co-ordinators to establish (or then monitor) norms of classroom practice in science. Beyond that, there seems some considerable irony that - regardless of the degree of diligence with which co-ordinator duties were undertaken - all remarked how the impact or outcomes of their work at classroom level was largely unknown. The classroom practice of colleagues remained a largely private realm. The reasons for this will be analysed later; at this stage it is important to note that the original submission's expectation that schools and co-ordinators could ensure science policies were implemented by all teachers was, ultimately, untenable in the five case-study schools, IF the assumption related to establishing consistency and equivalence in teaching approaches and curriculum understanding.

However, the cameos of co-ordinator practice show that the kinds of activity which were undertaken largely revolved around what one teacher called 'the administrative' aspect of science teaching, such as resource provision, or school planning and record keeping procedures. Significantly, these relate only to teacher activity which happens before or after classroom interaction with children. As well as that, the co-ordinator clearly had an increasingly important role in informing colleagues of developments relating to national/local requirements and recommendations for teaching primary science. These responsibilities also appeared to function as a way of keeping science in the collective consciousness of the staff: co-ordinators, so to speak, acted as advocates or lobbyers on behalf of their curriculum area. Hence, the role that consistently emerged was one that carried a general - and very important - provisionary, informational and advocacy function rather than having any specific responsibility for individuals' practice. Yet within this sphere of influence, significant differences in what can only be called 'standards of co-ordinatorship' began to emerge.

In order to fully appreciate this range, each of the main co-ordinator activities - and those 'ideal' practices that in actuality lay outside their brief - will be discussed in some detail.

Resources

As the cameos show, all but one school instituted a central science resource area immediately following the advisory teacher input, and the designated science co-ordinator in each case took clear and unequivocal responsibility for this. Sometimes this involved using the scheme's supply cover to 'research' into the most suitable items and arrangements for the centralization of resources, with visits to the LEA's Resource Centre or other schools.

Marked differences in the significance of this responsibility within a co-ordinator's repertoire were apparent by 1990. In one case, maintaining the availability of equipment was seen as the sum of co-ordinator activity by both co-ordinator and staff alike, whereas in other schools, it was but one of a number of organizational tasks. Similarly, the content of the resources areas varied from being primarily the storage of science equipment, to virtual 'mini' versions of the LEA's Resource Centre - with items such as prepared worksheets, teacher and pupil reference material organized into topics and themes, as well as equipment. The decision of one school to also institute a package of science equipment for each class *'things teachers need when children start to look carefully'* is a clear indication of the increasing centrality and integration of science within the curriculum. Consultation with colleagues over the acquisition of resources also varied: two co-ordinators were attempting to encourage whole-school or working party decisions on resourcing in the context of re-written policies and the planned two year cycle of National Curriculum related science topics, rather than merely asking or anticipating what individual colleagues thought they needed.

In sum, responsibility for resources often appeared as the lowliest 'servicing' function of the co-ordinator role, perhaps because in itself a resource area cannot guarantee any consistency in (or even the existence of) classroom implementation across the school. A number of teachers, even in 1989-90, said they were not selecting science themes or activities BECAUSE of the resources available to them in school:

> *I do know if I want resources, they're there. But it wouldn't make a difference to what I was planning to do, I'd get resources elsewhere.*

Yet despite the tenuousness of the direct influence of resources upon colleagues' practice, the way in which this aspect of the role is viewed and undertaken may perhaps be a useful indicator of the overall effectiveness of the co-ordinatorship. When co-ordinators conscientiously applied strategies for either expanding the resources area or drawing existing resources to staff's attention, it clearly fulfilled the important science-lobbying function and their efforts were usually much appreciated by staff. This appreciation was often accompanied by - or synonymous with - a good deal of professional respect. Familiarity with science resources was likely to convey, and also enhance, the co-ordinator's expertise in primary science. Though financial constraints were referred to in all schools, the evidence would suggest that, without a serious and on-going commitment to resourcing the school for science, a co-ordinator was unlikely to provide either the school or themselves with the best conditions for undertaking other staff development work.

Information and feedback

This aspect of the co-ordinator's role was undoubtedly seen as increasingly important in the light of National Curriculum developments. Where co-ordinators had invested in keeping abreast of information, through course attendance and so on, and when they had taken or were given the opportunity to provide thorough feedback, the outcome was a general acknowledgement of the value to the school:

> *we're very lucky, X is very good at keeping up with current information, passing it on very well so we all know about it ... she has helped us to be au fait and more knowledgeable about changes.* (Teacher)

*X's presentation of the courses was well prepared and thought out -
it made a big impact on the staff ... they realized she knew what she was
talking about, she was organized and confident and that got everybody
into that way of thinking.* (Headteacher)

*X's job was encouragement ... press-ganging people to concentrate
on science. She went to a lot of trouble, insisted on having meetings
and made her point. She duplicated information and was very
persuasive.* (Teacher)

However, it was also clear that co-ordinators could manage to convey
information (or, more accurately, their own informedness) in quite subtle
ways and, while doing so, continue to propel the staff's collective
consciousness of current science issues. Perhaps even more than
responsibility for resources, the role of information feedback emerged as
example of science co-ordinator as a 'lobbyer' for their curriculum area:

X usually manages to have some say at staff meetings about science.
(Teacher)

*X is enthusiastic ... whatever the staff meeting is about, she'll say
something related to science - she brings us back to thinking about
science. She's very conscientious about her position, and doesn't let
us forget the science.* (Headteacher)

*the staff have become more aware of what's going on [in relation to
National Curriculum]. Through informal discussion with X,
subconsciously they're becoming much more prepared themselves.
(Headteacher)*

However, the co-ordinator's role in feedback opens up the issue of both
the quality - and as Chapter Six suggested, the neutrality - of informational
messages as reconstructed and conveyed by co-ordinators. As the school
cameos demonstrate, there were quite startling differences in the response
and subsequent activity of the co-ordinators after the LEA course for co-
ordinators in the Spring term of 1989. One co-ordinator expressed a sense
of being *'more confident, because the courses have helped me to come
back and have something to say'* and she carefully prepared feedback *'on
the things I thought were important'*, followed by setting up a whole-
school planning and matching resources exercise using the National
Curriculum ring binder. Another, having fedback to the whole staff,
became actively involved with the prospective Year 1 team in developing
a topic referring to the statutory orders' programmes of study in the same

way as she felt the course had suggested. However, two co-ordinators revealed rather negative or discomforted attitudes to the course and, significantly, no joint planning whatsoever emerged in either of these schools until several months later. Though there were no doubt other factors involved in this delay, it reveals that the use which co-ordinators are prepared to make of information is a key issue in this aspect of the role.

A further aspect relates to the degree of 'entrepreneurialness' with which co-ordinators set about the business of obtaining information (and additional expertise) for later dissemination and support work. Major differences emerged during 1989-90 in the co-ordinators' efforts to attend science-related courses or liaise with advisory staff and LEA support groups. It is worth pointing out that there were said to be no official LEA courses for science co-ordinators at that time. Voluntary course attendance opened up the familiar problem of 'cascading' INSET experiences, especially in the largest of the schools: insufficient time to listen to feedback and the variable receptiveness of an audience of colleagues were mentioned. Using the co-ordinator as a medium for conveying additional classroom-related expertise to the school (as opposed to information on statutory requirements), could not be guaranteed to impact on colleagues' practice and hence its merits as a professional development strategy were felt to be somewhat dubious. First-hand experience of INSET was considered preferable.

Overall then, there was considerable variability in how or indeed whether the five co-ordinators undertook responsibility for information and feedback. A serious commitment to this aspect of the role was usually accompanied by other vigorous co-ordinator activity relating to whole-school planning and policy making. Quite simply, unless co-ordinators made efforts to acquire and up-date information and their subject expertise, it was clearly the case that they often had little to offer to staff, and hence a school's opportunities for development work were likely to be reduced.

Whole-school planning and policy making

Looked at over the three school years of the evaluation project, this aspect of the co-ordinator's role reflects the major increase in collective whole-school planning which has resulted from National Curriculum requirements. The science policies contracted by the original ESG scheme in the three retrospective schools tended to be drafted 'quickly' by the co-ordinator, sometimes in consultation with the head. As the cameos show, in 1989-90, co-ordinators were operating within either working party, cluster or whole-staff discussion, attempting to organize school-wide, science-related topic-cycles and schemes and sometimes to reappraise existing policy statements.

Again there were marked differences in the contribution made by the five co-ordinators, and concomitantly each school was at very different stages of development in a whole-school approach:

> *[We' ve brainstormed and worked in twos deciding on topics] but ... generally, there' s been no specific meetings about science, about how we think we' re going, what else needs doing or where we think we' re at - if we' re doing a topic we dig for ourselves... The structure of the science curriculum is not successful - I don' t think my having a greater influence is possible with only a small staff.* (Co-ordinator)

> *the [science] working party is talking about deciding if we should choose certain areas for certain years, and record keeping.* (Co-ordinator)

> *During this last year, the [science] working party has got a policy revised and reprinted and that takes account of non-statutory guidance along with the Orders. We' ve got the record system [and resources] sorted out ... and are reviewing [commercial] schemes at the minute - which is a long process.* (Co-ordinator)

The advantages of the science co-ordinator's familiarity with alternative models of National Curriculum planning, garnered at courses within and beyond the LEA were very evident. Equally, there was more progress when preparation for these staff-planning activities was undertaken by the co-ordinator:

> *I felt it was important to have, in a way, a lesson plan in quite some detail and reference material available as well ... I' d spent quite some time beforehand going through the document and guidelines ... doing plenty of planning beforehand makes a smoother day, other people' s interests aren' t necessarily the same as your' s and they' re not going to want to do all that beforehand.* (Co-ordinator)

However, it is important to stress at this point that the evaluation focus is not to adjudge the work of the co-ordinator as such, but to look at it from the perspective of how a staff's subsequent implementation of science was affected. The professional development potential of such planning is the issue to be addressed. When the focus was on policy statements and recording/planning procedures, several teachers still tended to minimize its relevance to their practice:

Up to Christmas, the co-ordinator's role was organizing the paperwork - record keeping and what we're supposed to be teaching from the National Curriculum. I know X said all the right things but I must admit that I didn't personally take it on board to the extent it made a great impact on me ... it was the nature of the work, it wasn't particularly exciting, there's nothing exciting about organizing your paper work anyway. (Teacher)

the policy seems much the same as we've always had ... you don't keep looking at such a document. (Teacher)

On the other hand, most teachers were generally positive about either contributing to (or receiving) schemes, themes and topics involving peer planning. They welcomed the increased exchange of ideas relating directly to the classroom delivery of science. However, it might be important to distinguish this 'craft-knowledge trading' from professional development per se. Such activity is perhaps best viewed as a sophisticated form of resource provision, rather than automatically advancing science skills and knowledge:

I think they're using [the scheme] as a fund, in with what they already did - I don't think its drastically changed what anybody did previously. (Co-ordinator)

Beyond that, for some co-ordinators and teachers, school-wide discussion and planning for National Curriculum had raised awareness of the fundamental issues of progression, continuity and the nature of children's scientific skills and understanding. The strong impression was that these remained in the minority. In most cases, whole-school planning activities seemed designed to resolve the issue of progression and continuity ON BEHALF of staff at two levels: FORMALLY i.e. written procedures for the planning and recording of statutory requirements and PRAGMATICALLY i.e. providing specific ideas or topics for classroom implementation of the ring binder. Enhanced understanding of science practice may occur incidentally. However, without direct responsibility for providing staff with additional expertise, one of the most active of the co-ordinators recognized where her influence ceased:

> *I would say I've had an impact on the planning that goes on before and the recording afterwards, not in classroom practice as such ... I can see around there is more thought going into the kinds of activities - and I think people are now more aware of the fact children learn skills gradually ... May be not doing anything about it, but at least some thought being given to it.* (Co-ordinator)

In sum, it seems possible to conclude that a co-ordinator's contribution to policy-making and planning could not guarantee consistency and equivalence in the quality of science practice across the school, but it was likely to make an important difference to the amount and quality of discourse surrounding that practice.

Informal support and advice

'Offering informal support and advice' regularly features in the rhetoric of a co-ordinator's role. However, the evidence from teachers and co-ordinators in the case-study schools would suggest that, quite often it had, in actuality, very little significance for classroom practice.

In interview, teachers regularly asserted they knew they COULD ask for help, but were then hard pressed to find examples of occasions when they had sought advice, beyond the location of resources. Many clearly felt sorting out classroom science was entirely their own responsibility:

> *If you need help, X will help. I don't go to her a lot - it's something I'm going to have to do myself, something you've got to get on and do - people don't come to me about [my curriculum area].* (Deputy head)

> *No, personally I don't ask: if I'm doing a topic I dig for myself. If you can't find what you want MAY BE you'd ask then ... [but I haven't, no].* (Teacher)

> *She has such good ideas it's a shame we don't make more use - that we don't have more than a quick word, such as "What can I do that might link with this?". That's the only way everyone uses everyone's specialism.* (Teacher)

They ask me very little. I think they know that if they want something I'll do my best to get it ... they don't look to me for science knowledge, they don't look to me for leadership. (Co-ordinator)

I don't think they want advice - they want to know where the resources are and they want to feel those are there to support whatever they're doing, but I don't feel the staff are seeking any more from me. (Co-ordinator)

Such responses indicate how, with one or two notable exceptions, the teachers had no conception of an in-house consultant on matters of science practice, and some of the five co-ordinators recognized this as one of the major problems for them. It meant taking the initiative in the role of informal advisor could be extremely sensitive:

Some people may not admit they're having difficulty and so you've to broadcast things in a more wide-ranging manner, you make it a very general statement that "if anyone's interested in whatever, this is happening". It's very difficult because you don't want to pick somebody out or feel you're victimizing anyone. (Co-ordinator)

Beyond the delicacy of the advisory role, there was the further issue that colleagues' practice was generally not known to the co-ordinator:

... it's hard for me to offer assistance when you don't really know exactly what happens within a classroom and how that classroom is organized and managed. (Co-ordinator)

Hence, any informal advice and support mentioned usually turned out to be practical (and optional) suggestions for additional activities on the teacher-chosen themes, based on evidence gathered by unofficial sorties to classrooms (usually after school) or through informal conversation in the staffroom.

Thus, 'offering advice and support', like other aspects of the role, was undertaken with varying degrees of commitment and energy by the five co-ordinators. However, the general reticence of teachers to come forward with issues they wanted advice on, as well as co-ordinators' lack of familiarity with colleagues precise 'needs' in science practice, suggests that this aspect of the co-ordinator role cannot be a serious contender as a strategy for staff development, without additional modes of operating in the school being available.

Enhancing co-ordinators' ability to give more in-depth support and advice would clearly result from greater opportunities to monitor, observe and work alongside colleagues or offer INSET workshops tailored to colleagues' current practice-related needs. As stated at the beginning of the chapter, none of these options were generally available, and the reasons for this lacuna are now briefly considered and further discussed later.

Monitoring

Co-ordinators stated that their brief did not and could not include any sort of monitoring role. As the cameos show, in one school there had been discussion between the co-ordinator and individual members of staff on 'where everyone was up to, what they expected of the scheme, resources they needed and what they saw as their strengths and weaknesses'. However, this appeared to be a one-off occasion, with the co-ordinator garnering information prior to engaging in a cluster planning exercise. The rest of the co-ordinators variously indicated that they had not the opportunity, predilection or status for such a role, which was often envisaged as having a coercive rather than diagnostic function:

> It's not my job as science co-ordinator to force people to do 20 per cent science, or even 15 per cent or 10 per cent .. it's not my responsibility to make sure they're doing it and I'm certainly not going to patrol. The most I can do is encourage and support. (Co-ordinator)

> I could go through [teachers' science plans], check them all off, see that they're doing what they're supposed to be doing, and OK it. But as far as I'm concerned at the moment I think that sort of job has authority and I haven't got any authority. (Co-ordinator)

> It's impossible, with 100 per cent contact time, to monitor anything. (Co-ordinator)

> I don't feel I've enough confidence in my ability [to monitor] ... I don't know how much science goes on. I know how much I do, I know some people do more and some do less. (Co-ordinator)

Teachers also tended to interpret questions on monitoring as referring to a form of authoritative surveillance and felt it was their heads' role to ensure science was undertaken. One head envisaged 'having to rely on my co-ordinators to let me know what is happening' in the future, but in 1989-90, monitoring clearly lay outside the accepted role of a colleague.

Working alongside

Though there was only one brief example of the co-ordinator working alongside among all five case-study schools in the period under review, most respondents were positive about its potential value. However, there were considerable differences of opinions about the purpose of working alongside, and the co-ordinator's role within it. One co-ordinator summarized the variations in teacher attitude very shrewdly, in effect anticipating some of the inter-personal problems which this form of professional development was likely to raise:

> *I can identify some people who would like me to come in and maybe work with children, or work with them and some children and give some advice. I can identify people who'd like me to come in and look at the work they're doing and see if it's alright. And I can identify those who wouldn't want me anywhere near their classrooms.*
> (Co-ordinator)

Some interviewees indeed indicated they envisaged the working alongside role as no more than a specialist support teacher, especially useful in relation to impending assessment requirements. Two co-ordinators were adamant that the working alongside aspect of the role did not appeal: '*I prefer my own classroom situation*'. Another noted that her own pupils were likely to be disadvantaged by her absence for support work.

Not surprisingly, it was heads who particularly acknowledged the value of working alongside as a form of professional development, but three out of the five stated that current staffing and inevitable staff absence made regular covering for co-ordinators a practical impossibility. There were also intimations that one head preferred to retain any working alongside option for himself, '*then I can also see what is going on*'. Another indicated that the need to keep equivalence between subject areas prohibited the adoption of the working alongside strategy:

> *I could go in and cover, but if I do it for science, I have to do it for maths and English - nobody else is spare.* (Headteacher)

Two heads stressed they would not like to see 'demonstration lessons' undertaken by the co-ordinator.

In sum, this range of opinion and attitude testifies to working alongside being perhaps a far more complex and problematic professional development strategy than it at first sight appears. Apart from organizational difficulties, it is possible that the sensibilities and status of the classteacher, other co-ordinators and even the head may all be challenged by its introduction. It is perhaps significant that the one example within the sample of five schools was the science co-ordinator working with a probationer.

INSET delivery

Delivering INSET, such as workshops for staff, was even less likely to be considered as part of a co-ordinator's role than either monitoring or working alongside. Only one co-ordinator volunteered it as a practice she would wish to undertake, but was equally realistic about its likelihood:

It's not possible because of the climate where people are reluctant to give over and above their directed hours doing workshop sessions, and there's a limit to the number of Baker Days ...

This suggests that the transmission of co-ordinators' specialist expertise was not readily perceived as an appropriate subject for a public platform within the school. Another co-ordinator stated:

On certain areas I could probably do a lot - may be 90 per cent of what's required to help a few of the staff in areas they're weak on, but it's got to be organized - but I can't put [a workshop session] forward if nobody says they want it.

Other teachers indicated they saw the benefits of having the classroom work of their science co-ordinator more accessible to them or being shown examples of activities they themselves could undertake with a class, but this seemed to still fall short of anything approximating to training. As one teacher put it, '*it's difficult to accept a colleague as a specialist, I prefer someone more neutral like an advisory teacher*'.

Having outlined the extent of co-ordinators' work, two further issues relating to the school self-sustaining component of the ESG scheme remain. First is the question of whether there were other kinds of INSET or development activity in science being undertaken by the schools (or individual staff members) which did not involve the co-ordinator directly. Second, there is the issue of what LEA support for development work was available and taken up by the schools. These other two possible sources of influence on practice were also the focus of discussion during the final phase of fieldwork, which covered activities undertaken in the first two terms of National Curriculum implementation.

INSET AND OTHER DEVELOPMENT WORK

INSET attendance relating to primary science was evident in the five schools during the first two terms of 1989-90. Two teachers from the sample of 15 had attended an LEA technology course, as had two of the co-ordinators. Several respondents mentioned that they felt their National Curriculum training had given no new insights on primary science: significantly, the only teacher in the sample who spoke of this INSET as a particularly positive learning experience for her science practice was an ex-probationer who had not been involved in the original school-based input. Only one co-ordinator made regular attendances at the LEA's science self-help group, as well as INSET taking place beyond the LEA. Two teachers mentioned the Early Years group within the authority as a valuable forum for conveying ideas on infant science practice.

At school level, there was no additional input on science specifically, other than the planning and policy-making strategies which schools and co-ordinators set up themselves. As the cameos reveal, one of the five schools had some advisory teacher involvement in this policy making. Four of the heads reported INSET input at whole-school level was focusing on other areas of the curriculum - English, technology and maths - or on general cross-curricular 'topic' planning. Indeed, in both 'prospective' schools (i.e. those who had experienced the ESG school-based input four terms previously) it was sometimes implied that the focus was deliberately not science because of this advisory teacher INSET:

> *science is only one aspect of the curriculum, we've had a good bash at it ... it has assumed less priority than other subjects. Staff are not asking for more training, only resources - science did not appear on their [list of] INSET needs.* (Headteacher)

> *There hasn't been any concentration on science - there's been so many things going on and especially after we'd spent all that time on science anyway.* (Teacher)

Hence, the science co-ordinator's work can be seen as the measure of curriculum and professional development strategies undertaken within the five schools.

LEA SUPPORT FOR THE CO-ORDINATORS

On one level, co-ordinator activity being the extent of a staff's school-based input for science is precisely what the original ESG submission envisaged. However, the scheme's design also referred to an advisory teacher continuing to '*support, monitor and evaluate progress*' as schools and co-ordinators 'gradually' took responsibility for initiating development work. Quite clearly, the National Curriculum was bound to - (and indeed did) - affect this intention: even in 1988-9, the ESG advisory teachers were required to be much more involved in central training at the expense of their follow-up and on-going monitoring role. Nevertheless, the evaluation team continued to inquire about the kinds of LEA support given to co-ordinators. In 1989-90, two co-ordinators indicated that, although advisory teachers had visited the school, no discussion took place about their work, '*they only talk to me as a class teacher*', '*there was no focus on my co-ordinator role*'. A third summarized:

If I wanted help, I could get it, but they're not seeking you out.

However, PRO-ACTIVITY in obtaining advisory teacher support was seen to pay dividends by one co-ordinator:

support is available [but only] when we've asked them to come in, or when I've called down there ... it's always been sort of requested ... and I suppose, in a way, I've gone out of my way by going on courses, especially weekend courses ... But having the advisory staff makes a tremendous difference in that you know a name or a face to go looking for. There is someone you will know that has got some expertise who isn't necessarily based in school, who will come out to you and will have time to solve a problem, to work something out, to provide something for you ... a shoulder to cry on. There is a face you can go to. (Co-ordinator)

In conclusion, it might be interesting to speculate whether the present depiction of the co-ordinator's role might have been in any way different if there had been resources available to allow such liaison to occur consistently in each of the five case-study schools.

THE IMPACT OF THE CO-ORDINATOR:
A TYPOLOGY REVISITED

The role is having someone with a real interest in the subject, a real interest in teaching it ... that enthusiasm comes out in leading working parties, incidental talking to staff, writing guidelines ... We've got further than we would have if we hadn't got a science co-ordinator. (Headteacher)

I mean, my impact on people's classrooms is fairly negligible, my impact on personalities might be more: but on actual classroom practice I cannot judge ... (Co-ordinator)

The evidence presented so far suggests that the science co-ordinators from the five case-study schools were not perceived - or perhaps even expected - to have any direct impact on the classroom practice of colleagues. The role, even when undertaken with the utmost efficiency and commitment, was essentially one of SERVICING that practice and, in a more general sense, PROMOTING the subject area amidst the school's other curriculum demands. Co-ordinators, are, as one head put it, 'a support package'. The use which teachers made of that support, in terms of classroom practice, was by and large entirely discretionary.

An alternative way of expressing and understanding this limited influence is to apply the 'typology of INSET outcomes' developed in the previous chapter substituting the on-going work of co-ordinators for the main INSET input. In the final section of that chapter, eight of the identified outcomes were ordered into a hierarchy according to their likelihood of effecting change in classroom practice. Thus, lower (or third) order outcomes were those deemed to be least likely to impact on practice, whereas higher order outcomes were those which appeared to invariably accompany any hoped-for change in practice. The hierarchy of outcomes was presented as in the diagram (overleaf).

If the effect of co-ordinator activities is appraised according to this hierarchy of outcomes, it would seem that, at best, they are currently achieving third and second order outcomes. However, Chapter Six also suggested that there was a considerable interdependency between the different outcomes, and that lower order outcomes may have an important knock-on effect: hence they too can be seen to function as pre-conditions

```
┌─────────────────────────────────────────────────┐
│  ╭───────────────────────────────────────────╮  │
│  │              I N S E T                     │  │
│  ╰───────────────────────────────────────────╯  │
│  ╭───────────────────────────────────────────╮  │
│  │ 3rd Order PROVISIONARY : INFORMATIONAL : NEW AWARENESS │
│  ╰───────────────────────────────────────────╯  │
│  ╭───────────────────────────────────────────╮  │
│  │ 2nd Order MOTIVATIONAL : AFFECTIVE : INSTITUTIONAL │
│  ╰───────────────────────────────────────────╯  │
│  ╭───────────────────────────────────────────╮  │
│  │ 1st Order VALUE CONGRUENCE : NEW SKILLS & KNOWLEDGE │
│  ╰───────────────────────────────────────────╯  │
│  ╭───────────────────────────────────────────╮  │
│  │         I M P A C T  O N  P R A C T I C E   │  │
│  ╰───────────────────────────────────────────╯  │
└─────────────────────────────────────────────────┘
```

for changing practice. This would imply that the co-ordinator as 'support package' performs a vital propulsion role if second and third order outcomes are achieved. However, if neither they nor the school's other development strategies broach first order outcomes, the likelihood is that many individuals' classroom practice will remain largely unaffected. This explanation would seem to account for the fact that the evaluation's interview questions about the co-ordinator's impact on practice were met with consistently negative responses. By and large, teachers felt they '*got on and did*' science by themselves. However, the replies of teachers, heads and co-ordinators did corroborate that third and occasionally second order outcomes were thought to result from school's and co-ordinator's development.

Typical comments about the PROVISIONARY outcome of co-ordinator activity were, in some cases, accompanied by the inference that this was the limit of impact:

It's made it easier for them ... I hope I've managed to do enough to keep them supplied with ideas and equipment, that's all I can do. (Co-ordinator)

To be honest, she's had no impact on my science practice, she's made it easier to find things on the resources side. (Teacher)

However, the knock-on effect of INFORMATIONAL outcomes were clearly appreciated by one school with a particularly committed co-ordinator:

> *[The science co-ordinator] keeps abreast of developments, and what [she] can most usefully do is provide a basis of confidence, so it is a supportive role. We get the confidence knowing she knows what she's talking about [which comes from] courses, reading, thinking to help that curriculum area forward. That's a real benefit.* (Headteacher)

> *everyone's got confidence in her ability and knowledge, we know we can use her expertise, we do it informally.* (Teacher)

Hence, it seems that important AFFECTIVE outcomes can accrue from the co-ordinators' informational role but this directly depended on the degree of commitment, organization - and, of course, 'informedness' - involved in feedback and dissemination. Similarly, MOTIVATIONAL outcomes were referred to when feedback (both the formal and the informal lobbying kind) was undertaken seriously:

> *The way she has organized staff meetings has regenerated people's interest and enthusiasm for science ... you need a shot in the arm, promoting the excitement of the National Curriculum. It's good to make people refocus and revitalize.* (Headteacher)

> *These people who are co-ordinators are very enthusiastic about their subject and ram it down your throat at every opportunity. You can either say yes and carry on with what you're doing or you try harder. X was very persuasive, and I've tried harder.* (Teacher)

No doubt National Curriculum imperatives as well as co-ordinator persuasiveness were influencing this teacher. In one case, the National Curriculum had necessitated the co-ordinator making efforts to achieve the INSET outcome identified in the previous chapter as NEW AWARENESS:

> *I think the major challenge[s] have been to help staff realize a lot of things they've been doing - (and may have called it nature study or even maths) - is in fact science, and to find time to go through the guidelines with people and get people over this hurdle and panic of "oh crikey, I'm not doing any science". It takes a long time but I think we're getting there now [and] people are recognizing that when children are playing with musical instruments or looking at condensation on a window, it's science. It's only a little step then to them planning a science-based topic or some science-based activities.*

It's not such a big hurdle, the big hurdle has been recognizing what is science ...

... Yes, I think people forget the message [of the advisory teacher input], it was over three years ago and since then we've had this major bash on our heads - this is what science is - National Curriculum. I think some people's confidence was knocked and some was completely shattered and the thought of wading through this document ... if you've very little interest in the science, it must be easy to just pop it on the shelf and not consider doing it. The difficult thing is to rebuild people's confidence and to help them realize that a lot of what they're doing is science ... (Co-ordinator)

However, redefining existing practice - *'You're already doing it'*, may not always be applicable to some teachers' current curriculum and classroom management preferences. Chapter Six indicated that teachers' ability and confidence to effect real changes in their classroom practice also depended on their sense of VALUE CONGRUENCE with the new practices being advocated and on their sense of acquiring NEW SKILLS and KNOWLEDGE. The evidence presented earlier in this chapter indicates that these first order outcomes were generally not achieved or even attempted by the co-ordinator. Though, in some cases, co-ordinators appeared to have been instrumental in - or supportive of - colleagues' moves to incorporate more investigative science, problems with teaching approaches, curriculum predilections as well as science skills or understanding were still referred to:

I still don't think most primary teachers have enough expertise or experience to do primary science for 12.5 per cent of the time. I still think the basics are important ... perhaps you should put that down to my lack of expertise to have ideas for topic to cover science for 12.5 per cent of the time. (Teacher)

Science process is not getting done in some classrooms - it's contrived, tacked-on science or teachers are doing a mega-bang science topic and ignoring the possibility of science coming from other curriculum areas on an on-going basis. (Headteacher)

I'm still hesitant, but for the National Curriculum I wouldn't have thought about science at all. The problem is me, you have to keep reminding yourself there's the science in there ... it's a big leap to suddenly see science as important. (Teacher)

It makes it all more difficult, I prefer standing and teaching from the front. I don't like it, but we've to work in groups ... I can't think of much science for houses and homes, but you've to squash it all into a topic. (Teacher)

I only feel I do properly what I enjoy, so I choose natural sciences - things I find interesting myself. I have a block about electrical circuits. It's easier to do what you believe in - I don't feel confident about cogs and wheels so I've not done anything. (Teacher)

In the staffroom, one or two of [the teachers] were producing worksheets with no open-ended questions - yet they were crossing off in the tick box they were doing the science ... [they were] trying to do too much, too deep and much too directed, but, just by going through those things, I think they thought there were doing a good job. (Co-ordinator)

Everyone's doing their bit - some to a greater degree than others, some find it difficult, it's a bit of a muddle but they're trying their best. X is conscious of what's going on, but I don't think she knows exactly what people are doing. (Teacher)

Clearly, schools' collective consciousness of science has been enhanced (i.e. there are marked INSTITUTIONAL outcomes) in the wake of National Curriculum demands: 'In the staffroom, the talk is of little else than science'. It is likely that co-ordinator activity (particularly a committed lobbyist) could make a qualitative difference to this institutional outcome. However, individual teachers were still prepared to acknowledge difficulties: the high profile of science in staffroom discussion and classroom planning may disguise a residue of individual professional needs in the crucial areas of VALUE CONGRUENCE and NEW SKILLS AND KNOWLEDGE. As the last quote above reiterates, none of the five co-ordinators were strategically placed to properly identify, diagnose or provide for those needs. The reason for this absence of support is the focus of the final section in this chapter.

FACTORS AFFECTING THE CO-ORDINATOR ROLE

I think some people find it hard to tell the difference between me and the National Curriculum, because I usually impart National Curriculum knowledge about science, I'm probably the symbol of National Curriculum science.(Co-ordinator)

It's extremely difficult to be specific about the role of science co-ordinator because we have co-ordinators for every other subject - I don't think the co-ordinator role gives a teacher any particular standing in that curriculum area. (Co-ordinator)

This section addresses the issue of why the INSET work of schools and their co-ordinators were felt to have limited professional development impact on the actual classroom practice of colleagues. However, it is first important to stress that, from interviews and observations in the five case-study schools during Spring term of 1990, it was clear that statutory requirements were being conscientiously responded to, with more science underway in classrooms due to its featuring prominently in the topic planning of teachers. The issue here is not the AMOUNT of science being done across the school, but the school's capacity to influence and support the manner of its classroom implementation. On one level, the National Curriculum (and schools' and co-ordinators' efforts to organize for its implementation) has ensured that the LEA's ESG scheme's aim of science (policies) *'implemented by all teachers in the school'* has been fully realized. But the question of a consistent quality in classroom delivery across the school appears not to have been resolved by the schools' self-sustaining strategies. Some teachers' professional development needs in science were evidently not being met at school level, and identifying reasons for this shortfall is now attempted.

The discussion with heads, teachers and co-ordinators revealed three arenas which contributed to this limited influence on practice at classroom level:

* the wider educational context: especially National Curriculum innovation and its impact on school-development work and co-ordinator role;

* the school context: staff deployment, co-ordinator status and the traditional culture or social norms of the primary school;

* the individual context: attitudes of primary practitioners, strategies for teachers' learning.

The wider educational context

Pace of change

Though the National Curriculum has been a great incentive to primary science, the heads of the five case-study schools also indicated that the very pace of change and innovation resulted in a constant pressure to focus school development activities on other curriculum areas and implementation issues. The dilemma of quality versus quantity, or detailed and sustained development work in one subject at the expense of adequate coverage of the rest demanded a limit on the amount of school attention which science could afford to receive. Thus, although heads often recognized individual needs in relation to science practice still existed, none felt further whole-school input could be made at the present time. They appeared to accept that discrepancies and even deficiencies in teacher attitudes, skills and knowledge regarding science were a fact of life:

> we all have different strengths and likes .. not all staff respond to initiatives to the same degree, we're all at different levels of understanding .. staff show different levels of enthusiasm and that is translated into practice in the classroom. (Headteacher)

Given the variable quality of science practice among a school's staff, a remediation role, or that of 'professional development sweeper', might - if there are no further opportunities for whole-school development work or school-based INSET - thus logically fall to the co-ordinator. However, other factors, such as the lack of opportunity (and cultural resistance) for a classroom support role by co-ordinators, by and large militated against this.

National Curriculum and co-ordinator role

The National Curriculum was said to have heightened the profile of the science co-ordinator's role in some but, as quotations at the beginning of this section convey, not all of the schools. However, the sphere of influence of development work was often felt to stop short of classroom practice:

> *X's job changed when we got the National Curriculum folder through - into being far more formal and far more involved in paperwork and its organization, her role was to help people with all the administrative side - record keeping and so on.* (Teacher)

The most committed of science co-ordinators had helped to provide a policy, structure and themes, plus even ideas for classroom activities, as well as procedures for planning and record keeping to comply with statutory requirements. In the process, a great deal of valuable discussion on science practice had, no doubt, been generated. Yet these contributions to the development of the science curriculum were generally acknowledged not to address vital pedagogical issues like classroom organization and questioning skills or teachers' scientific knowledge. In addition to that, the fact that two of the five co-ordinators had in no way attempted this kind of development work suggests a considerable number of teachers without the benefits of incidental learning from discourse on science curriculum planning.

Beyond that the focus on infant science practice in the wake of Key Stage 1 may have left at least two of the five co-ordinators (who had primarily experience of older children) unable to offer the appropriate advice and support for classroom practice.

LEA support and the co-ordinator role

The characterization of co-ordinators' development work as offering a 'support package' or 'lower-order (INSET) outcomes' raises questions about how far the professional development of staff (in terms of classroom practice) was even considered to be schools' own responsibility. It may be that greater clarification of this role is necessary if schools are to tackle the crucial areas of VALUE CONGRUENCE and NEW SKILLS AND KNOWLEDGE. Although appreciated when sought out, the LEA's proactive support for co-ordinators both informally and formally was not greatly evident in the five schools in the year of 1989-90. Training for a professional development role may be an important component of INSET directed at curriculum managers such as heads and subject co-ordinators. This is particularly the case if schools, under delegated budgeting, are to seriously take on a self-sustaining INSET function and the task of advancing classroom practice across the whole school.

The school context

Staffing and development

All five co-ordinators were full time classroom teachers with no additional allowance for their role as science co-ordinator. Hence, the role carried no official status or remuneration. Often, the work-load of practitioner role (especially in the light of recording and other statutory requirements) meant any co-ordinator responsibilities were felt to compete with classteacher and whole curriculum commitments. In the two schools where heads provided non-contact time, co-ordinators indicated they used it to keep up with their classteacher work, rather than for co-ordinator activities. Co-ordinators described the 'time element' as a major constraint on their role:

my own commitment as a classteacher is demanding and exhausting enough without the other role. (Co-ordinator)

[when it comes to giving advice] I play a waiting game purposely - because I've got enough to do with my own class. (Co-ordinator)

It's rather time-consuming and it detracts me from what I feel I should be spending my time doing. I'm quite resentful of that really. (Co-ordinator)

Thus, lack of time and sometimes lack of incentive in the form of allowance payments for extra duties were mentioned by some of the co-ordinators as a limiting factor on the work they were prepared to undertake. Two of the case-study heads, in a later response to the evaluation, also corroborated the tensions between a co-ordinator/class teacher role; particularly in the current context of change. One wrote:

How effective can we expect a full time class-room practitioner to be in promoting the management of one area of curriculum change amidst so many curricular innovations and demands? The science co-ordinator in a primary school has a duty to maintain an equal interest in ALL areas of the curriculum and cannot concentrate on science to the neglect of other subjects.

It was evident that national and local policy recommendations advocating that all practitioners had a curriculum responsibility over and above their classroom duties could not, in reality, guarantee a full development role in each curriculum area.

The primary school culture

Beyond practical difficulties of investing time in a (single-subject) development role, co-ordinators were generally quite adamant that the practice of colleagues was beyond their responsibility. The traditions of classroom autonomy and the equivalent status of staff were recognized and respected in all cases:

> *in this school, teachers are not used to being advised, they're not used to coming to the co-ordinator to ask - they feel they're being imposed upon.* (Co-ordinator)

> *I don't know if I'm not asked - I'd hate to put my penn'orth in if it wasn't wanted.* (Co-ordinator)

> *in a small school, everything is extremely personal, it's particularly difficult being a class teacher as well. It's so easy to sound critical of the way people are working and it is resented.* (Co-ordinator)

> *in the hierarchy, I'M not in the position of being able to dictate, and I don't see it as my place to do so.* (Co-ordinator)

In abiding by these well-established informal professional relationships, co-ordinators placed themselves outside a genuine professional development role. Though a sense of being a 'supportive colleague' - 'I'd never see anyone stuck' - was adhered to, pro-activity in offering guidance to colleagues on their classroom practice remained inherently problematic. This problem was acknowledged in both large and small schools. However willing and/or able co-ordinators may have been in such a role, it seems (as the quotation from R. J. Campbell suggested) that the ensuing damage to the quality of staff relationships and the ambience of informality and reciprocity within the school was simply too high a price to pay. Perhaps for this reason, these co-ordinators tended to remain firmly in the more neutral and less threatening territory of CURRICULUM development (such as resource and policy provision), rather than enter the minefield of overt PROFESSIONAL development and thereby directly confront differences in curriculum understanding, educational values and pedagogical approaches. In the end, however, schools' self-sustaining INSET may need to recognize that the old adage of *'no curriculum development without professional development'* does not mean the two are synonymous: curriculum development in itself does not deliver professional development.

The individual context

Attitudes to the co-ordinator role

With the exception of one particularly talented and career-minded teacher, the co-ordinators in the sample did not see any major professional satisfaction deriving from their science responsibility. Two indicated that the class teacher aspect of their work gave them their greatest sense of reward, another suggested the role was merely a 'spare-time extra' tacked on and very much secondary to her classroom work. Hence, co-ordinators' own perceptions of the role often militated against them attempting a major professional development brief:

[when I agreed to do the job] I thought it was just a matter of looking after the facilities, I didn't know what was coming then. (Co-ordinator)

I can see that mobility and leadership is part of the job as other people see it, but it isn't what I want for me. I prefer to be in a classroom ... my enjoyment is more in teaching a group of children a wide range of skills and subjects in an integrated day ... I don't think that can fit in with the extra work if I'm going into other classrooms. (Co-ordinator)

Teacher learning

Beyond co-ordinators current (lack of) amenability or opportunity to offer an overt professional development role, lies the final question of how practitioners feel they are actually helped to advance their teaching skills. This would give some measure of how or indeed whether schools can provide such support. Some teachers in the sample volunteered their most successful professional learning experiences (in terms of a development or impact on their teaching) resulted from INSET which provided a direct and challenging engagement with the subject:

After going on [the technology course], forces, pulleys wheels all made sense. We went and we really learned something, it was very challenging. We had to graft quite hard and it really paid off. It took us above the level of the children. It was hard going (and we did it in our own time) but we learned a lot more. It made you very confident when you know you've actually learned something. (Teacher)

we learned [on the National Curriculum awareness course] ... that the exploration of science is 45 per cent. That hadn't sunk in, though we knew it from school. It changed the way I did science after that - because of all the discussion, information and hands-on experience we had. The other teacher [from the school] felt the same. We'd done nothing practical on Baker Days, just passing on information, administering paper work, things on recording and resources. (Teacher)

you need COURSES to mould your thinking, the opportunity to try it for yourself - X does her best but it's all second-hand. (Teacher)

The evidence on the schools' and co-ordinators' development work suggests that they are not currently in any position to offer this level of support or training to advance teacher practice.

Another opportunity for professional development was sometimes said to derive from interchange between practitioners. Where teachers could identify not just the acquisition of additional 'concrete ideas' for the classroom, but a genuine advance in understanding, it had resulted from in-depth, on-going and lengthy discussion with major contributions from teacher(s) with acknowledged expertise. Participation in working party or cluster planning, undertaken in school time, were said to have been a particularly valuable learning experience. Again, it is unlikely that opportunities like this can be provided for all teachers in the school.

CONCLUSION

It is worth reiterating that this study of the co-ordinator role and schools on development work is based on longitudinal research in only five primary schools. However, a very similar set of issues came to be raised independently in each. The problems of lack of STATUS, TIME and OPPORTUNITY for co-ordinators to take on an overt professional development or consultancy role were repeated in all cases. This might suggest that versions of co-ordinatorship recommended nationally for over a decade remain inherently problematic for the practitioner with full-time class and whole-curriculum responsibilities. The tensions between curriculum leadership for a specific subject area and a generalist class-teaching role were evident and may even have increased in the current educational climate. Similarly, the strong tradition of egalitarian informality within primary staff rooms remained a cultural stumbling block to co-ordinators undertaking a full professional development role.

However, it is important to acknowledge the positive aspects of co-ordinator practice which have emerged from the evaluation. Without doubt, examples of 'good practice' were evident: the 'lobbyer' role or that of resource provision were, in some cases, undertaken with thoroughness, skill and subtlety. Hence, an initial conclusion is that achieving what were defined as 'lower order' INSET outcomes must rank as valuable contribution by the co-ordinator to the school's science practice. Co-ordinators who find themselves having only limited opportunities for undertaking staff development activities may benefit from recognizing the qualitative difference even a modest co-ordinator role appears to make to the attitudes of colleagues - IF it is undertaken with diligence and tact. Duties like resource responsibility, and information feedback may be re-valued by some schools and incumbents of the role if the impact and importance of this kind of activity was made clear. There seems to be a possible demotivation when 'ideal' co-ordinator practice is represented as a much more interventive consultancy role while 'real' co-ordinators find they can only operate in a very much more humble way. There were also very significant contributions which some co-ordinators had made to school science policy, planning and recording in the light of National Curriculum. These could undoubtedly help some individual teachers' reflexivity and the quality of staff discourse but do not appear to guarantee a consistency of classroom practice within the school.

CHAPTER EIGHT

AN EVALUATION UPDATE AND OVERVIEW

INTRODUCTION

This penultimate chapter provides an update on science practice in the five case-study schools since 1989 and then offers overall evaluative comment on the Calderdale ESG scheme. As such it directly addresses the two major summative evaluation questions outlined in the original research proposal:

> i) what are the signs of change in primary science practice?

> ii) what factors contributed to the effectiveness of the scheme?

On one level, the vastly - and fastly - changing education context within which the scheme has unfolded suggests there is the same very short answer to each question: A Science RING-BINDER in every primary classroom! The National Curriculum imperative could be said to COERCE teachers into granting a permanent and prominent position for science in the primary curriculum, whereas previous LEA and school initiatives embodied in such a scheme as ESG PST could only COAX. As such, researching any 'lasting change' effected by a local ESG initiative has a rather overwhelmingly powerful factor or intervening variable to take into account.

However, the National Curriculum can also be seen as the apotheosis or a legislated continuation of such initiatives as ESG, and 'signs of lasting change' can be interpreted as the difference between science practice at the current time and how it was prior to and in the earlier stages of the ESG scheme. A question about signs of change was asked of teachers and heads in each of the case-study schools during the final phase of fieldwork in March 1990. Further to that, the interviewees were also asked to give an account of the ways in which they thought the ESG scheme may have helped (or even not helped) with the classroom implementation of the National Curriculum. In this way, their perceptions provided some purchase on the distinctive contribution to science practice in 1990 which the scheme may have offered. At the same time, the responses gave a clear indication of how the scheme as a whole was conceived by the schools: for instance, very often interviewees equated the ESG scheme solely with the school-based input of the two advisory teachers. A final issue for discussion was that of 'outstanding professional development needs' with regard to primary science, and analysing responses here was seen by the researchers as a way of inferring what the scheme may have NOT provided in the furtherance of science practice, and equally what teachers required more of.

The present chapter is in two parts. Part One looks at the accounts of changes in practice provided principally by the 1990 data, and provides a summative overview of outcomes. Part Two addresses the factors affecting the effectiveness of the scheme.

PART ONE

SIGNS OF CHANGE

> *The main change, as I see it, is that in some teachers' classrooms, science has moved from being non-existent. As a school, we've tried to develop it so staff see the benefit of science, understand the need and importance of it for children. But some still don't, they feel its an imposition, they don't enjoy it and don't feel its importance. Others do, and are much more confident - even enjoy it - but for some staff its tokenistic. But now they're being forced to do it, they've no choice and that's actually a good thing ...*
> (Deputy head)

The National Curriculum's impact on science practice between 1989 and 1990 was discussed with 20 teachers. Using the same four criteria as Chapter Six's report on classroom practice in the Summer term of 1989, it is possible to detect considerable developments overall in the teacher accounts of the science curriculum offered to children, but it was evident that marked differences between the practice of individual teachers remained. To illustrate this there is an update on the five individual teachers whose 'outcome-routes' formed the final section of Chapter Six, as well as an initial brief overview of changes perceived by the twenty teachers.

Changes to the amount of science undertaken

The sample generally indicated that more science was underway since the National Curriculum, or sometimes a particular enthusiast would suggest that it still featured as frequently in the classroom experiences offered to children as it had in the previous research visit in 1989. Whether the amount of science had increased or not, the National Curriculum was seen as a powerful imperative:

I don't think my practice has changed, I'm not spending more time, but the atmosphere has changed - its more rigid, I didn't used to feel I HAD to do it ...

We know its got to be there, whereas before it didn't really matter, you did SOME but there was no pressure ..

I'm doing more, but don't feel I'm doing enough - if it wasn't for the National Curriculum I wouldn't have thought about science at all.

Some teachers indicated, as under the ESG scheme, that a sense of doing 'more' science accrued from a reclassification of certain learning activities.

Exact quantification still proved difficult for some teachers, though interestingly it was those who expressed lack of confidence or enthusiasm for the subject who were more likely to specify the precise amount of time given to science.

Responses varied enormously.

... on a WEDNESDAY AFTERNOON FROM 1.10 to 1.55

... about half the week is spent on science

I'm doing 20% ...

About three hours a week, usually in groups so it's three afternoons of an hour.

It depends, sometimes a little everyday, sometimes I spend all day on a certain topic.

Once a week in the morning, I'll take a group at a time.

The children spend two hours a week on science specifically.

I'll do science as a topic for 5-6 weeks and then stop - I'll do topic all morning - two lessons a day.

I [usually] have a group doing science on a table in the paint corner
- it's hard to say - sometimes for the whole week or sometimes for two
days.

Clearly, some teachers were referring to the presence of science in the
classroom, some to the amount received per week by individual pupils,
while others interpreted the question as one about their own teaching
investment in science. Nevertheless, the conclusion of very varied
degrees of integration of the subject into classroom life and daily
curriculum of children seems very evident.

Changes to planning

Some teachers indicated that there was no change to planning, apart from
post-planning reference of their freely determined topics to attainment
targets, though the starting point of science in topic planning was
frequently referred to.

When you think of a topic, it's always 'Right what can I do for science,
THEN maths, English, art and craft' - science always comes first now.

One or two teachers referred to planning directly from the statutory orders
(e.g. sound, light) despite a sense of prescription that this was not the
recommended approach.

The universally accepted procedure and imperative of topic planning for
the delivery of science did not however necessarily equate with the
whole-hearted acceptance of its new value and importance in the primary
curriculum. As in previous years, there was a sharp division between
those who reiterated the need for and appropriateness of the integration
of investigative science/group learning into the curriculum and those who
felt considerable divergence from this view. Where teachers were least
comfortable with the mandated science component of the primary
curriculum, reference was often made to societal needs rather than
appreciating any intrinsic value it had to children's education and
development, as the following contrasting accounts illustrate.

I now recognize the importance of valuing children's science learning,
and am able to slough the need for so much writing. I think teachers
are going to have to learn the value of children fiddling for half a
morning rather than writing. I feel they're learning and remembering.
The children are doing less of certain things, but I don't feel what
they're doing [instead] is less valuable.

It's been brought to light for me the importance of early science activities which will be built on, and the importance of science as one of the core areas.

We're supposed to do as much science as maths and English - but I don't. To be honest, I'm doing less science than I should because I don't like science - we're told the country needs more scientists but I feel some staff are putting too much emphasis on science. You can't neglect the bread and butter subjects: number, grammar, spelling are very important to these children, I just carry on trying not to neglect their general education.

Formerly the two priorities were maths and English. I now see it as three-fold including science. At the back of my mind I know now I've got to do some, so I've come to terms with it, made up my deficiencies and found out it's not so bad .. but the children won't be competent in the things I value - being literate, numerate, appreciative of arts and music. We're in danger of too much emphasis on science and technology. The powers that be are looking at children when they're grown up not as children at the present. Science is very much part of the end product, children are being programmed through a system.

Other teachers acceded to the value of science but with some trepidation, often with an acknowledgement that it was they who 'needed to change' 'become more knowledgeable'.

I'm still just as anxious about the content, but that's something I'm just going to have to overcome, but I feel happier in that now I know what I should be covering: I do see the importance of science, I know we've got to [do it] and I didn't see the importance at the beginning. [Frankly], it frightened me all this messing around.

Everyone tackles topics differently, the historical aspect always hits me first. I still see things that way, but science is always in the topic now. You still have a bias to what you're interested in, but you can't push science away any more. I'm more confident, but I'll never be totally confident teaching science. It's your own education. My own basic science knowledge is poor .. it's harder to make yourself learn something you haven't got a clue about, and easier [when planning] to look up information on subjects you're already interested and enthusiastic about ... I enjoy the actual teaching because the children enjoy it, so instead of my enthusiasm carrying them along, it's theirs carrying me. I think most of my problems I can sort out myself - my attitude, my feeling that I don't know enough, but it's not going to happen overnight.

Others recognized simultaneously the value of science and yet the exclusion of previously valued aspects of the curriculum.

I can see better than before it's more important for hands-on practical learning, but yet at the same time, because I'm doing so much topic work, I know other areas are being neglected. The imaginative work - like poetry and free writing - has gone: I think 'oh it doesn't matter so much 'cos they're young, there's still time.' At the moment I don't feel I'm doing justice to other areas, but I am to science.

In sum, discussion of curriculum planning revealed that VALUE CONGRUENCE remained an important issue in National Curriculum implementation. Perhaps the 1990 data suggests that it was being increasingly recognized as such by the teachers themselves. Teachers were more able or willing to express and confront - if not always resolve - underlying differences between their established practice and beliefs and the mandates of the science component of the National Curriculum.

Changes to classroom management

This was still referred to as a major issue in the effective classroom delivery of science. One or two teachers referred to a new-found solution of whole-class activities, others commented on no change to their usual grouping strategies. The most 'formal' teachers still expressed considerable discomfort and difficulty.

For me the main difficulty is the organization - the other children crowding round. The children enjoy it because they don't have to do any writing. They need to be reminded they are doing work.

I prefer to teach science standing at the front. Splitting the children into groups for experiments, I find it difficult, some children can't [work that way], they act the fool. I prefer the class approach, I can control the responses, with 23 children in front of you, I know who's answering. If we're doing experiments, it's difficult to get round, I don't feel I have control over the groups.

Last year, I did a whole class - 'the science lesson' - now it's more in groups. The inspectors, I believe, say work in a group method. But children in this school get on more happily if it's formal. We're told by a level above school [to work in groups], but nobody's finding it easy to get to this ideal.

If you have a formal lesson, it's much quieter - with science activities, the noise level rises and I find it difficult 'cos I didn't like noise. But it's something I've got to come to terms with. We've got to move with the times ...

However, the compromise involved in provision for science as well as the 'rest of the class' activities was still referred to quite regularly, and even by the most proficient of classroom managers:

When it's science, I've worked in small groups, and made the other tasks easier, quite formal, so they don't need any help at all. It's sad for those who have problems with reading and writing, I think the quality of English work has suffered.

We need extra support, if someone was with the science group just to ask that little question, it would be so much more worthwhile. Children, particularly the poor ones, do miss out.

However difficult when you've got the rest of the class, I [have to] take the science group, otherwise I miss out. There has to be intervention, or the children will sit in a fog forever. That's a big responsibility. Also, I think sitting with the science group gives the work and the subject itself value to the children. [They think] it

must be important, if she's so interested in it and using quality teaching time on it.

Changes in the classroom interaction

It would be spurious comparison to take a teacher's single observed lesson, contrast it with a single other lesson observed almost a year later, and claim there was 'hard evidence' about changes to practice. Consequently, this section will refer mainly to teachers' comments and perceptions of change, (using classroom observation only as a contextualizing support material.)

A noticeable feature of the 1990 discussions was a clearer awareness of the whole issue of science discourse between pupils and teacher. Aspects of science process - perhaps through Attainment Target 1 embedding itself in the psyche of primary profession - were volunteered by a number of the teachers. This consideration of science process had not been such a feature in previous discussions with the research team.

I find things like hypothesizing difficult, trying to get children into that way of thinking. It's a difficult process for children to learn.

Primary science is a method of working, a way of children thinking - the ring binder brings that home to you.

I'm more child based than teacher based. I always thought I was child centred but I wasn't - I wasn't letting the children do the work - I'd go over and say, well almost tell them off, and then have to stop myself saying 'You should do X' to what might be another way of doing it.

I can see better that telling children things and saying this is true doesn't work - that they can't grasp the idea till they've done it for themselves.

The idea of the teacher not making statements, but questioning the children to make statements, that's definitely come from the National Curriculum.

However, awareness of a changing teacher role inherent in greater concentration on science process brought out some interviewees' internal conflict on issues like control as well as preferences in the timing and degree of teacher intervention.

I've now an increased preparedness not to know what the result is - for instance, I gave a group some equipment and told them they'd to tell the rest of the class how they knew there was air around us. It's good children learn for themselves rather than being told by the teacher, but in a school like this it's much easier to have a path from A to B to C, it's tempting still to go for the safe path rather than setting up a situation which leaves the children free to explore.

I'll never be one who just lets or leaves the children to investigate. I like to lead and to know. But that's me, because I'm not 100% happy. I'll set up an experiment but I'll talk with every group first, give them information, not just letting them discover. Children discovering, investigating - AT1 sounds frightening when you first read it, but it's there, it's what children will be asked to do, and they will benefit from it. It's not just the statement they need to know, is it, it's the method and process by which they achieve it - that's what's so different [from before].

You can be doing more science and still only fulfilling half of the National Curriculum .. the children have got to think. It takes them longer and even then they may not come up with the right answer. You've to try and put them right at the end somehow, as a class when they've all done it say, I don't think you can leave them with a wrong understanding of things.

The children may develop down the wrong path - the only way is to work and talk through the work WITH them. They have great difficulty with the concepts ... it's important they tell me their ideas, we can miss out on routes they could have possibly taken [to a better understanding] because I wasn't there to explore those with them. They don't have the same discussion technique when you're not there. When you're there, you can guide them, even without realising - your expression, tone or voice - that doesn't come from their friends.

The wide range of interpretations of the teacher role in science work is very apparent from these extracts. Comparing these descriptions demonstrates that the implications of the ring binder (and AT1) for teacher-pupil interaction are internalized quite differently - from the apparent abnegation of the first teacher to the subtle but constant guidance inherent in the last teacher's account of her preferred very interventionist way of working. It may be significant that the former was a non-specialist whose only encounter with science INSET was through LEA National Curriculum training days, whereas the latter was a science specialist with a sophisticated view of the need to extrapolate and develop children's scientific thinking derived from advanced courses at higher education institutions. In sum, the interpretation of messages and meanings about teaching primary science under the National Curriculum seems as varied as those which resulted from the ESG scheme.

Finally, greater attention to children undertaking science work was referred to by some teachers in response to impending assessment and recording obligations. More than one infant teacher referred to closer observation of informal science activities - such as waterplay, sand and construction work. Others interpreted questions on recording as an administrative task, done away from the classroom.

This brief and general overview of practice in 1990 testifies to the universal acceptance of mandatory science into the primary curriculum, albeit with a considerable - and inevitable - variance in the degree to which the practitioners concurred or were comfortable with its pre-eminence. It leads on to a consideration of the effects of the ESG scheme upon National Curriculum science.

VIEWS ON THE ESG SCHEME

A question about views of the scheme's significance for National Curriculum implementation was put to all teachers. As indicated in the introduction, the responses often suggested that the ESG scheme was equated only with the advisory teacher school-based input. Few references were made to the school self-sustaining component or the role of science co-ordinator. Significantly, in some cases, opinion about the value of the advisory teachers and their school-based input were still freely volunteered in both prospective and retrospective schools during the 1990 interviews.

The major recollection, or highest frequency of responses, from many of the teachers was the AFFECTIVE and MOTIVATIONAL outcomes which were often described as directly resulting from a third outcome identified in the typology - NEW AWARENESS. Teachers' 1990 depictions of what they saw as the value of the scheme suggests that it was the definitions and imaging of practice presented by the advisory teachers which remained an outstanding memory. It was remembered as a stimulating and reassuring demonstration of the subject's accessibility for many of the practitioners and this was perceived as a useful preparation for confronting statutory orders.

It was a definite help, it made us more relaxed about the whole thing - it looked so easy ... obviously there's a lot of work sorting out the work cards, but that's most of it done - it's up to the children then. They made it fun too. The message of child-centredness came from the two advisory teachers. The National Curriculum folder didn't say a lot to me - we had the course first and could understand the folder better.

I think the scheme made us focus more on science and that we were doing science when we didn't think we were. The advisory teachers were the start of helping me to feel more confident 'oh things aren't so bad as I thought, I am doing more science than I realized ... things aren't so difficult'. Had we just stopped there all that would have been lost I'm sure. The advisory teachers were the initial start of what came later.

[The scheme] helped definitely, it came before the National Curriculum. They did it so well they made science seem very exciting, very simple for us at the bottom end - you can easily do it too hard. [For instance the advisory teacher showed us all the science involved in turning bread into toast]. They made it feel important to us and put forward simple ideas, ones that we could do. In that way it was helpful.

[The scheme] helped, we had some good discussion in the evening. It helped take away the initial - not fear - but it made me feel that I was already organizing my classroom the right way to cope with National Curriculum. It backed me up that I was going the right way. They gave me a sense I was doing it, before maybe doing it without being aware.

It did help, it made the whole school aware ... It made me aware of what was coming - perhaps helped [me with] the physics element. It helped in a little way to give a little confidence to pitch in and try it, I'll concede that.

The only thing I can say is the fact that it made me very much aware that the National Curriculum was coming and we were going to have to do it, to change and become more scientific in our outlook for the children. It was them showing a way of thinking and saying that other people are doing this.

The INSTITUTIONAL outcome was also suggested, particularly by senior management. However, significantly, the following extracts indicate the scheme's value was not only an institutional development in science but more in aspects of 'good' primary practice by which science is deemed to be most appropriately delivered.

It helped staff with topic based approach. Without it it would have been difficult to get the topic base approach, staff would have tried to compartmentalize National Curriculum and teach it as separate subjects. I thank them for that, they persuaded the staff it was the correct thing to do to do topic approach which I don't think I could've done. I still refer to it. I'd taught like that all my life, but it was good it wasn't just me telling them to do something again. (Deputy head)

The work done in the evening sessions and the two advisory teachers working in classes influenced the group work we're doing now. There's no doubt about that. It helped bring a whole-school approach to topic or project work. That was its other main influence. And because you can't do the National Curriculum any other way, it helped us have a whole-school approach to the National Curriculum. That's what I wanted to make sure happened. (Headteacher)

These outcomes - MOTIVATION, AFFECTIVE and INSTITUTIONAL - are what Chapter Six has nominated as second order outcomes. Only two teachers directly recollected PROVISIONARY outcomes, acknowledging 'the equipment/resources' which accrued from the scheme. INFORMATIONAL outcomes were referred to by two other teachers as they recollected being made conscious that '*the National Curriculum was coming*' by the scheme.

A small number of teachers also suggested that advisory teachers provided PROTOTYPES for future practice within the provisionary outcomes.

Oh yes [a great help], the way she set out topics I've followed on - more help than anything else. Some of the ideas [e.g. writing in bulb for electricity, a raindrop for water] I base my workcards on hers. They were the major influence - she taught us such a lot - came into school with hands on experience, so well prepared, brought everything she needed, so very enthusiastic. She did a heck of a lot of good in this school. I don't think we'd be where we are now - I know I wouldn't. I can't praise her enough. She really did set up an impetus, it was due to her personality a lot. Even if there was no National Curriculum, I'd still be doing a lot more.

Such prototypes for practice '*I base my workcards on hers*', '*I got good ideas for things to do in the classroom*' was the nearest approximation to the first-order outcome NEW KNOWLEDGE AND SKILLS voiced by the sample in 1990.

On a more general level, the 1990 discussions revealed that good and bad memories remained. In 1990, teachers often voiced - and used identical language about - the same incident or opinion they had brought up the previous year as evidence of impact or lack of it (sometimes giving the researcher a distinct sense of *deja vu*). This would seem to powerfully suggest that initial impressions remain: impact has to be perceived to be successful fairly immediately or the input is destined not to be valued at all. Where the input was not valued (i.e. negative comments prevailed), practice and opinion on primary science remained most dis-congruent from that of the advisory teachers. Thus, while early engagement with (or attraction to) the INSET message may not equate with a sustained successful impact, the evidence seems to suggest it is an absolutely vital component. In other words, put bluntly INSET deliverers could adopt the maxim 'if you're not getting through, you're right, you're not getting through.'

OUTSTANDING PROFESSIONAL DEVELOPMENT NEEDS

When the sample of teachers was asked to identify its outstanding professional development needs in PST in 1990, by far the most common response was for *'more ideas'* for *'activities which could be undertaken with children.'* Two teachers mentioned classroom management *'seeing how other teachers manage.'* One mentioned their own *'personal development in technology and science knowledge'* and one requested a course reviewing the needs of second language learners in science.

The universal popularity of 'practical ideas' which can be instantaneously transposed or adapted to classroom use suggests the continuing predilection for a particular kind of INSET which has been defined elsewhere as the distinctive primary INSET culture. Significantly, this 'teaching-repertoire expansion' is precisely the kind of INSET need often recounted as being so ably met by the two advisory teachers and the original ESG school-based input. Thus, while the curriculum demands on teachers in the current educational climate had shifted enormously, teacher expectation as to the kind of assistance they might require to meet those demands appeared not to have significantly changed.

Though the CONTENT of projected science INSET was now often defined quite precisely to include new aspects of the science curriculum - e.g. Attainment Target 1, the physical sciences - the requested FORM of that INSET remained highly traditional.

More science courses to learn in a practical manner, more ideas, different ways of putting things across - a hands on course with cards to follow, [so you get] ideas and experiences to bring back to the children. [It's like] reading a book about driving a car doesn't help you to drive - it has to be practical work, not just listening. [If it's practical] you see the problems, you remember better. The ESG worked especially 'cos they did it with the children rather than just come in and talk to you.

For us to learn about areas of the national curriculum that I'm not competent or confident in, I want someone like the advisory teachers to come in and show us how very basic these things can be and [what sort of] activities can be done in these areas.

General science courses to give different ideas/ variations on a theme. It's always ideas you're looking for when you go on a course - things that haven't occurred to you, before. It's nice when someone says they did this and it worked really well, it can spark off an idea and you think 'I could have done that with that topic.

I'm looking for ideas, actual hands-on ideas, us getting a chance to play with [the ideas], accompanied by matching what we're doing to national curriculum. Also planning a topic we'd be able to use.

Contact with other schools, advisory teachers - referring to things actually done with children.

Finally, however popular as a FORM of INSET, there was some evidence that a small number of the teachers were increasingly recognizing that purely 'activity' driven science sat somewhat uncomfortably with the codification (and pre-eminence) which the subject was now afforded in the primary curriculum. For instance, one reception teacher, while still requesting INSET which provided *'ideas for activities in the classroom'*, also summarized her professional development needs in a much more profound way:

I'd like to know how we can give children cumulative science experiences, not just thinking of science things to do in class and hands on experience. [I'd like] to be able to build on the experiences so they can go at their own level as a group or individually, so they can develop. I don't find that easy, it doesn't come into my mind at all how I can develop children's conceptual development - I'd like help on that. It's not like that in other subjects. We can convince ourselves that we're giving them lots of experiences and they'll building on their own level, and they will up to a point, it's true. But if we only knew what area/direction we were going in.

224

Here, concerns over differentiation, progression and continuity surface in a way which seems markedly different from any expectation or INSET need expressed prior, during or immediately after the ESG scheme.

To conclude this section we look again at the five teachers whose outcome-routes formed part of Chapter Six. These updates may provide some useful illustration of the very different attitudes and differentiated needs which practitioners had in the first year of National Curriculum science implementation.

TEACHER A

PRACTICE:

Teacher A expressed considerable discomfort at the expectations inherent in teaching science under the National Curriculum. She openly admitted that her preference for '*class teaching from the front*' and her unhappiness with group work and mixed curriculum teaching related strongly to control issues. Moreover, she claimed that '*it's extremely difficult to even think of science experiments ... so quite a lot is done by talking about it from the front*' and reiterated a belief in the importance of 'the basics.' Consequently, science continued to feature as a timetabled, once a week, afternoon activity because '*I believe maths and English should be taught in the morning.*'

OUTCOME ROUTE UPDATE:

Teacher A represents an extreme form of VALUE DISCONGRUENCE or ideological intransigence. Though acknowledging she '*knew a little bit more about primary science - the object is to get the children to think,*' the considerable development work organized by the school for implementation of the National Curriculum did not provide sufficient support or incentive to encourage this teacher to adapt her practice and incorporate the required new pedagogic approaches and curriculum activities. The ESG scheme was still remembered as being '*useful for providing resources*' and '*enjoyable*'. Awareness that her practice and values were becoming increasingly at odds with national and institutional imperatives contributed to this teacher's decision to take early retirement.

SUMMATIVE COMMENT:

This teacher may represent an extremely formal attitude. The issue of affecting any change to practice here revolves around the need for a considerable investment in achieving the two first-order outcomes: particularly pedagogic SKILLS and VALUE CONGRUENCE. Teacher A hinted at this by defining her needs in terms of '*courses to mould my thinking.*'

TEACHER B

PRACTICE:

Teacher B stated she was '*sceptical about the amount of science that is expected*'. She described herself as '*still dabbling*' *with science, and acknowledged she* '*was not doing enough*'. Though 'more' science was being done, RECLASSIFICATION was said in part to account for this; '*I'm consciously trying to label more activities as science*'. Practical group activities were undertaken '*once a week*'; the one observed involved young pupils working with very advanced measuring equipment, to complete a teacher-devised activity and worksheets. These were acknowledged to be '*based on*' the format of worksheets provided by the advisory teacher - hence an example of PROTOTYPING.

OUTCOME ROUTE UPDATE:

Teacher B's continued lack of intrinsic (as opposed to mandated) MOTIVATION for teaching science was apparent, and the cause of this was located in a lack of KNOWLEDGE by the teacher herself. With virtually no support or guidance from the school science co-ordinator, Teacher B was left to make entirely individual, independent and even idiosyncratic choices about the topics and science work she would undertake. '*Dipping into*' a commercial scheme bought by the school (hence PROVISIONARY outcome) was said to be sometimes helpful. The assumption of VALUE CONGRUENCE through the ESG messages 'you're already doing it' appears to have dissipated in the face of National Curriculum demands. Teacher B stressed that the duration of the ESG input was '*not enough to get the message home about science*', or achieve '*a lot of improvement in real scientific thinking or being good in the classroom with it by having a range of ideas, activities and expertise*'.

SUMMATIVE COMMENT:

Teacher B defined her needs as '*a lot more training ... a long-term course*' *which would provide the* '*expertise to have ideas for getting science out of topics, particularly obscure ones [which I might like to do but] where no science jumps out at you.'* The emphasis thus seems to be not so much on knowledge empowerment for classroom interaction, but for the continuation of primary curriculum planning styles (where personal predilection determines choice of theme) and expansion of a teaching repertoire. Teacher B may thus represent a practitioner who still is engaging in 'curriculum domestication' (i.e. accommodating - or subverting - new curriculum demands to existing practice) and has still to address the full implications of teaching science knowledge and process to children.

TEACHER C

PRACTICE:

Teacher C interspersed her academic year with specifically science-based topics, usually of 5-6 weeks duration, with considerable parts of the school day and week being devoted to science work. Science was then left for a while. She had planned her most recent topic by using the statements of attainment on Sound at Level 3 and 4 and made those *'the objective of my topic.'* This planning approach was described as *'finding my own way through.'* Practical work, using a progression of workcards, featured heavily. She planned to use commercial assessment sheets *'for my own interest,'* at the end of the topic. Though still anxious about her scientific knowledge, and her capacity to support children in AT1, the continued conscientiousness in her attempt to implement the full implications of National Curriculum was very evident. *'The importance of science'* was said to be now recognized. Whole-class group activities on science was now a feature of her management of science learning in the classroom, partly influenced by a change of classroom. The teacher - in responsive mode - attempted to facilitate and support these investigative activities after an initial whole-class discussion.

OUTCOME ROUTE UPDATE:

This teacher's serious engagement with National Curriculum science now left her acutely aware of the need to enhance her own pedagogic SKILLS in developing children's learning in science process. *'Children discovering for themselves - achieving the aims of AT1'* was now identified as *'the hardest thing for me to develop'* because *'as a profession it's not what we have done.'* Her anxiety about new scientific KNOWLEDGE was said to be somewhat alleviated by the guidance offered by the ring-binder and the comprehensive scheme about to be provided by the school's science co-ordinator. However, '*the questions the children ask and I can't answer*' and the '*science knowledge involved in topic planning*' was still a cause for concern. Summative comment on the scheme was that the advisory teacher input had not been really helpful for National Curriculum implementation but would be '*very useful now.*' This teacher's previous outcome route had been identified as third order (PROVISIONARY, INFORMATION, NEW AWARENESS), and second order outcomes MOTIVATION, AFFECTIVE) in the short term only. Her summative comments on the scheme seem to confirm the sense of minimal long term impact on practice accruing from lack of first order outcomes.

SUMMATIVE COMMENT:

Teacher C's descriptions of practice suggests that recognizing - or acceding to - the importance and value of investigative science, i.e. VALUE CONGRUENCE has been achieved in the light of National Curriculum developments. Though the pedagogic SKILLS involved in science process may well have been ably demonstrated during the advisory teacher input two years before, Teacher C now recognized outstanding needs in this area. This suggests that the imaging of practice must coincide with a teacher's own sense of need before it can be fully appreciated and replicated. As she commented '*all that messing about*' had merely '*frightened her*'.

TEACHER D

Teacher D left the profession at the end of the Autumn Term 1989.

TEACHER E

PRACTICE:

Teacher E stated that she remained '*flexible*' about the amount of science activities undertaken in the classroom. However, she now clearly distinguished '*informal*' science (i.e. the generally unsupervised play activities which had always been a permanent feature of her classroom organisation) and '*structured*' science (i.e. topic-related activities which had more direction and teacher-investment). She acknowledged that she had become '*more aware*' of '*having a reason for*' the informal science activities and that children doing informal science were now observed more. Though '*more planning*' was now involved, her structured science could also be responsive to children's interests. Science could '*happen all day*' or be planned for '*just a bit each day.*' Classroom observation showed Teacher E operating efficiently in a small group discussion (again on natural science), drawing out mathematical concepts, vocabulary extension as well as children's observation skills. Teacher E considered that in early years teaching '*maths, language and science are all so interlinked*' and that '*good language teaching was closely related to science teaching.*' Science was now seen to be of equal importance as maths and English.

OUTCOME ROUTE UPDATE:

Teacher E commented on her increased confidence about the science underway in her classroom, citing both the ESG scheme and '*the [NC] file*' as the source of this confidence. As an early years teacher, she said she had no anxieties about her scientific KNOWLEDGE: the statutory orders had made her realize '*how much science I am doing, and what else I could do.*' The positive comments on the ESG scheme suggested that NEW AWARENESS (confirmatory), MOTIVATION, VALUE CONGRUENCE, AFFECTIVE and INSTITUTIONAL outcomes were particularly remembered. The scheme was described as helping her attitude to national curriculum science because of the '*good discussion in the evening sessions*' and because it made her feel confident she was '*already organizing the classroom the right way to cope with the national curriculum.*' The advisory teachers were also specifically mentioned as '*backing me up that I was doing science before, maybe doing it without being aware.*' Teacher E defined her professional development needs as '*contacts with other schools and advisory teachers - where we refer to things actually done with children.*'

SUMMATIVE COMMENT:

Teacher E's comments on the planning and observation of her informal science particularly suggest some enhanced reflexivity. Perhaps because she had come to feel buoyant about her capacity to implement national curriculum science in the early years, this teacher saw her professional development needs solely in terms of repertoire expansion. Indeed, there appears to be a very positive viewing of the ring binder as a provisionary resource in itself. Hence, the acquisition and exchange of proven classroom-related science activities remained her only INSET priority. It is worth noting that advisory teachers were closely associated with this PROVISIONARY outcome. Teacher E raises the issue of what kinds of support and additional KNOWLEDGE in science would benefit a highly skilled early years practitioner and indeed whether the practice-exchange/ discourse which she sought from science INSET could be classified as a form of NEW [CRAFT] KNOWLEDGE. However, it is at least possible that teaching pre-KS1 pupils coupled with the advisory teachers' confirmatory message of '*You're already doing it*' has meant that Teacher E remains essentially activity-oriented and as yet has not altogether addressed such issues as progression in science learning, the physical sciences in her 'structured' early years science curriculum and the full implications of AT1. The only very informal INSTITUTIONAL outcomes may be a factor here: organized whole-school discussion and planning for science was said not to have occurred after the advisory teacher input.

OUTCOMES OF THE SCHEME

This section presents the evaluation's final overview on the impact of the scheme as a whole, taking into account the conclusions and commentary provided by all previous chapters. Two caveats are raised first:

(i)   The feasibility of generalizing about the effects of the scheme must be tempered by the evidence which suggests it came to have a very varied influence upon the practice and attitudes of thinking of individual practitioners.

Certainly, the cameos of 'individuated outcome routes' presented in Chapter Seven and their update in the present chapter indicate considerably different responses and degrees of impact. Indeed, one of the main messages of the study is that INSET planning needs to take close account of the fact that in-service is experienced and assimilated in highly individual ways. However, highlighting discrepancies in individuals' subsequent practice allows some general conclusions as to the 'mean' influence of the scheme overall.

(ii)   The difficulty of extricating the specific effects of the scheme from all other influences has also to be acknowledged, especially the factor of the emerging national curriculum imperative.

It is particularly obvious that, in its later stages (1988 onwards), the scheme's messages on primary science were likely to be increasingly received as an 'advance warning system' on future teaching and curriculum obligations. A powerful persuader had been added to the coaxing repertoire of the advisory teachers and any subsequent school-based development work. It is at this point that the value of a longitudinal study becomes apparent. The evaluation's account of 'signs of change' during the Summer term of 1988 (written up in an earlier interim paper) gives some useful insights into teacher and school responses to the scheme BEFORE the implications of national curriculum imperatives were fully formulated or responded to by the primary profession. Although it may be to enter the realms of fanciful speculation 'what would it have been like if there hadn't been a national curriculum ...?, the outcomes achieved solely by the scheme can in some way be measured by even a very brief reference to earlier data. Such a comparison thus forms part of this summary.

Overall then, in answer to the summative question of the impact of the scheme, there appear to be two distinct aspects to its long-term success.

First, the scheme operated as a particularly effective promotion exercise in raising awareness about the nature - and accessibility - of primary science for the generalist practitioner. Undoubtedly, the message and imaging of science as a curriculum area which involved topic-based, practical, investigative group activities impacted upon every practitioner involved: there was consistency of the 'new awareness' rhetoric on these counts both across the sample and over the two year period of the research. In turn, the frequency of accounts of MOTIVATION and AFFECTIVE outcomes accompanying this NEW AWARENESS suggests that a key aim of the scheme, namely 'removing anxiety', had been ably met by the work of the advisory teachers and sometimes by the INSTITUTIONAL outcomes subsequent to their input.

However, some caution is required at this point. Removing 'anxiety' which had accrued from erroneous conceptions of primary science did not mean that **new** versions could be automatically implemented without discomfort, difficulty or challenge. The classroom management skills and curriculum values and predilections of some practitioners could result in considerable problems (and demotivation) being encountered at the point of solo-implementation. As such, the study highlights the significance of a VALUE CONGRUENCE (i.e. where the INSET message and a teacher's own beliefs underpinning practice come to coincide), as a major factor determining the degree of impact on classroom practice. For others, such problems with VALUE CONGRUENCE may have been minimized by the absorption of the message 'You're already doing it', and the reclassification of certain maths, language, art and play activities as science. In the pre-national curriculum period, a few teachers (usually of older children) rejected this reclassification rhetoric and still considered science was a specialism which the generalist practitioner was not equipped to deliver. This is one intimation that the scheme, by and large, did little to advance science knowledge. Similarly, as Chapter Six outlines, **changing** curriculum values and classroom management predilections was rarely achieved. Hence two major outcomes (NEW KNOWLEDGE and VALUE CONGRUENCE) which are associated with effecting change in practice were not a common feature of the ESG scheme.

Nevertheless, the positive effects of NEW AWARENESS, MOTIVATION and AFFECTIVE outcomes clearly initially stimulated many of the teachers to 'have a go' at new investigative science activities. The additional impetus provided by PROVISIONARY outcomes - particularly the advisory teachers' worksheets and also resources acquired by the _200 grant - should also be recognized here. However, such enthusiasm did not always guarantee sustained or substantial impact on practice. A comparison of the 1988 data on signs of change in the three retrospective schools and the 1990 accounts of practice clearly demonstrates this. The evaluator commented on the 'vagueness' with which many of the retrospective case-study schools' teachers recounted the amount of science they did in 1988 - with terms like '*it crops up*' used frequently. This suggests that the national curriculum and not the scheme was largely responsible for the regeneration of investigative science as a prominent, planned component in the primary curriculum in 1990. Pupil interviews often corroborated the infrequency of investigative activities in 1988, and teachers and heads themselves coined phrases like '*fall off*', '*flavour of the month syndrome.*' Thus there were accounts of initial INSTITUTIONAL outcomes with the whole staff responding enthusiastically to the higher profile of science. However, these too were often acknowledged to be generally short term as other curriculum and policy demands necessitated new institutional foci, and the co-ordinator role in itself could not sustain the momentum for professional development in science.

This suggests that WITHOUT the national curriculum, the ESG initiative may well have been destined to effect predominantly temporary changes to practice or only achieve a status for science as a permanent but comparatively minor and infrequent component of the primary curriculum - (a small number of individual 'pauline conversions' excepted). The reasons for such limited general impact will be discussed in Part 2 of the present chapter, but it is important to register that, in one sense, this conclusion is in no way surprising - or damning. The history of curriculum innovation initiatives is a catalogue of similarly limited and short-term successes. As long as ultimate control of curriculum content was exercised by individual practitioners, the issue of VALUE CONGRUENCE would be a powerful factor determining the calibre and durability of implementation.

However, such curriculum freedoms at individual classroom level are now tempered by national imperatives and, in that context, a further important achievement of the scheme may well emerge. The definition/imaging of national curriculum science as closely associated with existing good primary practice became another occasion for anxiety reduction (or an AFFECTIVE outcome). In the face of the national curriculum's impending arrival, the scheme (or particularly the school-based input) in its latter stages was said to offer reassurance, as well as INFORMATIONAL outcomes, about what the national curriculum might entail and how best to plan for the delivery of statutory orders at classroom level. The continuing clear advocation of topic-based approaches to science was often appreciated at this time. Subsequent consistency in national curriculum implementation at classroom level was clearly not achieved, but the process of engaging more positively with the orders may have been valuably begun.

The second major and positive outcome of the scheme must relate to the manner in which, during the course of the ESG initiative, advisory teachers became an acceptable and indeed highly valued form of INSET. As the next section on factors will demonstrate, that success is no doubt a testament to both the inter-personal skills, dedication and teaching talent of the two advisory teachers in question, and to the imaginative design of the scheme which deployed them in such a way as to ensure good primary science practice was thoroughly exemplified during a five-week school-based input. Indeed, as some of the comments on professional development needs outstanding in 1990 convey, advisory teachers were now regularly viewed as one of the best ways to advance classroom practice and national curriculum awareness. However, it was significant that the teachers who advocated advisory teachers as a form of INSET generally suggested that the future support which they would most welcome was the provision of *'new ideas'*, *'things to do with children'* in the classroom. Those teachers who felt acutely that their own KNOWLEDGE BASE in science was limited did not suggest advisory teachers as a remedy. Perhaps this confirms the lack of NEW KNOWLEDGE outcomes identified in Chapter Six.

In this way, it is possible to conclude that the scheme operated effectively within a particular primary INSET tradition, where practitioners predominantly welcome the presentation of learning activities that can be instantly appropriated and recycled into their own classroom work. It is clear that the form of INSET operationalized by the advisory teachers - e.g. working alongside, whole-school input - was highly innovative: these popular, instantly replicable learning activities with children were now, quite literally, brought right into the classroom and staffroom. However, it may be that one outcome of the scheme has been to perpetuate the belief among many practioners that professional development is synonymous with extending teaching repertoires. Obtaining 'practical ideas' was one of the predominant expectations of the scheme in both prospective case-study schools in 1988 and, for a number of interviewees in 1990, this expectation of INSET had not changed. It seems that advisory teachers had come to be projected by many practitioners as invaluable **interpretors** of national curriculum demands, who could translate difficult and threatening concepts into classroom activities which were easily understood and operationalized.

Overall, it is clear that the advisory teachers were often affectionately remembered as particularly able and approachable ambassadors for the advisory teacher role as well as the curriculum area of PST.

PART TWO

FACTORS AFFECTING OUTCOMES

In this section, the summative evaluation issue of identifying factors (facilitative and inhibitive) to account for the impact of the scheme is addressed.

In any such identification of factors there is a strong element of 'hindsighting'. Hence, from the vantage point of 1991, pointing up the shortcomings and strengths of a scheme instituted in 1986 obviously requires that the milieu for and in which it was devised is given careful consideration. As Chapter Six suggested, the ESG's 1986 remit to advance science practice in the primary school was a quite awesome professional development task, given the traditional autonomy of the primary practiner and the new and often threatening subject area which was to be integrated into existing curriculum design and classroom organisation. In this case too, the scheme's main INSET strategy, namely advisory teachers, was perhaps as equally new and potentially threatening as the subject itself.

However, hindsighting is also an inevitable outcome or arguably one of the PURPOSES of evaluation, particularly in the case of a longitudinal study. Hopefully, identifying facilitative and inhibitive factors provides insights which are of value to future policy and practice. This section in fact draws on two different 'hindsight' vantage points. An interim analysis of factors affecting the scheme's impact (which was written up in an interim report in the light of research into the scheme undertaken in 1988) is incorporated into the present 1991 summative analysis.

Before presenting the final audit of factors, it may first be helpful to quickly re-summarize the overall findings on the scheme's impact. It seems that the positive outcomes achieved by the scheme were predominantly NEW AWARENESS, MOTIVATION (albeit short term) and AFFECTIVE (reducing anxiety). There was little evidence to suggest that the scheme had effected an increase in teachers' scientific KNOWLEDGE. Neither, in itself, did it seem to achieve VALUE CONGRUENCE over certain crucial aspects of science practice, such as teachers' predilections on classroom management or, initially, their curriculum values. However, the impending national curriculum clearly lent weight to an inexorable process of revaluing the place of science in the primary curriculum. Implying any critical failure in the scheme's inability, by and large, to achieve these 'first order outcomes' may be a prime example of 1991 hindsighting. It is entirely possible that, in the context of 1986-8, the generally positive effects on the ATTITUDES of primary practitioners towards science ranks as a major achievement precisely because it was a main intention of the scheme. Nevertheless, given the evidence that the absence of NEW KNOWLEDGE/SKILLS and VALUE CONGRUENCE outcomes could adversely affect the subsequent quality of classroom practice in science, it is important to identify how and why these first order outcomes remained elusive whilst third and second order outcomes were achieved.

Overall, the factors affecting outcomes fall into three distinct arenas:

(1) the design of the scheme, i.e. the **planned** components and procedures outlines in the submission;

(2) the implementation of the scheme, i.e. the way it came to be operationalized, the actual content of the various inputs;

(3) the wider context, i.e. those factors which lay outside the control of the scheme's designers and implementers.

In each of these three arenas, facilitative and inhibitive factors emerge.

1. THE DESIGN OF THE SCHEME

Facilitative factors in the scheme's design

* *The emphasis on school-based in-service provision*

Teacher's perceptions of the relevance and usefulness of the input were clearly favourably influenced by its location in the classrooms and staffroom of their own particular school. The contracted whole staff involvement was an important MOTIVATING/INSTITUTIONAL component. The combination of working with individual practitioners and group-based evening sessions, which included feedback from colleagues, often began the important process of sharing discourse on science and classroom practice generally.

* *The processes and criteria used to select schools*

The selection process outlined in the scheme's design ensured some degree of receptivity or pre-condition of MOTIVATION. The chances of the input delivering beneficial results were increased by the fact that the staff, or sometimes more accurately the headteacher, had actively sought the services of the advisory teachers. Consequently, at a minimum, advisory teachers were generally in a position of entering schools in which a proportion of the staff, if not all, were willing 'volunteers' rather than reluctant conscripts. The setting aside of time for three preliminary visits provided opportunities for negotiating and consolidating the staff's commitment to the scheme.

* *The five week input with individual practitioners as well as whole staff*

The deployment of the advisory teachers to make a fairly substantial investment of five working days plus evening sessions in a particular school, at whole-staff level and at the more micro level of working alongside, had clear benefits in terms of generally developing a climate of trust, support and rapport. AFFECTIVE outcomes were more likely to accrue from opportunities to establish such an on-going *in situ* relationship with the 'trainers'. It was seen as a significant advance on solo, central-course attendance by many participants. As well as that, a five week input offered an opportunity for a quite thorough INTRODUCTION to the philosophy and practice of primary science. Hindsighting suggests though that it was an insufficient period of achieve major practice changes in many cases.

* *The resources accompanying a successful application to the scheme*

The £200 PROVISIONARY outcome was clearly a useful addition, and stimulus, to the development of the science curriculum within a school. As well as providing equipment and/or books, valuable practice-related discussion could be generated in the school's perusal of such materials.

Inhibitive factors in the scheme's design

* *Lack of synchronization between the scheme's school-based and general INSET components*

The general assumption by all interviewees that the scheme equated only with the advisory teacher school-based input confirm that its other planned components - most notably the general provision and also the school self-sustaining work - failed to link sufficiently to the momentum created by the advisory teachers' work.

Thus, although the general provision was often applauded and valued in its own right and clearly achieved NEW AWARENESS, PROVISIONARY, MOTIVATIONAL and AFFECTIVE outcomes, it tended to be organized on an *ad hoc* basis and rarely seemed related to a formally negotiated plan for the professional development of individual teachers. Again, with hindsight, this seems to suggest that the degree of co-ordination required to sustain the principle of an integrated, multi-form strategy for INSET delivery was probably beyond the human and financial resources of the scheme.

* *Miscalculation and under-investment concerning the co-ordinator role*

The difficulty which the self-sustaining component of the scheme had in continuing professional development in science was described in Chapter Seven. Hindsighting here suggests an erroneous assumption about the development capacities of the generalist full-time practitioner who was most likely to take on the co-ordinator role; although, of course, this was a strategy long advocated by national policy makers. The ability to systematically influence and develop colleagues' practice and scientific understanding from within the school's resources was refuted in all five schools by heads, co-ordinators and practitioners alike. Further inhibitive factors such as a lack of clear remit about the role's function, lack of status, non-contact time and subject expertise may have all contributed to this difficulty in broaching a staff development role. Some of these factors may have been better addressed by a greater investment in the training of co-ordinators and a greater clarification of (as well as on-going support for) their sustaining role. However, the traditional primary school culture seemed also to remain resistant to the principle of an 'expert' colleague closely involved in other staff's classroom practice or at least sceptical about its feasibility without vastly increased human resources. Chapter Seven suggests that important **curriculum** development work was done by some co-ordinators and they were able to maintain the second and third order INFORMATIONAL, PROVISIONARY, MOTIVATION and AFFECTIVE outcomes.

* *The rigidity of the school-based package*

While the five week input has been identified as a successful way of raising AWARENESS about science, there is strong evidence to suggest that this amount of INSET time was insufficient to effect any practice change for a number of practitioners, whereas others were able to 'take to' science very much more quickly. Overall, this implies that a standardized 'package' is not the most effective way to address vastly different professional development needs, although its sense of equivalence clearly made for a less exposing and threatening INSET experience initially. A standard time allotment for each client teacher and school may thus have helped AFFECTIVE outcomes as the expense of creating opportunities to respond flexibly to individual and institutional needs with regard to NEW KNOWLEDGE AND SKILLS.

* *Limited follow-up and aftercare*

Following on from the previous point, the intended six half-day follow-up visits were also unlikely to provide sufficient support for some practitioners' and co-ordinators' outstanding needs in sustaining developments. Indeed, in practice, this part of the scheme's design was a casualty of the heavy workload of the advisory teachers and a full quota of even six follow-up visits proved hard to sustain.

2. THE IMPLEMENTATION OF THE SCHEME

Facilitative factors in the scheme's implementation

* *The qualities of the advisory teachers*

A widely recognized factor, especially among teachers and headteachers, was the personality traits and professional skills of the two advisory teachers involved in the scheme. In particular, their enthusiasm and approachability were often referred to as the most important factors. Their classroom credibility as highly skilled practitioners and their ability to effectively disseminate good 'ideas' and practice for PST earned an authority-wide reputation. Their tenure was of sufficient duration to set up positive expectations among future client schools and teachers. The fact that they were women, not previous headteachers and had no advanced academic qualifications in science or technology granted further credibility for their messages about the accessibility of primary science for the generalist practitioner. They had considerable interpersonal skills and sensitivity to the challenges of effecting institutional and individual change within the unique culture of the primary school. Their total familiarity with this culture was clearly beneficial. They exhibited the capacity to 'read' and, within limits, adapt to the context and circumstances faced by individual teachers, as well as to the predominant teaching and learning approaches applied in particular classrooms. In sum, they proved a major asset to the scheme by ably promoting and personifying the 'You're already doing it' message.

* *Headteacher support*

While teachers tended to see the positive effects resulting from the quality of the advisory teacher input, the advisory teachers themselves and other central LEA staff frequently cited the support of the headteacher as the most critical factor shaping the degree to which the input would have a lasting effect. A genuine commitment to raising the profile of PST and the degree of consultation with staff prior to the school-based input were seen as making qualitative differences to the reception of the scheme. Similarly, sustaining the 'pressure' to change was seen as a vital role of the headteacher after the input, by supporting the work of the co-ordinator (e.g. facilitating further INSET or working alongside) amd more generally by encouraging a risk-taking environment that promoted innovative and creative teaching. Prioritizing further school initiatives in science helped avert the problem of 'overload' and 'flavour of the month' syndrome. However, though headteachers could help ensure that the higher profile of science remained, evidence suggests they could not ensure consistency in science practice at classroom level.

* *The conscientiousness of some co-ordinators in their support role*

Though the design of the scheme may have generally overestimated the professional development capacities of science co-ordinators, there was strong evidence to suggest that a qualitative difference in the awareness and attitude of staff towards science resulted from the subsequent activities of the science curriculum leader. The 'provisionary/lobbying' aspect of the co-ordinator role (identified in Chapter Seven) was sometimes undertaken with extreme diligence and tact and could make staff feel more confident and informed - and hence motivated - particularly about national developments in science.

* *Individual teacher's receptivity*

Another influential factor affecting the scheme's impact was the personality and receptivity of the individual teacher. From the 1988 data, it appeared to be the case that the most positive response to the advisory teachers' work came from the most enthusiastic, lively and forward-looking teachers. It was noticeable too that teachers with a recent initial or other in-service training were among the most attuned and receptive of participating staff. By 1991, the other major factor identified as accounting for receptivity was defined as the degree of 'value congruence' which existed between the practice imaged by the advisory teachers and that of the client teacher, particularly over key issues like classroom management and investigative learning. Connecting the two factors, teachers least in touch with current thinking on primary practice were more likely to hold different values to those of the advisory teachers, and hence be more resistant to their messages.

* *The accessibility and acceptability of the scheme's message on primary science*

Looking more specifically at the CONTENT of the ESG scheme, it is clear that the advisory teachers were proficient at delivering a very accessible version of primary science. Two key messages were (a) the value of teaching science through topics and (b) the belief that much of the teachers' existing curriculum could be redefined as science. This is the highly reassuring rhetoric of, in effect, 'change means actually no change' and it was found that most participating teachers were in sympathy with both these messages. In 1988, only a minority demurred and felt science should be treated as a separate subject with specialist teaching. Other key messages about group approaches and investigative learning were often similarly concurred with in principle, but were more readily acknowledged to be difficult to implement in practice. Thus, it is likely that the '*You're already doing it*' rhetoric minimized the sense of discomforting challenge to existing practice and was essentially reinforcing for many teachers. It was a highly effective strategy for promoting AFFECTIVE and MOTIVATIONAL outcomes.

Beyond that, the chosen FORM of INSET during the school-based input and the general provision, namely teachers themselves undertaking practical activities and the offering of provisionary outcomes such as worksheets in abundance, was also very popular. However innovatory the role itself may have been, these advisory teachers essentially stayed within the tradition of primary INSET which puts a high premium on receiving 'practical inputs' or 'ideas to do in the classroom.'

Inhibitive factors in the scheme's implementation

* *Lack of reflexivity*

A frequent finding in all case-study schools during post-observation interviews was that teachers found it difficult to explain precisely what it was they were trying to get the children to learn in their science work. They were very much more comfortable and forthcoming in talking about what they and their pupils were doing (e.g. the topic the activity linked into, the source of the workcards, the tasks set etc.). There were few detailed expositions of the intended learning outcomes for that lesson, still less on how the latter related with any sense of progression to the learning accomplished in earlier lessons and to that aspired to in future ones. This reflected the emphasis which underpinned the advisory teacher's planned input with individual client teachers, whole-staff and general INSET attenders. The corollary of the scheme being seen by teachers as usefully giving and showing '*so many ideas for things to do in the classroom*' was that it may have unwittingly fostered an 'activity oriented' approach to the teaching and planning of science. The over-emphasis on exemplification as opposed to extrapolation of good science practice during the working-alongside component of the school-based input, and the failure to provide observation criteria for client teachers may also have contributed to this lack of reflexivity. The subsequent focus of any teacher planning and delivery which was modelled on the advisory teacher's work was therefore more likely to be '*what can I give them to do*' rather than '*what do I want them to learn*.'

* *Limits to teachers' scientific knowledge*

Probably the most widely acknowledged obstacle to change in classroom implementation was teachers' admitted lack of confidence in their own ability, skills and knowledge to teach science, in spite of the more positive perception of science enthusiastically evoked by the scheme. In the light of the practical, activity oriented approach to INSET, it was perhaps not surprising that many teachers came round to the view that their knowledge of (particularly the physical) sciences remained inadequate to the task of teaching it well. The exceptions to this were most likely to be teachers of infant or early years pupils, though even here physical sciences were less likely to be broached. Although less tangible, it should not be presumed that the process of science or 'science method' instilled any greater confidence in teachers than the corpus of scientific propositional knowledge. Overall, many teachers' grasp of science process was also acknowledged to be deficient. This may in part result from the lack of extrapolation accompanying the good practice in science process that was demonstrated by the advisory teachers.

*   Limits to teachers' pedagogic knowledge and skills

A further obstacle to changes in PST classroom implementation resided in some teachers' lack of a thorough understanding of the underlying pedagogic principles involved in new approaches to teaching and learning science. Such shortcomings often appeared to be combined with a lack of a secure skills-base to apply new pedagogic approaches regularly in their teaching repertoire. For some practitioners, the understanding and application of general skills of teaching and classroom management needed broadening before developments in a specific area of the curriculum could progress to a significant degree. It was a matter of some frustration to the advisory teachers that the development of such skills, and the conceptual basis which underpinned them, were well beyond the scope of the PST input yet, at the same time, were probably essential if the imaged good science practice was to be replicated.

*   Limits to teachers' knowledge of change processes

Finally, in addition to the lack of confidence in their knowledge and skills relating to science and new approaches to teaching and learning, many teachers claimed they were unsure as to how to go about translating ideas about new techniques into practice. In short, a knowledge of the processes of implementing change in their classrooms was often limited. It is arguable that the implementation stage is the most critical and problematic in the in-service training process and therefore it warrants maximum support, carefully constructed implementation plans, and opportunities to share reflections on and knowledge about the transference of ideas into action. Within the scheme, there were few indications that teachers regularly received explicit knowledge and skills concerned with the implementation process, nor additional support and time to affect the changes or formal opportunities to review progress and problems with colleagues. The pattern of the advisory teachers' school-based work and intended follow-up may be seen to have embryonically offered such support and discourse. However, the lack of emphasis on reflexivity and lack of time for extrapolation also resulted in very limited analysis and understanding of the process itself. Beyond that, the low profile given to the issue of implementing change is entirely consistent with the rhetoric underpinning the scheme. For logically - and ironically - the message of 'you're already doing it' would preclude the necessity to understand and appreciate change processes. Again, the short-term gains accruing from the scheme's practitioner-friendly messages and approaches left longer-term and more fundamental issues largely unaddressed.

3.   THE WIDER CONTEXT

Facilitative factors

*   *Statutory Orders for Science*

The significance of the emerging national imperative on science practice as a coercive influence, particularly on the later participants of the scheme, is very obvious. In fact, teachers' accounts suggest there may have been a reciprocal relationship in that the ESG scheme offered considerable support and reassurance about the implementation of the science statutory orders. It suggests that the scheme may represent the kind of in-service investment actually needed to comprehensively raise awareness about the teaching of core and foundation subjects. Conversely, mandated curriculum change clearly prevents the kinds of decline and disappearance associated with previous, essentially voluntary innovation initiatives like the ESG in its early stages.

Inhibitive factors

*   *Initiative overload at school and LEA level*

Accompanying the positive influence of the national curriculum, is the adverse effects on schools, advisory teachers and other LEA staff of the sheer weight of initiatives and responsibilities accruing from ERA. At classroom and whole-school level, the focus on science practice had to be tempered by attention to other issues and subject areas. The same vitiating effect on developing science practice occurred at LEA level, with the ESG scheme's follow-up programme particularly suffering. Given the pace of change to which schools and teachers had to respond, it was common for the advisory teacher input to be seen as the **sum** of the whole-staff investment or focus on science, rather than a first phase, as the scheme's original design implied.

CHAPTER NINE

IMPLICATIONS FOR EFFECTIVE INSET

In this final chapter, we have attempted to draw out the study's main implications for the design and delivery of effective INSET.

Extracting the practical 'lessons' of a research project is a treacherous undertaking for most researchers who, through their professional experience, usually feel more comfortable with analysing history rather than making projections about future policies and practices. In pointing out what appear to be the key policy-oriented messages to surface from this study, we certainly feel as if we are treading on thin ice, and would therefore advise the reader to treat them with due caution.

However, unless evaluation projects engage with the thorny issue of the implications for policy and further developments, it is difficult to see how they can claim to deliver their promise that evaluation can usefully inform the improvement and enrichment of practice. Although, undoubtedly a good exposition and analysis of research data should allow the policy-maker and practitioner to draw their own conclusions from the evaluation, it also seems behoven on the researchers themselves to spell out what they see as the salient lessons for practice. Accordingly, set out below are eleven tenets which the preceding analysis would suggest is likely to characterize effective INSET.

These eleven tenets are pitched at a fairly general level of abstraction. No attempt, for example, is made to relate them to a specific set of political, educational and financial circumstances. To do so at a time of such rapid changes in policy contexts would, in our view, accord the lessons offered a very short and limited shelf life. For us, it seems important to frame - tentatively - the general principles and then allow policy-makers and practitioners to interpret and apply them, with the inevitable compromises, to suit the political and financial constraints inherent in the context in which they currently operate. In a similar way, it is intended that the lessons offered by the study could be applicable to a wide range of INSET planners and providers. It is felt, for example, that the eleven points are as relevant to INSET or curriculum co-ordinators in schools, as they are to those who manage INSET at the LEA level. Other audiences include national planners of INSET, advisory teachers, Higher Education providers and other researchers. With regard to the latter, it should be stressed that the points presented below have their foundations in the characteristics of successful INSET practices highlighted in previous studies, notably Fullan (1982) and Joyce and Showers (1982).

What are seen as the key implications of the research are derived from the interpretations of the successful components of the scheme, proposed remedies to certain weaknesses in the provision and, most importantly of all, the variety of possible practical applications of the line of analysis pursued in the report, especially the typology of outcomes. As outlined in the typology, it needs to be recalled that, for the purposes of this study, and hence the following messages for good practice, changing classroom practice has been taken as the ultimate goal of INSET. If school management competency had been the selected INSET goal, it is possible that a different set of tenets would have emerged. Thus, with the above caveats in mind, the eleven tenets are outlined below.

1.   Differentiation should be given uppermost consideration in all stages of INSET planning and provision.

As an overriding principle, all stages of the design and delivery of INSET should be based on the recognition that individual teachers have different professional development starting points, different training needs and priorities, different experiences of INSET leading to different forms of impact on their attitudes, thinking and practice. These differences in turn precipitate a further set of different needs for subsequent development. This point has constantly emerged in the evidence of the primary science scheme and was demonstrated very clearly in the cameos of individual teacher's outcome-routes. To repeat one example from many, the message of '*you're already doing it*' was very apt for one teacher, yet highly inappropriate and counterproductive for another. The illustrations of outcome-routes presented in Chapter Six highlight how unlikely it is that all teachers will need equivalent amounts of the same input to secure certain outcomes (e.g. some teachers display great motivation towards certain initiatives, while others need various forms of pressure and support to stimulate them; some teachers have already attained advanced knowledge in certain areas, others require substantial inputs). To account for these differences, it seems essential to recognize that effective

246

(including cost-effective) in-service programmes necessitate activities which are differentiated according to individual teachers' learning needs. This seems a particular problem for the design and delivery of school-based INSET, which often appears to focus on universal provision without sufficient acknowledgement that in-service teacher education calls for as great a commitment to differentiated individuated teaching as that demanded in most primary and secondary classrooms.

Thus, it is ventured that the more INSET planners and deliverers take account of differentiation according to individual teachers, the more likely it is that the related in-service activities will be effective. In so far as differentiated INSET requires, inter alia, a detailed identification of needs and finely tuned forms of delivery, it clearly will not - in the short-term - be as cheap to mount as uniform mass training programmes. In the longer-term perspective, however, in terms of meeting the criteria of eventually impacting on teachers' classroom practices, differentiated INSET is considered to offer a more cost-effective option. The introduction of teacher appraisal schemes may present a useful opportunity to carry out thorough audits of teachers' professional development needs and priorities in order to provide a platform for more differentiated INSET activities.

2. Developing and applying the kind of typology proposed earlier, INSET outcomes should be given a high profile in (a) the identification and negotiation of individual professional development needs and (b) the planning of INSET to meet the specified outcomes.

Much has been written about the processes of identifying and negotiating professional development needs e.g. Weindling (1987), Hall and Oldroyd (1988), Galloway (1989), McBride (1989). However, as yet, little of this has focused on the content or conceptual framework in which professional development needs should be couched. In the main, substantive areas (curriculum/ pedagogical issues) and forms of INSET delivery have constituted the two principal organizing categories (e.g. Teacher X's needs are technology in the form of advisory teacher consultancy; Teacher Y's needs are profiling through a residential course). In addition to these categories, it is suggested here that the inclusion of a third factor - INSET outcomes - would focus attention directly on what effects (and sequence of effects) the proposed INSET is required to produce in order to support a particular change in classroom practice.

To illustrate this suggestion, it is hoped that the cameos presented in Chapters Six and Eight highlight the potential value of using the typology to diagnose an individual teacher's current state or pre-disposition towards certain outcomes as part of the identification of INSET needs process. For example, rather than merely identifying the 'topic' a teacher is interested in covering (e.g. assessment), along with the preferred form (e.g. advisory teacher input) - the use of the typology would allow a more exact identification of need (as learning outcome) within the topic. Taking 'assessment' as an example, the typology would encourage the INSET planner to ask such questions as:

-    does the teacher want PROVISIONARY OUTCOMES (e.g. a booklet of possible record-keeping systems)?

-    Is it the case that teachers want to develop their KNOWLEDGE AND SKILLS in the process of carrying out observational assessments?

-    Does a headteacher feel that many staff are not convinced by the need for pupil involvement in assessment, so an INSET input aimed at developing VALUE CONGRUENCE would be beneficial?

By thinking through the precise nature of the needs in terms of intended or desired outcomes, it is suggested that the application of the typology can make a valuable contribution to the identification and negotiation of professional development needs. Overall, a three-way classification of needs is proposed, including intended INSET outcomes, substantive areas and forms of INSET.

Having identified an individuated outcome route through appraisal and negotiation, a series of learning activities could be earmarked and organized to target the specific professional development needs and priorities of the individual teacher. In this way, it would be necessary for the INSET designer and planner to give attention first and foremost to the intended outcomes of the INSET, and their relative position vis a vis the overall goal of impacting on classroom practice, rather than, say, the details of the form or delivery of the in-service inputs. In other words, it is suggested that the design of effective INSET requires planners to decide the most appropriate forms of INSET by first determining which particular outcomes are most usefully to be encouraged for which particular teachers. Is, for example, the purpose of the INSET activity to offer information, raise awareness or ultimately, effect changes in teachers' classroom practice? By raising such questions at the planning stage, the typology of outcomes offered earlier could be used as a means of formulating more precisely the learning goals which the proposed in-service provision is seeking to achieve.

3. If the ultimate goal is changing classroom practices, then for many teachers, INSET involvement will need to be sustained and substantial.

If impacting on teachers' classroom practice is the ultimate intended outcome for a particular in-service provision, then the research conducted here would seem to confirm that a single INSET event taken in isolation is unlikely to achieve it for many teachers. Similarly, the findings indicate that the most likely scenario for affecting practice involves a sequence of knock-on effects - and not always a linear sequence, cyclical patterns also emerge - from one outcome to another (e.g. the advisory teachers stimulated Teacher D and produced a motivational outcome. This led to her to enroll on a course which increased her scientific knowledge and skills, which in turn impacted on her practice). Consequently, because of the improbability of single-event INSET activities impacting significantly on practice and because of the scope for inter-dependency and continuity between different outcomes, it is considered that INSET provision would be better planned as a sustained package of activities rather than as discrete events. In this way, it should prove possible to select the most suitable forms of INSET (e.g. workshops, advisory teachers in the classroom, self-directed learning packs) to match the intended sequence of outcomes.

Other writers have made similar observations about successful INSET by making the case for 'follow-up' or 'after-care' provision. While certainly subscribing to the principles underpinning notions of 'follow-up' or 'after-care', we have avoided the use of these terms on the grounds that they imply a single major input with subsequent minor ones. This not only down-grades the significance of the subsequent activities - with the consequential increased risk that they will not even occur - but also inadvertently reinforces the concept of single-event INSET activity by promulgating the view that the subsequent activities are 'hang-overs' from the one main input. Instead, to avoid such misleading impressions we suggest that it may be more helpful to INSET designers to think in terms of sustained sequences of learning activities.

Obviously, the requisite quantity of in-service activity depends on the distance to be travelled between the starting point of an individual teacher and the intended destination in terms of the outcomes aspired to. If, as in this case, the intended effect is a change in classroom practice - and it is worth recalling what an enormous INSET challenge the developments in primary science have demanded (Whittaker 1983) - this research is consistent with other studies in pointing out that the level of in-service provision required to support classroom change is substantial for many teachers. While a few teachers in this study were well placed to make speedy additions and alterations to their practices, it is salutary to note that most only achieved third and second order outcomes from a scheme which focused intensively on the staff of one school for one day a week for five weeks. As a result, it is important to stress that, if the aim of changing classroom practices is to be taken seriously, the level of INSET funding allocated should reflect the well-documented finding that for many teachers, effecting such change calls for a substantial degree of in-service training and support.

4. Coherence, continuity and progression in in-service training activities should be conceived and structured from the learner's perspective rather than that of management.

This recommendation requires the existence of national and local systems for financing INSET, management structures and in-service delivery mechanisms which permit the organization of INSET provision that fosters continuity and coherence in teachers' professional development and learning.

The proposal stems from the commonplace finding that teachers' involvement in professional development activities rarely allowed them to concentrate on a focused sequence of learning that was pursued to the point of it having a significant impact on their practice. The numerous references to in-service training initiatives coming and going like 'flavours of the month', suggest that many teachers felt 'battered' by one new

INSET imperative after another. In these circumstances, INSET was driven largely by an externally-imposed agenda from national bodies, the LEA and the school management rather than personal individual needs. Such conditions are highly inconsistent with, and unsympathetic to, the need to achieve a degree of progression through different outcome-types in order to produce a meaningful impact on a teacher's repertoire in the classroom.

We see the amelioration of this problem of lack of coherence in INSET activities residing in a greater emphasis being placed on designing INSET according to individually negotiated professional development plans. Although a more integrated and less atomistic approach to INSET funding and management at national, local authority and school levels would undoubtedly help, greater co-ordination from the provider's perspective only may not go far enough to reduce the degree of incoherence experienced by teachers. Consequently in addition, it is proposed that individual professional development needs and plans are used as the main source for devising a sequence of learning activities, into which externally-driven needs and agenda for INSET (including national, local and school priorities) are fused. Accordingly, the processes of identifying priorities and devising individual INSET plans would be derived through a negotiation that would endeavour to find a coincidence of needs, reflecting both personal and external/ institutional sources. One of the advantages of including INSTITUTIONAL-STRATEGIC outcomes in the typology is that it ensures that the school's management 'needs' can be registered as an important target of intended outcomes within an individual teacher's INSET plan and outcome route.

5. When planning INSET activities and recruiting teachers to attend them, the issue of motivation of teachers to participate warrants careful forethought and preparation.

The advisory teachers in this scheme recognized and acted upon the importance of MOTIVATION as a crucial INSET outcome for changing practice. Their success in motivating many teachers to adopt more positive attitudes towards primary science, especially in the short term, deserves particular acclaim. In spite of this, there were clear signs that many teachers' initial enthusiasm gradually declined and that of the few who sought out further in-service training opportunities, a high level of sustained motivation towards improving their practice in this area of the curriculum was a common trait.

Given the importance of the motivational factor, it would seem essential that the design and delivery of effective INSET should go forward in tandem with the implementation of successful strategies for positively rewarding teachers who engage in INSET in order to improve their teaching. The case for a positive reinforcement system would seem particularly convincing in the current context of compulsory INSET. Resources may be wasted by selecting unmotivated teachers for in-service activities which in themselves do not set out to achieve increased motivation as one of its outcomes. Consequently, in order to provide the necessary pre-requisites for effective INSET, management ought to seek out ways of rewarding teachers who participate in INSET to extend their teaching and subject expertise. Likewise, to complement this, INSET providers should be quite clear about the levels of motivation assumed by any given in-service event and the degree to, and means by which, the event itself will aim to strengthen motivation in specific directions.

6. The content and delivery of INSET should not dilute the pressure on teachers to effect changes in their practice.

While offering teachers reward and support for their efforts to introduce changes, INSET designers and deliverers should not evade the necessity of maintaining the expectation of developments in teachers' behaviour in the classroom. As described at several points in the analysis of the scheme, teachers were often reassured by the messages that they were 'already doing science' and that even major 'changes' like the National Curriculum could be incorporated into their existing approaches. For many teachers, these messages successfully allayed their fears but, in some cases, they resulted in a response of 'minimum disturbance' so that in some classrooms where change was warranted, the status quo was maintained. A domestication of imperatives and pressures to change had occurred.

From the advisory teachers' point-of-view, it is easy to understand why an emphasis was placed on 'reducing anxieties'. It was accentuated in the submission, but, probably more importantly, it coincided with the important 'be friendly' technique deployed by the advisory teachers. 'Being liked' is an essential part of gaining credibility with teachers, whereas stressing the pressure to experiment with change is potentially confrontational, and may jeopardize the hoped-for friendly rapport.

Much of the effectiveness of in-service training inevitably rests on the quality of the relationship between the 'teacher'/ facilitator and the learner/inquirer. The conclusion that we draw from the study is that a friendly and supportive rapport between the two is a valuable requisite, but not a sufficient condition of effective INSET. 'Being liked' is not enough, though for some teachers the 'likeable approachability' of the advisory teachers marked a big improvement on some other INSET experiences. However, in order to avoid minimizing the challenge to change, the INSET relationship has to be capable of initiating and maintaining the pressure on teachers to experiment in altering classroom behaviour. Expressed in terms of a 'critical friend' role, the former must not be sacrificed to achieve the latter. Furthermore, school managers clearly have a pivotal role to perform in nurturing a climate and ethos in which INSET relationships that are both 'critical' and 'friendly' can be built up and used to good effect.

7. Effective INSET is likely to take an eclectic approach to forms of INSET delivery, which should be selected to match the intending learning outcomes and the preferred learning mode of the individual teacher.

Using the maxim of 'horses for courses', there are certain forms of INSET delivery which most teachers would find compatible with certain INSET outcomes. The advisory teacher inputs, for example, were very effective in producing PROVISIONARY, NEW AWARENESS, MOTIVATIONAL, AFFECTIVE and (short-term) INSTITUTIONAL-STRATEGIC outcomes, yet seemed limited in their capacity to bring about significant increases in NEW KNOWLEDGE AND SKILLS. For a few teachers, the latter were more successfully developed through courses in Higher Educational Institutions, though problems were sometimes said to have ensued with those courses in extending their influence to classroom teaching repertoires. The science co-ordinators, often disseminating the content of central activities, were found to be successful in sustaining INFORMATIONAL and PROVISIONARY outcomes, both of which were supported by the self-help group. Illustrating how one form of INSET can be used to reinforce the impact of another form, the residential courses were seen as valuable consolidation experiences for those who attended them after being involved in a school-based input. The most suitable form - or combination of forms - for affecting VALUE ORIENTATIONS raises an important and, in this study, unresolved question.

8. **To capitalize on the attainment of other INSET outcomes, the provision of in-service support and training at the stage when teachers apply new approaches in their classrooms would seem to be highly desirable.**

For many teachers, the hardest part of any sequence of in-service learning is the application of the newly acquired skill into their teaching repertoire. Paradoxically, research shows that it is precisely this phase which receives the least support or attention. The findings of this study were no exception. During the week between advisory teacher visits, teachers were expected to implement the activities demonstrated to them in the working alongside session. During this week and the months after the school-based input, few teachers received any additional support in the classroom or were observed carrying out science experiments in such a way as to be provided with feedback on their performance. Moreover, as described in Chapter Five, there were very few opportunities for teachers to have detailed discussions on the problems and successes they had encountered in trying to implement the demonstrated activities.

The significance of the lack of support at the transfer and implementation stage of change in classroom practices counts as one of the major contributions to the analysis of INSET provided by Joyce and Showers (1982). These authors highlight the need for teaching about the transfer or implementation process as an explicit focus of any in-service programme. In our study, not every teacher appeared to need such support in that they successfully implemented change without it. Many teachers, however, did appear to require greater support and deeper understanding of the classroom implementation issues involved than was provided. Without adequate provision and support at what should be the climax of the learning outcome route, there is the clear risk that all the achievements in the earlier outcomes are rendered of limited value, because faulty implementation in the classroom does not allow them to be brought into play in an effective manner.

9. **In view of the manifest problems primary schools face in providing for professional development through curriculum co-ordinator roles, there remains an essential role for the LEA as an external agency in supporting the identification of needs and the design, delivery and evaluation of effective in-service training.**

The evidence on the work and impact of the science co-ordinators in the case study schools raises the whole question of how or if co-ordinators can be helped towards a fuller professional development function within the school. Certainly, there was evidence of at least three of the five co-ordinators having the requisite classroom expertise and subject understanding in science to offer useful support to colleagues - indeed, sometimes their classroom science work was explicitly portrayed by other staff as a model of good practice. Equally certainly, there was evidence of a colleague 'market' or need for further support in the area of science in each of the five case-study schools. Thus, a finding from this study suggests that, within a single school, professional development needs and their solution can seem to lie conveniently close to one another but apparently are often unable to connect. On top of that, it appears that often school-based INSET cannot fully address some individual teachers' remaining professional development needs in the core areas because other National Curriculum subjects and LMS requirements demand new foci for any whole-school work.

If this substantial residue of differentiated INSET need (in a curriculum area already on stream) is viewed as a significant problem - and there are strong indications that teachers would still benefit fron enhanced understanding of both the process and content in the science orders - there seem to be two different remedies:

(i)   to invest in more training for the co-ordinator to undertake a professional development role in the school;

(ii)   to invest in centralized courses that cater for different levels of expertise and accompanying professional development need.

More training for co-ordinators is by now such a commonplace recommendation, it must rank as little more than a policy cliche. However, it may be of some value to suggest that this training could also focus on a clarification of the likely outcomes of different co-ordinator modes of working. If this clarification was extended to heads and school staff, meeting individuated professional development needs may in turn be part way resolved by the fact of making the whole issue quite explicit.

However, making the whole issue quite explicit may still leave co-ordinators and schools unwilling or unable, due to the lack of resources to fund the work of the co-ordinator, to take up a professional development role. At this point, it may be that the LEA remains the most appropriate conveyer of expertise and support - from remediation to enhancing an already advanced level of classroom practice. The evidence would suggest that currently, school-based development work still leaves an LEA with a vital and irreplaceable professional development role.

The value of the LEA INSET role was amply demonstrated in this evaluation, especially through the contributions of the advisory teachers. The whole-school focus and impact, for example, was highly commended by headteachers and staff alike. It would seem that the quality of such inputs was totally dependent on the availability of outside professional experts in in-service work. Effective in-service provision should continue to have recourse to the substantial experience and expertise of advisory teachers as an indispensable vehicle for sustaining professional development in schools. In addition, we would recommend that their work in schools be extended to include a role in the negotiation and identification of INSET needs.

10. The primary INSET culture could be strengthened by supplementing the strong practicality ethic with increased opportunities for shared critical reflection on curriculum and pedagogical issues.

Consistent with their own training and considerable teaching experience, the two primary science advisory teachers operated within what may be termed a primary INSET culture, which accentuates a strong preference for practical products and ideas that are immediately applicable to teachers' daily routine. In working within this culture, the two advisory teachers inherited its strengths and weaknesses. The former included a valuable practical experiential start which quickly accorded the advisory teachers credibility with teachers in schools. As mentioned at a number of points in the book, one apparent weakness of this culture was a lack of shared opportunities and tradition for critical and reflective discussions on teaching and learning.

In the absence of such opportunities, it may well be that certain aspects of teaching are not amenable to development and change, in particular those which are more deep-rooted and complex than practical additions to daily routines. Hence, without suggesting any diminution in the practicality strengths of the primary INSET culture, it is proposed that all those concerned with in-service activities in primary schools may find it profitable to take deliberate steps to extend the scope for more discursive and reflexive elements. In particular, observations or video recordings of teachers in the classroom followed by detailed discussions of underlying pedagogical issues could be more widely used. This approach has many similarities with what was called the zetetic mode of INSET in Harland (1990).

11. Professional development processes and outcomes should be evaluated on an on-going basis at both individual and institutional levels.

Reminiscent of one of the main tenets of chaos theory - the so-called butterfly effect - (a butterfly stirring the air today in Peking could transform storm systems next month in New York), the evidence garnered on teachers' outcome-routes indicated a fairly high degree of unpredictability in the nature and sequencing of outcomes. This is particularly the case when following the effects of a single input or programme over a long period of time. It is arguable that the unpredictability could be reduced by a series of short-cycle INSET interventions over the same period of time, thus increasing the scope to determine and predict outcomes. The unpredictability of outcomes, however, reinforces the need for INSET planners to monitor and evaluate carefully the impact of their provision over time. Without such monitoring, there would be little direct information on the most appropriate INSET to mount in the future. The typology of outcomes, perhaps in conjunction with teacher appraisals, could be used as a framework for evaluating the extent to which the needs identified previously as intended outcomes have been met for individual teachers.

The typology could also be used as a tool for conducting an audit-type analysis of a school's or LEA's annual INSET provision. It would be advantageous to ascertain, for example, whether a school's annual INSET programme was heavily biased towards informational and awareness-raising outcomes which, as evidenced by some teachers in the study, may ultimately have negligible impact on practice. Taken together, evaluation at the individual and institutional level could be used to analyse the degree to which the overall institutional provision is effective in meeting the differentiated professional development needs of individuals - the point which was emphasized in the first tenet as an overriding principle for successful INSET.

REFERENCES

ASE (1990) *The Advisory Teacher - A Collection of Perspectives* Hatfield: Association for Science Education

BIOTT, C. (1990) *Semi-Detached Teachers: Building Support and Advisory Relationships in Classrooms* Basingstoke: The Falmer Press

BOLAM, R. (1987) 'What is effective INSET?', *Annual Members' Conference* Slough: NFER

BROWN, B. and CONSTABLE, H. (1989) 'Exploring Impact: An investigation into the teachers' view of the influence of in-service education' in Constable, H. and Brown, R. (eds.) *Researching INSET* Sunderland: Sunderland Polytechnic

CAMPBELL, R. J. (1985) *Developing the Primary School Curriculum* London: Cassell

COCKCROFT REPORT: GREAT BRITAIN. DEPARTMENT OF EDUCATION AND SCIENCE (1982) *Mathematics Counts* London: HMSO

DAY, C. (1986) *A Survey of the Provision and Management of DES Regional Courses in England and Wales 1978-83* Nottingham: University of Nottingham School of Education

DE BOO, M. (1988) 'Supporting science: Reflections of an advisory teacher', *Education 3-13*, October

DIAS, O., HARLAND, J. and WESTON, P. (1988) *Professional Practice: Implications for Teacher Development and Support* Slough: NFER

DIENYE, N. E. (1987) 'The effect of in-service education', *British Journal of In-service Education* Vol. 14, No. 1, pp 48-51

EASEN, P. (1990) 'The visible supporters with no invisible means of support: The ESG teacher and the class teacher' in Biott (op.cit)

FULLAN, M. (1982) *The Meaning of Educational Change* New York Teachers College Press

GALLOWAY, S. (1989) *Identifying INSET Needs: The Case of Solihull Schools*, Warwick: Centre for Educational Development, Appraisal and Research

GREAT BRITAIN: DEPARTMENT OF EDUCATION AND SCIENCE (1978) *Primary Education in England: A Survey by HM Inspectors* London: HMSO

GREAT BRITAIN: DEPARTMENT OF EDUCATION AND SCIENCE (1982) *Education 5-9: An Illustrative Survey of 80 Schools in England* London: HMSO

GREAT BRITAIN: DEPARTMENT OF EDUCATION AND SCIENCE (1983) *9-13 Middle Schools: An Illustrative Survey by HMI* London: HMSO

GREAT BRITAIN: DEPARTMENT OF EDUCATION AND SCIENCE (1986) *Local Education Authority Training Grants Scheme: 1987-88,* Circular 6/86

GREAT BRITAIN: DEPARTMENT OF EDUCATION AND SCIENCE (1987) *LEA Training Grants Scheme: Monitoring and Evaluation - a note by the DES*

GREAT BRITAIN: DEPARTMENT OF EDUCATION AND SCIENCE (1989) *Aspects of Primary Education: The Teaching and Learning of Science* London: HMSO

GREAT BRITAIN: PARLIAMENT, House of Commons (1986) *Achievement in Primary Schools: Third Report from the Education, Science and Arts Committee,* Volume 1 London: HMSO

HALL, V. and OLDROYD, D. (1988) *Managing INSET in local education authorities: Applying Conclusions from TRIST* Bristol: National Development Centre for School Management Training

HALPIN, D., CROLL, P. and REDMAN, K. (1990) 'Teachers' Perceptions of the Effects of In-service Education', *British Educational Research Journal,* Vol. 16, No. 2, pp. 163-77

HARLAND, J. (1990) *The Work and Impact of Advisory Teachers* Slough: NFER

HENDERSON, E. S. (1978) *The Evaluation of In-service Training* Beckenham: Croom Helm

HODGSON, F. and WHALLEY, G. (1990) 'Evaluating the effectiveness of in-service education', *British Journal of In-service Education,* Vol. 16, No. 1 Spring, pp 10-11

HOPKINS, D. (1989) 'Identifying INSET needs: A school improvement perspective' in McBride (ed.) *The In-service Training of Teachers* Lewes: The Falmer Press

IPSE (1988a) *Initiatives in Primary Science: An Evaluation Report* Hatfield: Association for Science Education

IPSE (1988b) *Initiatives in Primary Science: An Evaluation, The School in Focus* Hatfield: Association for Science Education

IPSE (1988c) *Initiatives in Primary Science: An Evaluation, Building Bridges* Hatfield: Association for Science Education

JONES, C. (1988) 'Advisory or support teachers in primary education?', *Education 3-13,* October

JOYCE, B. and SHOWERS, B. (1982) 'The coaching of teachers' *Educational Leadership,* October.

JOYCE, B. and SHOWERS, B. (1980) 'Improving in-service training: the messages of research' *Educational Leadership,* Vol. 37, No. 5, pp 379-85

KINDER, K., HARLAND, J. and WOOTTEN, M. (1991) *The Impact of School-focused INSET on Classroom Practice* NFER: Slough

KRUGER, C., SUMMERS, M. and PALACID, D. (1990) 'INSET for primary science in the National Curriculum in England and Wales: are the real needs of teachers perceived?', *Journal of Education for Teaching,* Vol. 16, No. 2, pp 133-46

LOFTHOUSE, B. (1987) 'Advisory teachers in primary education', *Education 3-13,* October

McBRIDE, R. (1989) *The In-Service Training of Teachers,* Lewes: The Falmer Press

NATIONAL CURRICULUM COUNCIL (1989) *Framework for Primary Curriculum: Curriculum Guidance 1* York: NCC

PARSONS, C. (1990) 'Evaluating aspects of a Local Education Authority's in-service programme', *British Journal of In-service Education,* Vol. 14, No. 1, pp 48-51

PETRIE, P. (1988) 'Primary advisory teachers: their value and their prospects', *Education 3-13,* October

PRIMARY SCHOOLS RESEARCH AND DEVELOPMENT GROUP/ SCHOOLS COUNCIL (1983) *Curriculum Responsibility and the Use of Teacher Expertise in the Primary School* Birmingham: University of Birmingham Department of Curriculum Studies

RODGER, I. (1983) *Teachers with Posts of Responsibility in Primary Schools* Durham: University of Durham, School of Education

STRAKER, N. (1988) 'Advisory teachers of mathematics: the ESG initiative', *Journal of Education Policy,* Vol. 3, No. 4, pp 371-84

SULLIVAN, M. (1987) 'Working and learning in other people's classrooms', *Education 3-13,* October

WEBB, R. (1989) 'Changing practice through consultancy-based INSET', *School Organization,* Vol. 9, No. 1, pp 39-52

WEINDLING, D. (1987) *Diagnosing INSET Needs: A Review of Techniques,* Slough: NFER

WHITTAKER, M. (1983) 'Whom are we trying to help?: In-school work in primary science' in Richards, C. and Holford, D. (eds) *The Teaching of Primary Science: Policy and Practice* Basingstoke: The Falmer Press

OTHER PUBLICATIONS

Other in-house publications available from the NFER include:

The Work and Impact of Advisory Teachers

Developing the Arts in Primary Schools

The Changing Role, Structure and Style of LEAs

About Change: Schools' and LEAs' Perspectives on LEA Reorganization

Enabling Teachers to Undertake INSET

A Survey of School Governing Bodies

Towards Effective Partnerships in School Governance

Foreign Languages for Lower Attaining Pupils

Staff Appraisal: The FE Pilot Schemes

Charging for School Activities

Education: Guide to European Organizations and Programmes

Four Year Olds in School: Quality Matters

Vocational Education Opportunities for Students with Speech and Language Impairments

SACREs: Their Formation, Composition, Operation and Role on RE and Worship

Copies of these publications are obtainable from:

Dissemination Unit, NFER, The Mere, Upton Park, SLOUGH, SL1 2DQ

Printed by The Chameleon Press Limited, 5–25 Burr Road, London SW18 4SG